Unification of Artificial Intelligence and Psychology

Petros A. M. Gelepithis

Unification of Artificial Intelligence and Psychology

Volume One - Foundations

palgrave
macmillan

Petros A. M. Gelepithis
Brain and Mind Sciences Faculty
School of Medicine
University of Crete
Irakleion, Greece

ISBN 978-3-031-68318-3 ISBN 978-3-031-68319-0 (eBook)
https://doi.org/10.1007/978-3-031-68319-0

This Palgrave Macmillan imprint is published by the registered company Springer Nature Switzerland AG
The registered company address is: Gewerbestrasse 11, 6330 Cham, Switzerland

For
Margarita
our daughter

"Πάντα χωρεί και ουδέν μένει"
"Everything changes and nothing remains still"
Heraclitus c. 535 BCE – c. 475 BCE.
(As stated in Plato's (~385-379 BCE) *Cratylus* p. 74, 402a).

"Never doubt that a small group of thoughtful, committed, citizens
can change the world.
Indeed, it is the only thing that ever has."
Margaret Mead 1901–1978.
(*Although it is widely attributed to Mead, its source remains a mystery (Keyes 2006) and The Institute for Intercultural Studies*).

Preface

The book you are holding is the first of a two-volume monograph on the *Unification of Artificial Intelligence and Psychology*. It unifies the topics of representation, meaning, thinking, communication, and understanding. The second volume extends this unification to four pivotal topics of cognitive science: knowledge, consciousness, emotion, and human nature. Each volume is self-contained and ends with a listing of the chapters in the other one.

Such a unification requires the establishment of a novel, fully explicated, theoretical construct—*noémon system*—that replaces all the inadequately developed concepts that historically have been used as constitutive notions of cognitive science. The *space* of noémon systems encompasses an awe-inspiring variety of noémon species and an increasing variety of artificially noémon entities and hybrid noémon systems. As such, it is a superspace of the space of phenomena addressed by cognitive science. The theory of noémon systems (TNS) described in this two-volume monograph is envisaged as the first step towards an emerging science of noémon systems.

Emotions, whether consciously experienced or unconsciously operating, can be very powerful motivators. When I finished reading my first book on the history of evolution, I wondered: What the new species of *Homo sapiens* would be? Earlier on, around the age of 8, a little blue car was placed on the table in the underground space of the wooden hut my family of seven were taking our meals. I was asked to watch without touching under any circumstances: the curvy blue car moved, reached the edge of the table, stopped, and reversed! It then started moving in a variety of patterns: a square, a circle, an 8, … I was flabbergasted. My research interests were born out of these two experiences. They constitute my root motivation for this monograph.

Finally, a word to the reader and prospective reader.

The task of unifying Artificial Intelligence and Psychology is huge and I stand to be corrected by all those scientists and philosophers who know in more detail each one of the foundational topics of either discipline that I treat in this two-volume monograph.

Either volume should be useful to scientists and non-technical philosophers working on the interfaces of psychology, AI, philosophy of mind, and neuroscience for their novel common approach and distinct results. In addition, most of them—as well as postdoctoral researchers and graduate students—will find illuminating the *interdisciplinary* reviews, in-depth coverage of topics and principles, and theoretical syntheses provided. Understanding them is facilitated by brief definitions of less well known terms. Such reviews and theoretical syntheses *cover a major gap identified but not addressed by in the corresponding literatures.*

Hellas, Greece Petros A. M. Gelepithis

The original version of the book has been revised. A correction to the book can be found at 10.1007/978-3-031-68319-0_5

Acknowledgements

I received the most invaluable help in writing this two-volume monograph from Mike Elstob. His penetrating and revealing comments in reviewing the full manuscript as well as most of its individual chapters improved this book beyond my expectations. Mike's broad and deep knowledge of noémon systems, coupled with his immense kindness and appropriately-excellent steering capabilities greatly improved this book. Last but not least, Mike's strong belief in the value of my endeavour and his encouragement to finish it helped me enormously.

I am hugely indebted to Peter Hacker for his 12 months long invitation to the Faculty of Philosophy, University of Oxford. Our weekly talks challenged, added, modified, or/and strengthened my ideas. Above all it was always a pleasure to discuss with Peter. My warmest thanks go also to St John's College for electing me to membership of the SCR. I found the latter's environment uniquely appealing and edifying. The same applies to the academic, cultural, social, and political environment of the University of Oxford. Staying there was both unforgettable and instrumental to my intellectual development. A paper I deposited at ORA, (the Oxford University Research Archive), outlined my noémon systems approach to the study of biological and artificial minds and was the basis for this two-volume book.

Thanks are also due to two scientists a few decades ago. The first, George Rzevski for allowing me the freedom of demonstrating the worth of my idea for setting up the first MSc course in AI in the UK that earned me the freedom of pursuing my *own* research interests in the non-research oriented Kingston University, London. His kindness and generosity compete with his professional achievements. The second, the late, Donald Broadbent for his invitation to the Department of Experimental Psychology, University of Oxford as a visiting scientist. It opened myself to a research environment I had only thought of possible and motivated me to pursue my research—for one year I was not alone.

Coming back to the recent past, I want to thank the anonymous reviewer for pointing out certain omissions in my treatment which I happily attended to. Also, my friends Yiannakis (John Papayiannopoulos), John Kontos, and Pantelis Moukas for interesting early talks on aspects of this book. Thanks are also due to Miss Dialektopoulou for painstakingly splitting the initial single book references into references corresponding to a two-volume monograph. My gratitude goes to Matoula (M. Demetriou) for sealing me away from distractions and providing the warmest and most suitable work environment for more than two years. In addition, sometimes surprisingly, discussions—on certain aspects of this two-volume book—with her always turned out to be helpful. I fondly greet her.

Finally, my apologies to all contributing authors whose names do not appear in the index (i.e., 3-author or 3-editor contributions). This is due to the et al. policy. Of course, the names of all single, 2-author, or first-author contributions do appear.

Contents

Acronyms

AI	Artificial Intelligence
AIS	AI System
ANNs	Artificial Neural Networks
ARE	Autonomous Robot Entity
BSC	Biological Species Concept
CHC	Construction of Human Concepts
CTC	Cumulative Technological Culture
CUP	Communication—Understanding—Primitives (system)
DAC	Darwin's Argument for Continuity
DaTE	Darwin's Theory of Evolution
D_L	Darwin's List
DoI	Domain of Investigation
ESS	Extended Evolutionary Synthesis
$^{ext}R_H$	External Human Representations
FHK	Formalisability of Human Knowledge
FLN	Faculty of Language in the Narrow sense
H	Historic *Homo sapiens*
HRI	Human-Robot Interaction
I_A	Individual I of a particular animal species A
$^{int}R_H$	Internal Human Representations
KRR	Knowledge Representation and Reasoning
M	Dynamic System of All Meaningful Neural Formations
MBI	Mind-Brain Identity
MMP	Memory-Meaning Postulate
MS	Modern Synthesis (theory of evolution)
N	Neural Formation

NCC	Neural Correlates of Consciousness
N_m	Meaningful N
NS	Nervous System
NoS	Noémon System
PriNS	Principle of Noémon Systems
PSN	Pivotal System of Notions
PSSH	Physical Symbol Systems Hypothesis
R_o	*own*-Representational System
S	Space of Noémon Systems
S_c	A Stimulus within its Context
TNS	Theory of Noémon Systems
WHuLa	Written Human Language

List of Figures

List of Tables

CHAPTER 1

Introduction: The Approach

"Don't bite my finger, look where I'm pointing"
(widely attributed to Warren McCulloch; not able to trace it down to any of his published manuscripts I am in possession).

"Biology today is no more fully understood in principle than physics was a century or so ago." (Woese 2004, p. 173).

Unification of any discipline, and a fortiori of more than one disciplines, best proceeds by integration of the constitutive notions, foundational principles, and approaches of the disciplines concerned.

Psychology's constitutive notion is 'mind'. Artificial Intelligence (AI) uniquely aims to *design* intelligent systems (essentially to *design* 'mind'), and its constitutive notion 'designed intelligence' is closely related to that of psychology. Until recently, intelligence was the all-encompassing performance measure of mind and to a considerable extent it is still conceived to be so.

This chapter prepares the ground for the unified study of noémon systems by presenting the TNS approach to it. Specifically it:

A. Demonstrates the desirability and necessity of unifying AI and psychology.

P. A. M. Gelepithis, *Unification of Artificial Intelligence and Psychology*,
https://doi.org/10.1007/978-3-031-68319-0_1

B. Establishes the necessity for an alternative approach that synthesises the positive elements of earlier approaches along with ignored notions and principles.
C. Discusses and formulates recommendations on choosing the appropriate methodology for building unified theories of noémon systems.
D. Argues for a non-formal axiomatic approach against the programming and continuous systems approaches to theory construction.

In particular, Sect. 1.1 provides a brief review of the foundational notions and principles of core disciplines of cognitive science as well as of the major unification approaches and AI-based foundations of cognitive science.

Section 1.2 introduces the notion of 'noémon system'—the constitutive notion of TNS. It is a common theoretical construct that replaces the ill-conceived and un- defined constitutive notions of cognitive science. Noémon system is completely defined and fleshed out in the chapters of this book.[1] It captures the essence of the evolutionary continuum of both biological and artificial minds.

Section 1.3 briefly: (i) argues that any mature unified theory of animals and robots should fulfil at least four criteria in addition to the standard ones of explanatory and predictive power; and (ii) justifies the choice of the non-formal axiomatic approach of the TNS against the dominant programming and continuous systems ones.

Figure 1.1 juxtaposes psychology, AI, cybernetics and TNS in terms of their domain of investigation (DoI); type of approach; and progress.

Two final points are in order. First, barring physics and chemistry that have achieved successive unifications, no other discipline has achieved any worthwhile unification. In particular, AI, de facto, goes through cycles of development culminating in partial unification of some of its various subfields in the form of successive 'robot generations'. The latter notion can be a robust criterion of AI's progress but it is not currently used as such. Interestingly, Cybernetics, the father of AI, had unsuccessfully attempted to unify the study of animals and machines. Neuroscience appeared to be in a reasonable state of integration with its neuron

[1] A definition is complete if and only if all of its definiens are expressed in terms of primitive notions—defined in Chapter 4.

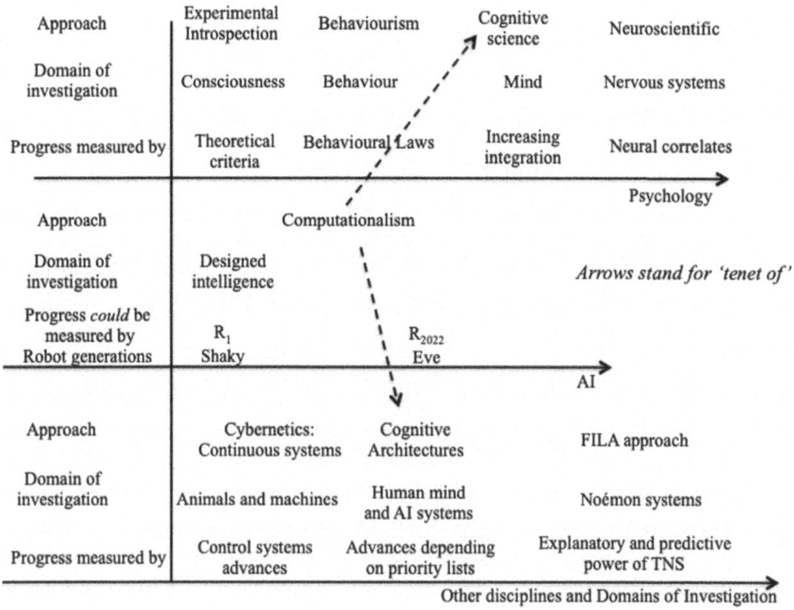

Fig. 1.1 Bird's eye view of psychology, AI, cybernetics and TNS

doctrine, but its unification seems to be receding. Finally, psychology is in the worst state of all despite some significant work to that end.

Second, each of psychology's four successive paradigms, namely, experimental introspectionism, behaviourism, computationalism, and biological reductionism, (with these last three paradigms being applicable to biological minds in general), identifies an indispensable characteristic of human minds and gives nearly exclusive prominence to it. This exclusiveness is a mistake; unification of psychology along the lines of any single of the four approaches characterising its history is inadequate. Since each paradigm identifies an indispensable characteristic of human mind, all four of them need to be combined for a unified account of it and of certain animal minds. Computationalism, being the exclusive paradigm of AI, suffers from the same inadequacy.

1.1 Brief Review of Core Disciplines of Cognitive Science

This section has a dual objective. First, to review psychology, AI, cybernetics, and neuroscience from the perspective of their constitutive notions and principles. Namely, 'mind', 'designed intelligence', 'communication' (ignored by the founders of cybernetics to its eventual demise), and the neuron doctrine (Sect. 1.1.1). Second, to provide a brief overview of unification approaches and review the AI-based foundations of cognitive science in the form of cognitive architectures (Sect. 1.1.2).

1.1.1 Review of Foundational Notions and Principles

Wilhelm Wundt (1832–1920) established psychology as a scientific discipline distinct from philosophical and literary approaches to mental phenomena. In particular, he defined psychology as "the science of immediate experience" (ibid., p. 9) with a distinct methodology. Specifically, the space of inquiry of the new science was the vast domain of consciousness (bewusstsein); the methodology he argued for and widely practiced was introspection assisted by experimentation. As he defined it, psychology is a natural science irreducible to biology.

Jointly, Wundt and William James (1842–1910) established its first paradigm until John Watson (1878–1958)—by excluding introspection as valid psychological method and focusing only on S-R sequences- transformed it into an objective, albeit quite restricted, science. Behaviourism (Watson 1913; 1924) became the dominant paradigm of psychology for at least forty years.

The so called cognitive revolution that overthrew behaviourism was gradual and started quite some time before its well-formed appearance (Neisser 1967*2014) and its establishment in the late 1970s and early 1980s. Its roots appeared in the early 1930s. Bartlett (1886–1969) introduced his notion of schema as a model for explaining both the organisation and active modification of sensory and linguistic information by humans (Bartlett 1932). Turing (1936) published his idea of universal computing machine (later to become knows as universal Turing machine). McCulloch & Pitts (1943) showed that networks of simple neuron-like units can compute any logical function. Rosenblueth et al. (1943) introduced the idea of feedback (essentially a formalised special type of homeostasis. Norbert Wiener (1948*1961) published *Cybernetics:*

or Control and Communication in the Animal and the Machine. Donald Hebb (1949) wrote his classic neurophysiological account of mind and Ross Ashby (1960) wrote the first edition of his pioneering *Design for a Brain* in 1952. Many of these and other contributors to the cognitive revolution belonged to the Cybernetics movement that in the 1970s started giving way to AI and cognitive science that were formally established in the mid 1950s and 1960s respectively. Before moving on, the following three paragraphs make certain points about cybernetics that are worthy to be kept in mind.

In the 1940s, early Cyberneticists like Warren McCulloch, Grey Walter, Ross Ashby, Rosenblueth, and Wiener thought it possible not only to create thinking machines but also to unify certain phenomena common in the study of animals and machines. It flourished for nearly four decades from its beginning in the early 1940's.

Their former objective was taken up by AI that adopted and extended most of its innovative ideas. Nevertheless, their latter aim, their unification vision, survived primarily in the form of the subtitle in Wiener's classic: *Cybernetics: or control and communication in the animal and the machine.* The study and applications of control won over the study of communication. The latter was picked up and continued to be studied by numerous, non-communicating, disciplines that used, and still use, it as a mere orienting construct (cf, Sect. 4.1). The necessity of developing a comprehensive theory of communication was simply ignored; the demise of the Cybernetic vision followed unavoidably (Gelepithis 2004 for details and related remarks). As we shall see below cognitive science adopted a more restricted unification aim.

Presently, Cybernetics has moved far away from the original aspirations of its pioneers and part of its name (i.e., Cyber) has been appropriated to become the first part of compound new names depicting the futuristic, commercial, and criminal aspects of life in the twenty-first century (cf, cyberorganism, cybercrime). What has been left of cybernetics may arguably be called a fringe exercise in pursuing obscure ideas lacking both the novelty and rigour of the pioneering ideas and methods of the field.

The above introductory remarks to the study of animals and machines only serve in highlighting some of the complexities of these physical systems. Back to our story.

The cognitive revolution proper was approaching. Around the time of the formal birth of AI in 1956, psychology started being liberated from the bonds of the behaviourist school of thought that had rejected the study of some of the most interesting of the traditional mental phenomena and linguistics started being transformed by Chomsky's (1959) scathing critique of Skinner's *Verbal Behavior*. The societal and cultural impact on mind had, unfortunately, the least impact on the cognitive revolution. Vygotsky's (1934*1986) work was virtually ignored until its second edition in 1962, and G. H. Mead's (†1934*1962) posthumous social behaviourism was not appropriately received. The work of AI-ists exemplifying and, at least indirectly, arguing for the computational approach to mind was quickly picked up by psychologists working on thinking and cognition. The ensuing call for the cognitive (or information processing) approach (Neisser 1967*2014), essentially that of AI, led to the dominance of the computational paradigm. Within psychology, information processing (equivalently cognitive) psychology became its most visible and influential area. The actual name 'cognitive science' was selected over at least two other alternatives by the Sloan Foundation in 1978 that needed a name to refer to the new interdisciplinary research programme to bridge mind and brain they were funding (Miller 2003). The program itself did not succeed but it greatly contributed to baptise and establish cognitive science as a discipline.

It was promising that each and every of the disciplines that were taken to constitute the original conception of cognitive science:

> "by historical accident, had inherited a particular way of looking at cognition and each had progressed far enough to recognise that the solution to some of its problems depended crucially on the solution of problems traditionally allocated to other disciplines." (Miller 2003, p. 143).

But despite this felt necessity, (of unifying their individual approaches) the eventual outcome was disciplinary progression and therefore failure to unify.

However, things started getting interesting. For the first time psychology and strong AI share a common paradigm: the computational approach to mind. It is useful at this point to distinguish between the two forms of the computational approach to mind and AI's design stance. Collectively, they constitute the foundational hypotheses of theoretical AI:

1. The cognitive simulation hypothesis: a computational system is capable of modelling intelligence (weak, or narrow AI).

2. The computational mind hypothesis: the human mind is a computational system (strong AI).
3. The AI constructability hypothesis: artificial general intelligence (AGI) can be realised.

It should be noted that the AI constructability hypothesis, as stated, is ambivalent. Its realisation may refer to either:

3.1 Construction by humans (the AGI hypothesis); or
3.2 Emergence without having being constructed by humans (the *own-AI* possibility).

The former hypothesis has been shown to be subject to the limits of human constructability (Gelepithis 1984; 1991). The latter eventuality does not impact on traditional psychology and therefore it will not concern us further in this chapter. However, because of its considerable discussion both within AI and the public sphere, I comprehensively discuss it in Sects. 2.2, 3.2.2, 4.3. For further discussion from the perspectives of consciousness, emotions and human nature one may respectively consider Sects. 3.3.2, 4.3.2, and 5.2.1 of the monograph's Consequences volume (Gelepithis 2024b).

The cognitive simulation hypothesis has been a reality for quite some time now. What is more important is the determining and increasing impact of AI on all aspects of human society. Already the performance of AI systems vary from higher than human in formalised cognitive domains down to considerably lower than human levels of performance in common sense domains of human conduct. An additional fact that is usually overlooked should be mentioned: there are domains of robot action that lie outside the possible range of human behaviour (e.g., robot space explorers).

In contrast, the computational mind hypothesis remains an unsubstantiated claim. Turing (1950), in his seminal paper Computing Machinery and Intelligence, dispelled a number of irrelevant objections to machine intelligence but he did not explicitly develop an argument for machine intelligence. His belief in an omnipotent programmability rather hindered fundamental discussion on the *nature* of human language, the *nature* of human-machine communication and the *nature* of machine intelligence.

Five years later the Dartmouth conjecture, concerning the AI project, was explicitly stated:

> "The study is to proceed on the basis of the conjecture that every aspect of learning or any other feature of intelligence can in principle be so precisely described that a machine can be made to simulate it." (McCarthy et al. 1955)

Turing's belief and the Dartmouth conjecture reinforced each other and papers and monographs repeating, but not providing evidence for, them started appearing with increasing pace. The mathematical foundations of AI were not cross-examined against foundational issues in the study of mind like the ones stated in the previous paragraph. These mathematical foundations pivoted around the notion of Turing machine (Turing 1936). Specifically, a Turing machine U may be defined as a machine comprising an *infinitely long* tape movable (forward and backward) through U, and U being able to read, write, and erase 'symbols' from such a tape. In sharp contrast to this mathematical notion, a computational system, C, is a system comprising a *finite* tape movable (forward and backward) through C for a *finite* interval of time, and C being able to read, write, and erase 'symbols' from such a tape. Failing to distinguish between a Turing machine and a computational system can only lead to mistakes.

Turing machines, physical symbol systems, Markov algorithms, artificial neural networks, and recursive functions are equivalent, that is, they define classes of functions which have turned out to be the same. This single class of functions has been termed the class of computable functions and the systems realising them universal computers. Can it be shown that this is the largest and only class of functions that can be possibly realised by physical systems? We do not know. Nevertheless, answering this question to the affirmative has become known as the Church-Turing thesis. It is worth adding that it is very widely believed that any 'reasonable' definition of the notion of 'algorithm' will be equivalent to those we know. If that turns out to be the case then the Church-Turing thesis will become a theorem. Finally, for the meticulous reader I should add that originally the Church- Turing thesis was referring only to the equivalence of Turing machines and effective procedures. It was later on that the other equivalencies were shown.

This valuable work provides a strong foundation for narrow AI albeit without providing any support for the strong AI claim. Actually, work on the theoretical foundations or philosophy of AI is grossly inadequate. From the early 1990s when realisation of this state of affairs was first admitted:

> "AI has virtually no tradition of the careful criticism and comparison of ideas, of sifting them for their antecedents or their coherence in a standard scholarly way, so as to extract general principles." (Partridge & Wilks 1990 p. xi).

Through a repetition of this admittance 20 years later: "[AI] still lacks a firm foundation" (Froese & Ziemke 2009, p. 474), to the 2020 Special Issue "On Defining Artificial Intelligence" of the *Journal of Artificial General Intelligence*, the situation has not improved. Actually, its very definition has been an item of hotted debate and of a variety of unsupported suggestions (Appendix-1). Wang's (2019) recent definition of AI that led to JAGI's special related issue updates Appendix-1 without modifying its conclusion, namely, no complete definition of AI has been published so far. The relevant chapter 2 definitions address this lack.

In summary, computationalism revived the study of mental states by adopting a formal, syntactic approach to human thinking that was assumed to be the universal paradigm of mentation. In other words, computationalism claimed to unify animal and machine thinking by reducing the former to the latter. But, for the identification to be valid several challenges need to be addressed by a computational theory of mind. They include:

(i) Account for the complete system of functions of the human nervous system and its subsystem of mental phenomena like consciousness, emotions, and motivation. In particular, any such complete theory of mind should be able to account for the distinction between conscious and unconscious states or processes.

(ii) Given that 'mind' is situated, the computational paradigm should be able to account for the societal influences on the former's development and evolution.

(iii) A new equivalence must be shown: the class of situated human brain/mind functions is equivalent to the class of computable functions.

The lack of progress along these requirements coupled with the increasing evidence against the computational approach to mind led cognitive science to an inevitable identity crisis of multiple origins.

The latter include: Hunt's (1989) questioning of psychology's autonomy vis a vis neuroscience; Bechtel et al.'s (1998) cautious pessimism; Cromwell & Panksepp's (2011) remark on the lack of a usable shared definition of 'cognition'; and the different perspectives on the status of cognitive science as a single science as it is clearly reflected by the the two major encyclopaedias on cognitive science (Bechtel and Graham 1998; Wilson and Keil 1999). They exemplified, respectively, the schism between those aiming for a unified science of mind (sometimes called cognitive science) and those pursuing mind research along disciplinary lines collectively known as cognitive sciences.

Gradually, the cognitive science (or information processing) approach started losing its dominant status in psychology. Currently, its place has been taken up by cognitive neuroscience. The latter's strength draws upon two sources. One, the fast- forward marching neuroscience. Two, the adoption of narrow AI's techniques. This confluence is quite useful; narrow AI techniques can help tremendously neuroscience. Nevertheless, there is also, to some degree, adoption of the computational mind hypothesis. The latter is a dead-end methodology. As Brooks remarks:

> "I believe that we are in an intellectual cul-de-sac, in which we model brains and computers on each other, and so prevent ourselves from having deep insights that would come with new models." (Brooks, 2012, p. 462).

More importantly, equating brains and computers is a gross mistake based on ignorance of facts. My briefest review below of the fundamental principles of neuroscience reveals some of that ignorance from the latter's standpoint.

Before that let me step aside for a couple of paragraphs to comment on evolutionary psychology's failed claim to dominance facing neuroscience's imposing accomplishments.

Evolutionary psychology emphasises gene-level selection, adaptations and mind modularity. In addition it adopts the computational approach to mind, seeing the latter as a set of if-then rules variously called evolved psychological mechanisms (e.g., Buss 2009), or psychological adaptations; The term cognitive modules is also used but it is a rather misleading term as it points to a limited range of psychological mechanisms. The use of the latter term is a clear indication of the influence of the basic premise of cognitive science on evolutionary psychology. This is how an award-winning textbook in evolutionary psychology describes a psychological adaptation:

> "An evolved psychological mechanism exists in the form that it does because it solved a specific problem of survival or reproduction recurrently over evolutionary history." … "An evolved psychological mechanism is designed to take in only a narrow slice of information." (Buss, 2009, p. 50).

This description of an evolved psychological mechanism is accompanied by the premise that most brain and mental processes are unconscious.

The key objective of evolutionary psychology is clearly stated by Tooby & Cosmides (2005, p. 5):

> "Evolutionary psychology is the long-forestalled scientific attempt to assemble out of the disjointed, fragmentary, and mutually contradictory human disciplines a single, logically integrated research framework for the psychological, social, and behavioral sciences—a framework that not only incorporates the evolutionary sciences on a full and equal basis, but that systematically works out all of the revisions in existing belief and research practice that such a synthesis requires".

Although this grand objective is vigorously promoted under different names, for instance, a meta theory "that can shed light on all questions of psychology" (e.g., Carmen et al. 2013), its actual results even in cognitive and cultural psychology are left wanting. Modern human mind is far away from that of the Pleistocene period. It has evolved in ways producing results that cannot be explained by evolutionary psychology. Actually, they are not even addressed. One such development is the increasing artificiality of modern humans. Evolutionary psychology's actual foundational notions are inadequate for addressing even such obvious facts—let alone in meeting its stated grand objectives. The proponents of this approach have not shown how their foundational notions would solve even a single of the major psychological issues falling outside the restricted range of selected Pleistocene problems. Let me come now to the currently imposing paradigm of cognitive neuroscience.

The rise and partial opposition of neuroscience to computationalism characterises the first quarter of the twenty-first century. With respect to psychology, its dominance is both overwhelming and comprehensible albeit hardly fully justifiable. More unexpected, although scientific fad can go some way in explaining it, is neuroscience's influence well away from psychology into economics and ethics to name but a couple of fields. Obviously, Eric Kandel's (2006, p. 264) succinct point: "genes also are servants of the environment" has not been taken into account. This point also applies to the excessive claims of neuroscience itself.

Let me focus now to probably the briefest possible review of cognitive neuroscience. For a comprehensive, book-length, review of the philosophical foundations of neuroscience see Bennett & Hacker (2003).

Presently, cognitive neuroscience is characterised by the *practicing* neuron doctrine. It consists of the following two principles:

> *Principle-1*: Neurons are the basic units of information processing, of plasticity, and cognition.
> *Principle-2*: Neurons either *excite* or *inhibit* other neurons.[2]

It should be noted that there are several different descriptions of the practicing neuron doctrine that may not be exactly equivalent to each other.[3] For instance:

> "The neuron doctrine defines nerve cells as structural, functional, developmental and trophically independent units, and the law of dynamic polarization defines the nerve cell body and dendrites as providing receptor surfaces for incoming messages, whereas the axon serves as the output of the nerve cell." (Guillery 2005, p. 1281).

The *practicing* neuron doctrine is characterised by four fundamental inadequacies:

I-1: Failure to account for new data on brain research;
I-2: Neglect of semantics;
I-3: Fragmentation; and
I-4: Confusing fundamental conceptual distinctions.
I consider them in turn.

[2] This principle is sometimes called the logic of nervous systems.

[3] Nevertheless, these principles constitute a more comprehensive statement of the neuron doctrine than any other I am aware of.

I-1: Although cognition is definitely *part of* nervous systems, what evidence- based reasons do we *currently* have to assume the neuron as the unit of cognition? From a historical perspective, the emergence of the neuron doctrine could be justified if not unavoidable. Nevertheless, currently, a growing number of experimental results indicate that:

(a) astroglia, and probably microglia too, play significant role in the processing that takes place in complex nervous systems (Giaume et al. 2010; Lallouette et al. 2014; Scemes & Giaume 2006; Rusakov & Dityatev 2014).

Such data have already led a few scientists to assert that: "Information processing in the brain results from continuous interaction of two cellular circuits: neuronal and glial." (Abbracchio et al. 2009 p. 23).

(b) "We do not know much about how this [synaptic] diversity is determined, nor what it means for the neural networks in which these synapses participate." (Sudhov & Malenka 2008, p. 471).
(c) "apart from the properties that distinguish neurons from other cells, the rules for belonging to the class of neurons under the neuron doctrine are far more rigorous than are the rules for belonging to the class of cells under the cell theory." (Guillery 2005, p. 1284).
(d) Synapses do not constitute structures between two neurones but they are tripartite, and most likely tetra-partite, structures incorporating astroglia and the ECM respectively (e.g., Navarrete et al. 2014; Dityatev & Rusakov 2011; Rusakov & Dityatev 2014).
(e) According to Guillery (2005, p. 1298): "a single nerve cell can operate as more than one distinct functional unit." Is a single functional unit equivalent to a multifunctional unit?
(f) Finally, the classical view is challenged by the fact that action potentials subject to waveform modulation as they travel down an axon (Sasaki et al 2011).

My conclusion is that the neuron doctrine concerning, at least, mental processing *of* nervous systems need to be replaced by a much wider conception. Most likely it will also necessitate asking rather unusual questions for the overall action of the human nervous system. For instance, how extrasynaptic release affects the key integrative actions of nervous systems, that is, their behaviour and disease. This difficulty is augmented not only by the multiplicity of release sources but also by both the much longer time-course (months even) and the much wider spatial distribution of the chemicals produced during extrasynaptic events.

I-2: The issue of semantic neglect has several aspects. One, semantic neglect does not consider the nature of 'information'. To start with, although 'information' is a notion with a vast literature in a number of disciplines including physics, philosophy, biology, AI, psychology, and sociology there is no widely accepted theory of 'information'. There is only the very restricted, still very useful, theory of the syntactic aspect of information (Shannon & Weaver 1949). It is useful for the designed transmission of formal (i.e., syntactic) codes but as Shannon himself noted it is inappropriate for semantic and pragmatic problems. The assumption of cognition as *syntactic* information processing goes against the accumulating evidence of biological organisms as 'meaning' manipulators (chapter 3). This syntactic theory of information along with the assumed distinction between the content of cognition and the physical substratum (inherited from the computational distinction between software and hardware) is uncritically adopted by neuroscientists.

Two, although it is unanimously assumed within computational neuroscience that organisms compute, the precise meaning of 'computation of living systems' is lacking. It is assumed that the computer science notion of 'computation' is identical to the notion of 'computation of living systems'. But the latter has not been even defined, let alone shown to be identical with 'computation'. Moreover the complexity of living systems does not permit unsubstantiated metaphors from the level of cells to that of cognition. In addition, the neural coding metaphor has been severely criticised on the grounds of incompatibility with the causal structure of the brain and semantic representation (Brette 2019). In summary, ignoring the semantic nature of animals is akin to the behaviourist prohibition of mind. Unfortunately, Brette does not account for the phenomenon of semantic representation. It is a complex issue that is thoroughly addressed in Sect. 2.2 and Chapter 3.

I-3: The third inadequacy of current cognitive neuroscience has been at least partly inherited by psychology: it is badly fragmented. Although big data and new or more elaborate techniques are necessary for its progress, their interpretation and integration require new concepts and ideas. The latter are sorely missing.

> "The ever-growing volume of big data in neuroscience demands not only advanced analytics and sound statistical inference, but it also calls for theoretical ideas that can unify our understanding of brain structure and function." (Bassett & Sporns 2017).

The lack of theoretical ideas seem to go hand in hand with a lack of a dual requirement: direction and objectives (Adolphs 2015). Actually in his brief and substantial paper he states 23 unsolved problems of neuroscience grouped in five classes. The most interesting single question posed is: "What counts as an explanation of how the brain works? (and which disciplines would be needed to provide it?) ".

I-4: Confusing fundamental conceptual distinctions is particularly pronounced with respect to the notions of dualism and monism. Let me explicate.

Cognitive neuroscience assumes, that neurophysiological mechanisms *underlie* cognition and attempts to specify them for a variety of cognitive phenomena. Since the end of the twentieth century, the most well known instance of this effort is the quest for the so called neural correlates of consciousness (NCC). The NCC quest is misguided because it essentially rests on the discarded metaphysical assumption of dualism. Mechanisms are mechanisms. They *materialise* functions; they do *not underlie* functions. It is exactly the same with mental mechanisms and functions. Mental mechanisms are NS mechanisms. NS mechanisms materialise mental functions. There is nothing new in this thesis; It is the well known mind-brain identity theory (e.g., Armstrong 1968; Bunge 1980; Feigl 1960; Place 1956; Smart 1959). It is thoroughly materialist without committing itself to a further hypothesis like the radical neuron doctrine or, worse, the dominant neural correlates approach. A broader version of the NCC approach has been argued by Searle (2007). Namely, mental processes are *caused/produced* by the firing of neurons (Searle 2007 for a brief argument). I hold that the NCC viewpoint and the broader neural correlates of mental phenomena (NCM) approach have to be recognised as misleading metaphors. See monograph's Volume Two–Consequences; chapter 3 on consciousness for detailed critical discussion (Gelepithis 2024b).

Sometimes, the mind-brain identity (MBI) hypothesis, despite being considerably supported by modern neuroscience, is derogatively called "metaphysical materialism" (e.g., Bennett & Hacker 2003). Despite their constructive and useful work just stated, baptising the MBI hypothesis "metaphysical materialism" betrays lack of a substantial argument against. For a still excellent introduction to the main variants of MBI and equally excellent discussions see Borst (1970). For some important recent work see Chalmers's (2002) collection of readings. Quite often, the MBI hypothesis is called identity theory. I will not use this alternative name because it misinterprets the notion of theory. The MBI is a hypothesis and needs theories and data to support it or point out its weaknesses.

The quest for mental mechanisms underlying NS mechanisms has no place within a materialist weltanschaaung. Mental mechanisms can only be special types of NS mechanisms. As such whenever a mental mechanism is identified or postulated we should provide empirical conditions differentiating it from *other* NS mechanisms.

Of course the latter claim presupposes acceptance of a version of the venerable tradition of reductionism or, more generally, materialism. Its earliest recorded treatment can be found in Aristotle's Posterior Analytics (4th c. BCE*1984). Biological reductionism is its most recent form. Külpe's (1893) claim for it suddenly appears justifiable. Freud's project (1895*2001) might now have looked feasible for Freud himself. The elimination of psychology is on the table. Neuroscience's potential appears all-embracing:

> "So we might well wonder whether the breakthroughs and near hegemony of current neuroscience could have the ultimate potential to assimilate the rest of psychology and, thus redefined, turn it into a traditionally linear, cumulative "hard science."" (Hunt 2005, p. 369)

Kandel, echoing Hippocrates is certain:

> "each mental function in the brain—from the simplest reflex to the most creative acts in language, music, and art—is carried out by specialized neural circuits in different regions of the brain." (Kandel 2006, p. xii).

Very few voices seem to indicate otherwise by arguing that "psychology as a science cannot survive other than as a science of behavior." (Catania 2013).

Külpe (1893) was probably the first who provided the basic work for the foundations of biological reductionism. In response to that position,

Wundt elaborated his thesis for the independence of psychology from biology on the following grounds:

(i) mental phenomena are "unapproachable by means of experiment"; (ii) there is necessity of purely psychological constructs like value, meaning, and purpose; and (iii) psychical causality is different from physical causality.

Although the first two of the constraints of Wundt's argument do not hold the weight they used to do, the third one can still hold well on the basis on neutral monism. To my knowledge the strongest case for the latter has been made by Bertrand Russell in his *The Analysis of Mind*.

The debate is still on. For a clear and substantial introduction to the issue (Brigandt & Love 2017). With the advent of imaging techniques, a tiny part of black- box psychology becomes subject to mediate experience. This factual basis enables one to claim that eventually the human mind can be described *solely* in terms of neuroscience. Gold & Stoljar (1999) named this assumption the "*radical* neuron doctrine" and argued that it is impossible. For a peer-reviewed discussion (Commentary to Gold & Stoljar 1999).

My view on this debate differs from both Külpe's and Wundt's views. I hold, contra Wundt, that human psychology cannot be independent of biology and, contra biological reductionism, human biology depends on biology, human culture, and Earthian ecology. I call this view evolutionary non-reductive materialism. It implies that both human psychology and human biology need to be re-defined in much broader terms.

In summary, current cognitive neuroscience is characterised by the following four major inadequacies that, jointly, demonstrate the inadequacy of current neuroscience for the study of mind. One, 'the neuron as unit of cognition' hypothesis is incompatible with an increasing amount of new neuroscientific data. Two, cognitive neuroscience has neglected the semantic character of biological minds. Three, current cognitive neuroscience is badly fragmented and in need of new conceptual breakthroughs. Four, barring consideration of mental mechanisms as fundamentally different from neural mechanisms, neuroscience should provide NS conditions that differentiate the mechanisms of mental phenomena from other NS mechanisms. In other words mental mechanisms are identified with a subsystem of NS mechanisms. Of course, ontological reductionism does not entail either the methodological or epistemic forms of reductionism.

I come now to this sub-section's conclusions. First, we have four types of psychological data: introspective, behavioural, neuroscientific, and simulation-based. The problem is that we have no theory to relate the huge number of these four types of apparently incompatible data. And we do not have such a theory because so far the vast majority of our attempts were characterised by a single paradigm and the very few interdisciplinary efforts focused on peripheral mental phenomena. The repeated failures of the single-paradigm approach point clearly to the need of at least disciplinary paradigm unification.

Second, all efforts to define the constitutive, or assumed constitutive, notions of psychology and AI have failed. Such notions primarily include 'mind', 'intelligence', 'cognition'. Such notions are closely related to a host of other fundamental, undefined notions. Some of them delineate *core* phenomena of both psychology and AI (Sect. 1.3).

Third, all mental phenomena, especially human ones, depend both on ontogeny and phylogeny. It follows that a theory of mind should be compatible with the extended evolutionary synthesis (Sect. 2.3.1) and, at least some of, the results that support it.

Fourth, advances in A-Life have blurred the distinction between biological and artificial minds much further. This points to the *desirability* of a radical re-definition of both psychology and AI.

Fifth, I say that although current neuroscience is demonstrably inadequate for the study of biological mind, it is possible that a future neuroscience will not need the vocabulary of individual psychology—of either the scientific or folk kind. Nevertheless, the vocabulary of any future neuroscience will keep falling short of addressing phenomena emanating from human culture, hybrid human-robot societies and, a fortiori, of *possible* societies of genuinely autonomous robots (Sect. 2.2).

Sixth, the progresses in narrow AI, neuroscience, and in the emerging hybrid field of the interface of AI and neuroscience create unprecedented phenomena and point out to the possibility of AGI or hyper-intelligence by chance *and* own robotic development.

Jointly, the last five conclusions also point to the *desirability* of developing a well defined theoretical construct that will be the constitutive notion of both psychology and AI. Sect. 1.2 makes a case for the necessity of a novel unified theoretical construct for the study of animals and robots.

1.1.2 Unification Approaches and the AI-Based Foundations of Cognitive Science

Unification of ***human*** knowledge is one of the major, and probably the most difficult, objectives set by ***human*** scientists. Its roots are traced back to the early Greek natural philosophers. Thales of Miletus argued for a simple unified description behind nature's manifest diversity and it was continued with Parmenides and Heraclitus through Demokritos and Empedocles to Plato and Aristotle. Of course the extent and depth of human knowledge has become incomparably larger than in the times of pre-Socratics and classical Greek philosophers. As a result of this growth, many disciplines and numerous areas of research within each of them have emerged. Consequently, unification of concepts and principles ranges from integration of areas within a discipline to integration of traditionally distinct disciplines. The best example of the former type of integration are the three unifications within physics: From Newton through Maxwell to Weinberg & Salaam. The most striking instance of the latter type of integration is the very limited still useful integration achieved by cybernetics.

Recently, a call for the synthesis of all human knowledge, that is, unification of the so called hard and soft sciences, has come from Wilson (1998 and 2014). A less general, but still very broad, framework proposal for the unification of economy, psychology, anthropology, biology, sociology, and political science is that of Gintis (2007). Both proposals have not produced any discernible results.

At the discipline level, the oldest calls for unification are those in philosophy (e.g., Boole 1854*1958; Putnam 2004) and sociology (e.g., Parsons 1937; Baldwin 1986). Nevertheless, the most interesting development, from the perspective of this book, emanates from biologists favouring integration of several new fields like genomics, developmental biology, multilevel selection, niche reciprocity, and inclusive inheritance with the standard evolutionary synthesis of the 1940s into a new paradigm. Of course the gradual (no pun intended) replacement of the latter by an extended evolutionary synthesis is a research programme in progress (e.g., Gould 1980; Laland et al. 2015; Pigliussi & Müller 2010;) and in debate (e.g., Laland et al. 2014; Noble 2015) with extant proponents (e.g., Wray et al. 2014) of the modern synthesis (e.g., Huxley 1942*1974). Progress in advancing a cumulative extended evolutionary synthesis (see

Sect. 2.3.1) is in sharp contrast to the micro-theory proliferation characterising psychology. More importantly, the recognition of the necessity to incorporate cultural, developmental, and inclusive inheritance elements in evolution will positively enhance existing, and create new, links between biology and psychology. Let me now briefly introduce the debate on the possibility of unifying psychology and indeed whether psychology is a science.

From its inception as a distinct scientific discipline, psychology was plagued by the question of its status. In Sect. 1.1 we saw the origin of this debate in the positions of Wundt and Külpe. A few years later, James' concluding remark in his *Psychology—Briefer Course* is most revealing:

> "A string of raw facts; a little gossip and wrangle about opinions; a little classification and generalization on the mere descriptive level; a strong prejudice that we *have* states of mind, but not a single law in the sense that physics shows us laws, not a single proposition from which any consequence causally can be deduced. We don't even know the terms between which the elementary laws would obtain if we had them. ... This is no science, it is only the hope of a science." (James 1892, p. 468).

It should be noted that apart from lamenting psychology's state, James equally clearly stated one of the key requirements of psychology as a mature science (then called simply science), namely, laws. I will return to this point in Sect. 1.3 Compare also Table 1.1 in that section.

By now the debate has moved away from the scientific status of psychology to the possibility of its unification. James' indirect call for the latter was not addressed. Actually, psychology's fragmentation kept getting worse by the emergence of new disciplines studying mind in an ever increasing number of specialised topic areas, using an ever increasing number of tools, and producing an ever increasing amount of diverse data and micro-theories. The result is a morass of experimental, observational, and clinical data as well as thousands of associated micro theories that are hardly related in any fundamental way. A revealing example in the form of a question is provided by Sutton (2004). After listing 22 fields that deal with phenomena under the label of 'memory' he raises the question: to what extent workers in these fields study the same phenomena? In addition, although researchers quite often pursue similar questions, lack of crosstalk among them results into duplication of efforts and loss of exchanging valuable disciplinary insights concerning common phenomena and key concepts. This state of the art constitutes one more major stumbling block in the development of psychology as a mature science. We need to remove this major impediment too. I address it in Sect. 1.3 under the third of the criteria (C-3) that a mature, unified theory of mind should fulfil.

Before continuing with my outline of unification efforts, it will be useful to clearly distinguish between work on the foundations of cognitive science and research on the unification of psychology. In practice, the two expressions refer to studies that can overlap albeit they are usually distinct and, in the latter case, they may interact. The following three paragraphs illustrate the distinctions.

Two of the earliest studies on the foundations of cognitive science were by Pylyshyn (1984) and Simon & Kaplan (1988). Both should be seen as attempts to state some of the fundamental assumption of the field. In particular, the latter is only of historical interest for their views on (computational) intelligence and specifically their belief of a single set of mechanisms that could explain the diverse set of behavioural activities that common sense takes to come under the name 'intelligence'. The former is an in-depth discussion of some of the themes of cognitive science under the assumption that 'cognition' is a natural domain like those of chemistry and biology. The notion of 'natural domain' is understood by Pylyshyn as a domain for which

> "it is possible to develop theories based on a special vocabulary or reasonably uniform set of principles independent of the principles of other sciences—that is, principles with considerable autonomy". (ibid. p. xi).

Although I entirely agree with the above thesis (see Sect. 1.3, criterion C-3), I strongly disagree with the suggestion that 'cognition' constitutes a natural domain. The only definite such domain is *H. sapiens*. Even individuals of a species cannot constitute natural domains as their inescapable individuality captures only part of the nature of the species they belong.

My second work type (Branquinho 2001) is a collection of thirteen essays that clearly reflect three things: (i) the crisis in cognitive science or sciences as I have already pointed out in Sect. 1.1; (ii) the emergence of the situated approach; and (iii) the trend toward fragmentation rather than unification in cognitive science. Collectively, this set of readings provides interesting and illuminating discussions on specific topics of the science of mind that far exceed the narrow confines of cognitive science—barring of course a redefinition of the content and methodology of it. Such topics include the relation of cognition (identified with intelligence) to life (Boden 2001); Open issues in how brains represent space (Farber et al. 2001); Reviewing well-known theses of perennial problems like the referential theory of meaning (Higginbotham 2001). The specifically cited work has been almost exclusively selected because they represent instances of studies from the following three relational areas respectively: mind to the world; mind to brain; and mind to language.

My third choice are two recent textbooks on the foundations of cognitive science (Dawson 2013; Leahey 2022). I selected them because they are both a useful addition to the textbook series on cognitive science and they demonstrate the stagnation of the field with respect to new ideas. For instance, Dawson builds his textbook around three so called types of cognitive science, namely, symbolic, connectionist, and embodied that study three supposedly distinct conceptions of mind as a "physical symbol system", "information processor but not as digital computer", "and controller of action" correspondingly.

Let me return now to the research for the unification of psychology. It is interesting that although the case for its unification has been convincingly and repeatedly made (cf., Staats 1981, 1999; Newell 1990; Kimble 1994; Sternberg & Grigorenko 2001 (despite warning for the existence of many, competing 'paradigms'); Henriques 2008; Cleeremans 2010; Grilner 2014—about neuroscience overall, not specifically for the neuroscientific perspective of psychology), several opposing viewpoints have also been aired (e.g., Koch 1981: inherent disunity of the field to be accepted as a fundamental constraint; Kukla 1992: goal of unification is questionable; Hunt 2005: Psychology's fragmentation and hyperspecialization can be understood in terms of its self-referential basis). Eventually, the debate faded away due, to a significant degree, to Newell's *Unified Theories of Cognition* that also codified the then assumed foundations of cognitive science, established the cognitive architectures approach to unification and urged multiple theories of cognition as candidates of psychology's unification.

Newell's book is based on his William James Lectures delivered in the Spring of 1987 at Harvard University. On accepting delivery of those lectures he set himself the task of "urg[ing] on psychology unified theories of cognition". Explicitly stated:

> "Psychology has arrived at the possibility of unified theories of cognition–theories that gain their power by positing a single system of mechanisms that operate together to produce the full range of human cognition.
> I do not say they are here. But they are within reach and we should strive to attain them." (Newell 1990, p. 1, and p. 508).

Newell, following the rather standard practice of that period, uses the term cognition as coextensive with mind. This is evident from the way he specifies the eventual contents of *a* unified theory of cognition (ibid. pp. 15–17). Nevertheless, I see no reason for conflating these two notion; I will use 'cognition' to refer to a small, as yet unidentified, part of 'mind'. The latter term is defined in Sect. 2.1.

Newell's monograph provided an excellent service to the scientific community in three respects. First, he developed a convincing argument for both the urgent need and the advantages of developing unified theorie*s* of cognition (UTsC). Second, he reviewed, what the dominant belief of the community considered to be, the foundational notions of cognitive science from the perspective of AI. One may not agree with Newell's set of foundational concepts but he has to agree with his emphasis on specifying and defining the set of concepts he considered to be foundational for cognitive science. Finally, he presented a very interesting and detailed theory, (viewing mind as the control system of an organism or artificially intelligent entity), that illustrated the feasibility of his argument. The theory, called Soar, is in the form of a cognitive architecture and Newell insisted that UTsC should be formulated in terms of architectures.

These positive contributions should be counterbalanced with the following two inadequacies of his approach. One, he put two much emphasis on the AI perspective, especially in the form of cognitive architectures. Two, he urged for as many UTsC as possible and that goes against the very idea of a genuine unification. It actually weakened the call for a genuine cumulative unification of psychology. (Below, in our discussion of Newell's overall approach we will understand his reasons for this choice).

To a large extent in response to his book the relevant cognitive science community moved along two distinct pathways of research action.

The first one, kept only the multiple cognitive architectures suggestion and flourished in terms of numbers. Indicatively, Kotseruba & Tsotsos (2020) in their technical survey of 84 cognitive architectures state that their estimated number is approximately three hundred, of which at least one-third of their associated projects are active. The technical cause for this mushrooming was partly due to one of Newell's working hypotheses. Specifically, Newell proposed the Physical Symbol Systems Hypothesis (PSSH) as a law of qualitative structure, and the knowledge level as a working hypothesis. The addition of the latter as the top level of the usual computer architecture, (built from the electron level up to the programming one), made the notion of cognitive architecture even more attractive. Despite the fact that Newell gave an answer to what should count as a unified theory, researchers used their own criteria (in accordance with Newell's suggestion for multiple unified theories) without any regard for comparison except for work done or theories developed within their own narrow domain.

For instance, at quite a specialised level, we have theories that integrate issues within a single phenomenon like reading by Sadosky & Paivio (2007) that followed a harbinger on this type of unification (Just & Carpenter 1987); and thought (e.g., Davidson 2001). The necessity for a cumulative unified theory of mind was de facto ignored. In other words, the emperor of fragmentation simply changed his clothes.

The second pathway was that that Newell himself, his collaborators, and earlier harbingers of unified theories followed. In our age of fast food and quick profit, it comes as no surprise that it had a few new adherents. The major recent such programmes are four (see Gelepithis 1999 for review of earlier programmes including Edelman's theory of neuronal group selection and Arkin's AuRA).

One of the strongest and earliest candidates within the cognitive architectures approach that is still under development has come to be known as the ACT-R theory of human cognition. It started off as a semantic memory model (Anderson & Bower 1973) and went through several transformations from stressing the UTC approach (Anderson 1983), through the adaptive and rational elements of human thought (Anderson 1990 and 1993 respectively), to investigating the neural plausibility of ACT-R (Anderson et al. 2004). Dancy et al. (2015) provide an extension of ACT-R.

More recently the CLARION and Sigma architectures have been proposed. The former (Sun 2002, 2016) is promoted as a UTC but frankly I cannot see this claim coming anywhere near either Soar or ACT-R especially in terms of its associated theoretical foundations. Although it does account for several psychological data in the form of tasks like the

Tower of Hanoi and the process control, it is greatly wanting in explaining fundamental mental phenomena.

The Sigma proposal (Rosenbloom 2013) sounds more impressive but it is even less developed. More damaging is the fact that it is proposed as a grant unified architecture in contrast to mere UTsC as envisioned by Newell (1990). Rosenbloom of all people should have been more careful in making such comparisons (ibid. p. 4). Newell's proposal was aiming exactly to what Rosenbloom calls grant unified architecture. The former, in sharp contrast to the latter, was acutely aware of the huge problems ahead and discussed them in relative detail.

I would like to end these brief comments on UTsC by saying a few words about Soar's development and a new collaborative initiative. Since 1990 Soar has been augmented in terms of its scope (e.g., Laird 2012) but not strengthened in terms of its foundations. More recently Laird et al. (2017) aimed to bring together the Soar, ACT-R, and Sigma architectures into a simple overall architecture that "reflects a significant point of convergence, consensus, and progress" (ibid. p. 23). Their overall objective:

> "is to begin the process of engaging the international research community in developing what can be called a standard model of the mind, where the mind we have in mind here is humanlike." (ibid. p. 14).

This is a laudable aim. The three programmes singled out for initial collaboration are, in my opinion, the strongest ones and the call for the wider community to join forces is highly commendable. My only critical point is that the sought consensus seems to be destined to be on the foundations already described by Newell (1990) with no suggestions for any further elaboration or extension of those foundations. It would be a pity if the programme was limited only to technical advances. Conceptual advances we need more.

Despite its dominance, the cognitive architectures approach to the unification of psychology is not the only game in town. It will therefore be fair to at least mention illustrative cases of alternative conceptions for the unification of the science of mind.

Such conceptions vary remarkably producing a bewildering variety of theories, frameworks, and meta-frameworks vying for attention. They all are useful in one way or another and their aims make it impossible to classify them. For instance: Hagoort (2005) presents a framework for connecting psycholinguistic models to a neurobiological account of language and names processes like syntactic combinations unification. Lieder & Griffiths (2019) on human rationality; Petocz & Mackay (2013) philosophical framework of situational realism; Lickliter & Honeycutt's (2013) metatheoretical assumptions aiming to integrate the study of developmental and evolutionary mechanisms; Clark's (2013) argument for the predictive coding framework; Kimble's (1994) behavioural approach; Langton's (1995) A-Life conception; Freeman's (1999) brain-inspired non-linear dynamics; Sternberg & Grigorenko (2001) urge the use of many methodologies for studying a single phenomenon; Henriques (2003, 2011) presentation of a theory of 'knowledge'; Eliasmith (2013) semantic pointer architecture; Petersen & Sporns (2015) argue for cognitive architectures as networks of networks; Butz (2016) proposed "a path toward a sub-symbolic computational theory of cognition"; and Ceruti & Damiano's (2018) rather tenuous genealogy of embodied condition.

Such a variety may remind one of Marsh & Boag's (2014, p. 49) remark:

> "individual theorists seeking to court others to their frameworks with promises of comprehensive singular unified theories."

As it should have become obvious from the above brief outline, Newell's work on the foundations of cognitive science was far from being the only one. Nevertheless, it was the only one that dealt, in a comprehensive and systematic way, with all of the presumably foundational notions of cognitive science interpreted and defined on the basis of the *then* dominant paradigm of AI. Therefore, a review of these notions is necessary as, jointly, they set an important milestone in the quest for the unification of psychology and AI, that is of course part of the wider objective of a unified science of Homo.

The rest of this section provides a brief critical review of the AI-based foundations of cognitive science.

Newell as I remarked earlier reviewed and extended the dominant conceptual foundations of cognitive science. Let me briefly outline below a critical review of these foundations. They are based on the following twelve "key terms that lie at the foundation of cognitive science": behaving and knowledge systems, representation, machines and computation, symbols, architectures, intelligence, search and problem spaces, preparation and deliberation. Of these, three characterise his view for a unified theory of mind: knowledge systems, symbols, and architecture. The rest are either derived ones like 'intelligence', or well known ones like 'machines' and 'computation'. Taken together they constitute the basis of all work on cognitive architectures and, more widely, of the second level of theoretical foundations of at least symbolic AI. Below I review these three foundational concepts starting with the notion of 'knowledge'.

The idea that intelligent systems are made of multiple system levels is central to Newell's work on the development of unified theories of cognition. Within such a hierarchy of system levels the knowledge level is considered to be just another level without any philosophical or foundational significance. At the same time it is claimed that a description of the human being in terms of a knowledge (level) system is particularly important (Newell 1992, p. 426), and the proposed knowledge-level systems theory is indeed a theory of knowledge (Newell 1990, 1992).

So, what is a knowledge level system? I doubt if I can summarise this notion better than Newell himself, so here it is:

> "A knowledge system is embedded in an external environment, with which it interacts by a set of possible actions. The behavior of the system is the sequence of actions taken in the environment over time. The system has goals about how the environment should be. Internally, the system processes a medium, called knowledge. Its body of knowledge is about its environment, its goals, its actions, and the relations between them. It has a single law of behavior: the system takes actions to attain its goals, using all the knowledge that it has." (Newell 1990 p. 50).

The key term in the above passage is of course knowledge so we need to be as clear as possible about its meaning. Newell accepts that the analysis of knowledge has a long philosophical history but he is rather dismissive of the contribution of philosophers to this notion at least as far as AI is concerned. His claim is that cognitive science at large, and AI in particular, requires

> "a concept of knowledge that is used simply to describe and predict the response functions of a system." (ibid. p 46).[4]

[4] A response function (of an organism) is defined to be any function (in the mathematical sense) whose domain is the environment's stimuli, and range the organisms' actions. (Newell 1990 p. 43).

His proposal follows exclusively from the AI *practice* and dismisses the traditional philosophical view. As he remarks, with an extraordinary modesty, his contribution consists of having observed the standard way of using knowledge systems in computer science and artificial intelligence and having made it explicit (Newell 1990, p. 51). Specifically:

> "what is here called *knowledge* is called *belief* by the philosophers, who reserve *knowledge* for something akin to *justified true belief*." (ibid. p. 53).

So, 'knowledge' is essentially identified with belief. But then one can hardly see any reason for talking about knowledge level systems. Such a usage can only cause confusion without offering anything in return and should therefore be avoided. Of course, 'knowledge' can be, and is being, used in Newell's sense, that is, as a new technical term. In other words, knowledge is characterised as the medium of a system level. In this case, though, it is not true anymore that Kn (i.e., knowledge according to Newell), is the same as belief. For, beliefs are characterised by their semantic content and Kn is devoid of meaning. The latter feature leads one to avoid addressing some of the most fundamental issues in both the theory of knowledge and the study of knowledge representation in AI (its most fundamental and notoriously difficult area).

In summary, Newell's theory of knowledge has two significant drawbacks. The first, is that his support for his definition of knowledge is *solely* based on the fact that it is *exclusively* derived from the AI practice. Although I am quite happy to go along with Newell on the merits of the AI practice and even accept that it is an indispensable knowledge source in the quest for the nature of (human and machine) knowledge, the AI conception of knowledge as belief without semantic concept is mistaken. Second, Newell's definition of 'knowledge' is *externally* inconsistent, that is, it is inconsistent with the homologous results of the other disciplines concerned with knowledge. What we do need is to *integrate* the practice of *all* the disciplines concerned with 'knowledge'. The third inadequacy concerns his principle of rationality, that is, the single law of behaviour of a knowledge level system. In a nutshell, the proposed principle is too restricted, not allowing, for example, processes like curiosity.

Let me now come to the notion of symbol as it is used in AI. It is closely linked to 'knowledge' as defined above and fundamentally related to one of the versions of a universal computational system (Sect. 1.1). This version and, fundamental hypothesis of explicit AI, is the ***physical symbol system hypothesis***. This assumption was originally introduced in 1976:

> "A physical symbol system has the necessary and sufficient means for general intelligent action." (Newell and Simon 1976, p. 116).

Where a physical symbol system (or, simply, a symbol system) is a system composed of a memory and operations, and characterised by the properties of sufficiency and completeness (Newell 1990, pp. 76–77).

In particular, the memory of a symbol system consists of structures containing symbol tokens which are modifiable at some level of granularity. Operations are the means for composing memory structures from other memory structures. Some of the memory structures are called programs and determine the modifiability of specific memory structures. Sufficiency simply refers to the sufficiency of memory (and consequently of the symbols it is composed of). Completeness refers to two distinct requirements. First, a requirement referred to as complete composability, "the operators must make it possible to construct any symbol structure". Second, a requirement referred to as complete interpretability, "symbol structures must be possible that determine any arrangement of operation actions and the interpretation processes [i.e., the processes of applying the operators] must be able to evoke the operations given the symbol structures." Finally, and most importantly, a symbol is defined as a pattern that provides access to distal structures.

Newell's point of departure is the physical law according to which processing is always local (for otherwise there would be action at a distance). It follows that anything involved in a processing task should be local too regardless of the complexity or simplicity of the task at hand. The important thing to remember is that the required structure, let us call it structure-acquisition, is an internal operation happening in the internal memory of the system. Therefore, the key question needed to be answered convincingly is: How does a symbol represent something external? As Newell put it:

> "How does it ever happen that a symbol actually *refers to* or *denotes* or *designates* or *stands for* or is *about* something outside the system itself?" (Newell 1990, p. 78).

For Newell the answer is straightforward. Symbol systems realise knowledge systems. Such realisation is possible through the implementation of what Newell calls *The representation law*. Namely:

> "decode[encode(T)(encode(X))] = T(X) where X is the original external situation and T is the external transformation". (ibid. p 59).

It should be noted that encoding is meant to be seen as creating internal situations and transformations from the 'corresponding' external ones, and decoding is meant to be seen as creating an external situation from an internal one. In other words, 'encoding' and 'decoding' are assumed to be inverse functions of each other. This relation is subsequently assumed, without further support, to capture the essence of representation (Newell 1990 p. 59; and 1992 p. 426).

This brings us back to the notion of knowledge. For, since "[k]nowledge is about its domain which is external to the system being characterised.", symbol systems are about things outside the system itself. Straightforward-sounding indeed. Still, all the inadequacies characterising Newell's conception of knowledge are carried through to his notion of symbol. It should be noted that a view, variously known as situated action, situation cognition, or situativity theory, has also challenged the symbol system hypothesis. Situated action emphasises the role of the situations in which intelligent entities find themselves and hence the role of the context and the social and cultural setting.

I come now to the notion of 'architecture'. Its pivotal importance stems from the fact that it is the chosen vehicle for the formulation of unified theories. It is defined in terms of a symbol system, namely, an architecture "is the description of the system in whatever system-description scheme exists next below the symbol level." (ibid., p. 81).

Drawing upon the standard computer architecture ranging from the medium of electrons through bits to programs, Newell added the knowledge level on top of this in order to address the problem of meaning (although the word is nearly an unbroken taboo in AI). As we saw he used knowledge to bypass 'meaning' and claimed equivalence of knowledge system to the Dennett's (1978, 1988) intentional system. It has to be kept in mind that an architecture is a relatively slowly changing structure.

The human cognitive architecture closely parallels the above-described computer architecture. It is actually conceived to be made of several bands, each consisting of usually three levels. For instance, the cognitive band is taken to consist of either three (Newell 1990, p. 122) or four levels (ibid. p. 140). Nevertheless, the essential point is the claim "that humans are symbol systems that are at least modest approximations of knowledge systems." (ibid. p. 113).

Newell is well aware of some of the difficulties of this conception. For instance the amazing plasticity of the human nervous system and the essentially formal nature of the proposed architecture. Still paradigms are powerful and the computational approach to mind is still ongoing despite the rise of cognitive neuroscience. One probably has to say *because* of the current prominence of the latter (Sect. 1.1). A clear example of aiming to retain both the traditional, symbolic-AI, notion of mind and the neuroscience of brain is the integrated connectionist/symbolic architecture of Smolenski & Legendre (2006). It is an impressive piece of work within the realm of cognitive architectures but without a contribution onto the theoretical foundations of cognitive science.

In summary: First, unified theories of cognition cast in terms of computational architectures (whether symbolic, connectionist or hybrid) cannot address fundamental phenomena like meaning, communication, consciousness, and emotion. By and large they also cannot address more complex psychological and social phenomena presupposing the aforementioned ones. Furthermore, to develop a cumulative theory of 'mind' (i.e., the evolutionary continuum of biological and artificial minds), we need to specify criteria that fulfil both established criteria of theory evaluation and specific criteria reflecting the requirements of our object of investigation. Second, although formal approaches like cognitive architectures do have several advantages they also restrict their user by their formalism. In the study of mind our knowledge concerning phenomena like the ones stated above are not yet suitable for formal approaches. We need alternative ones. Section 1.3 addresses both of the above two critical points.

1.2 Necessity For a New, Common, Constitutive Notion: Noémon System

This section identifies some of the characteristics of the evolving space of biological and artificial systems, argues for the necessity of a well defined theoretical construct to replace the ill-conceived and un-defined constitutive notions of the disciplines studying animals and robots, proposes such a theoretical construct: 'noémon system', and spells out its crucial relationship to the TNS.

In the history of the study of 'mind', and for periods of varied length, certain clusters of mental phenomena have been conceptualised as coextensive with it. The major such clusters come under the names of 'consciousness', 'intelligence', and 'cognition'. In all cases their corresponding constitutive terms had not been defined in any widely accepted way. Such usage is misleading and will be pointed out and justified whenever it is encountered.

The earliest biological 'mind' may turn out to be part of the domain of Bacteria (e.g., Majumdar & Pal 2017) and possibly Archaea (e.g., Charlesworth et al. 2017). Nevertheless, supporting this claim through the notion of 'communication' as horizontal transfer of genetic material (e.g., Soucy & Cogarten 2017) weakens the case for an Archaea mind (see also chapter 4). If we are looking for certainty, biologically-intelligent systems appeared at least half a billion years ago. Much later, certain social species started developing aspects of artificiality to the extent of becoming keystone species (e.g., the Castor genus). Still until the 1940s, although we kept discovering new types of BISs, our progress with respect to the construction of artificially-intelligent systems was limited to philosophical and fictional investigations. It is with the advent of early Cyberneticists that the monopoly of biological minds started being questioned and extremely simple devices claiming rudimentary intelligence appeared. AI, Cybernetics' successor, gradually made artificially-intelligent systems the commonplace they are today.[5] Thinking started being exhibited by AI systems albeit not with characteristics identical to those of biological thinking (see Sect. 3.2.2).

[5] The two major approaches of AI, namely symbolic and connectionist, are based on two of the innovative ideas of early Cyberneticians concerning the building of thinking machines. The former is based on ideas concerning symbol processing (e.g., Shannon 1950), the latter on artificial neural networks (e.g., McCulloch & Pitts 1943).

Let me introduce certain major elements of comparison between biological and artificial 'minds' (actually BISs and AISs). First, for more than 20 years now, the performance of an increasing number of AI systems exceeds that of humans in a good number of domains in the range of behavioural and mental phenomena. In addition, the gap between humans and AI systems, in terms of both performance and range of phenomena exhibited, keeps shrinking in both dimensions (Fig. 1.2).

I had to distinguish between autonomy and human-designed autonomy because of the possibility of a true robot autonomy (see Sect. 2. 2). I should also note that both types of autonomy bring in the issue of consciousness that is fully covered in chapter 3 of the Consequences volume of this monograph (Gelepithis 2024b).

The following few examples provide an indication of the steadily diminishing gap between humans and machines in the case the gap is still in favour of the humans and simultaneously of the increasing gap in

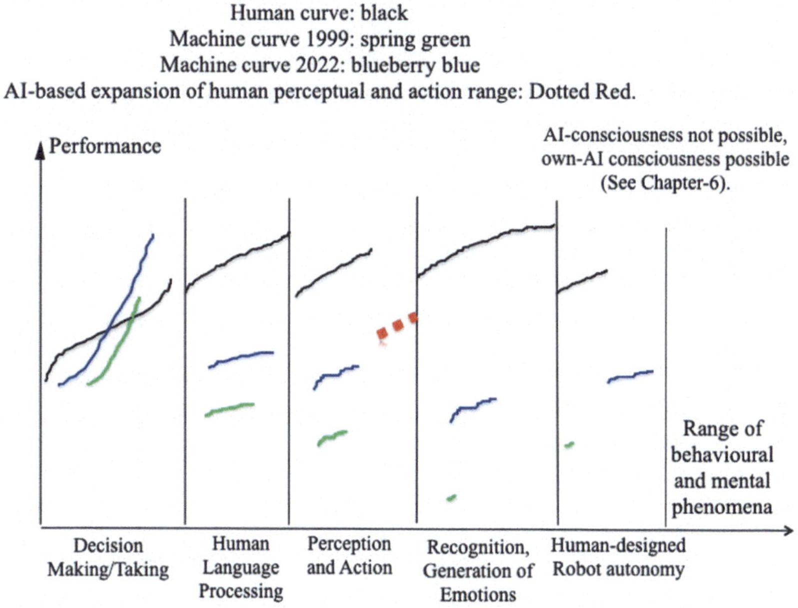

Fig. 1.2 A 2022 comparison of historic humans and AI systems (based on Gelepithis 1999c, 2001). See also text.

the case machines have already exceeded human performance. The reader should notice the red machine curve falling outside the range of human behaviour in the perception and action domain. It corresponds to AIS and robot behaviour with no human counterpart.

Mirhoseinir et al. (2021) developed an AIS that compares favourably against human designers along all key metrics in designing the physical layout of a computer chip (chip floor planning). As an indication the time was smashed from several months of intense effort to less than six hours. In "a large survey of machine learning researchers on their beliefs about progress in AI" (Grace et al. 2018), it was predicted the automation of all human jobs within 120 years with Asian respondents to expect it considerably earlier. Finally, a key finding of the survey (ibid., p. 733) was the thesis that "[S]ociety should prioritize research aimed at minimizing the potential risks of AI." This is repetition of an old call—still it is welcome.

The second element of comparison concerns the classification of biological and artificial minds in terms of the following *apparent* characteristics: (i) living; (ii) individual system; (iii) artificial and (iv) collective system. They determine four quadrants (Fig. 1.3 depicts them, with examples). Because I will repeatedly refer to the space determined by these four dimensions I will use S as an abbreviation. For reasons that shall be clear after my fifth comparative point below, I name S the space of noémon systems.

Brief comments on some of the intelligent systems of S will clarify comparisons and point to the evolving character of S to be discussed in the next two elements of comparison. Let me start with some examples from the domain of individuals (quadrants 1 and 4). I single out two instances. First, Shakey (Raphael 1976) instantiating the first generation of robots (in the sense introduced in the introduction to this chapter, Fig. 1.1). The second refers to individuals of the common octopus (Octopus vulgaris). They possess nervous systems with approximately 500,000,000 neurons most of which are found in their tentacles and their behavioural repertoire is tantalising (Godfrey-Smith 2017 and references cited there).

Moving to the domain of complex systems (quadrants 2 and 3). Animal species with an artificial component abound: From the well known case of a termite colony, to tool-using species of crow (Rutz et al. 2016); chimpanzees using sharpened sticks for hunting (Mannu & Ottoni 2009); tool use by wrasses (Bernardi 2012); and cultural transmission of tool use by dolphins (Krutzen et al. 2014). Complex AI systems like robot swarms

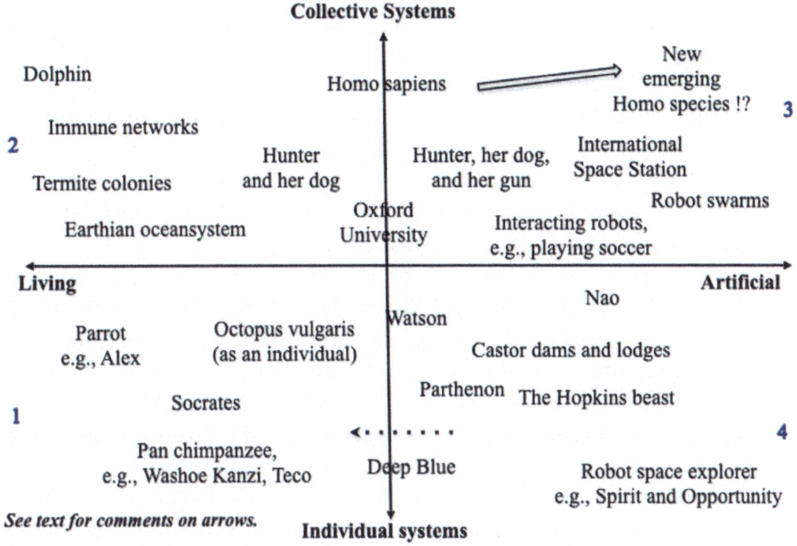

Fig. 1.3 Examples of noémon systems (*revised from Gelepithis 2001, σ. 20*).

and soccer teams make slow but steady progress. Recently the notion of liquid brains has started being investigated (e.g., Solé et al. 2019). An interesting example of intelligent species without artificial components are dogs who form lasting biologically hybrid systems (e.g., a hunter and her dog).

This example brings me naturally back to the 4th quadrant. A simple and usually effective bio-artificially hybrid system is a hunter his dog and his gun. Within the same quadrant, the most complex hybrid system is, currently, the International Space Station. It involves individuals from the class of noémon species, the class of robots, and the class of tools contributing to qualitative changes. I should add here a substantial difference between members of quadrants 1, 2, and 3 on one hand and members of quadrant 4. The former are characterised by autonomy whereas the latter does not. Is should of course be also noted that certain members of 4 (e.g., the Spirit robot explorer) does exhibit a limited form of human-derived autonomy.

The third element of comparison is related to the evolution of S that is characterised by two interacting parameters. The slow and random biological evolution and the fast and designed artificial evolution (currently and primarily, the artificiality of historic humans and their products). The latter can easily be seen in the accelerating increase of the number and diversity of artificial systems and in particular of artificially-intelligent systems. In the year 1000 CE there were no AI systems around although there were of course simpler human organisations and plenty of artificial systems like houses, bridges, and beehives. In the year 2024, S is substantially different (cf, Fig. 1.3 again).

Presently, the most significant subspace, for the future course of both human society and the *evolving* S, is that of human-robot systems. The cause of its accelerating growth and evolution is the confluence of several research and development programmes of planetary significance. They include: facing climate change; biotechnology; space exploration; the socially-determining advance of narrow AI and the quest for AGI; and the study of the human mind/brain. The steady increase of AI and hybrid systems (e..g., Kaufman et al. 2020) is poised, eventually, to overcome in number, sophistication, and significance non-hybrid ones. All five programmes stated above are interrelated in quite interesting ways and this is something we need to take seriously in consideration as a society for the future of our species and, in particular, *for the betterment of the lives of all of us*. Presently, we do not despite the fact that humanity is at crossroads. For a discussion, the reader may consider the companion volume of this book (Gelepithis 2024b).

The fourth element of comparison is both factually-based and speculative. Taking the first human heart transplant in December 1967 as an indicative reference point, *Homo sapiens* increasingly and significantly enhance the capabilities of individual members of our species (e.g., Bess 2008; Kaku 2014; Gu et al. 2020). The issue of human enhancement is one of the new problems characterising large parts of the evolving and expanding space of biological and artificial minds. In particular, the boundary between enhancement and medical treatment is rather arbitrary and the corresponding risks similar. This invites attention and calls for examining the need for regulation; models for regulation started appearing (e.g., Boden et al. 2011*2017; Maslen et al. 2014).

How far in the future does modification of our own species to a new species of *Homo* lie? Joint advances in biotechnology and AI already produce significant individual modifications. Gerald Edelman (1992, p. xiii) wrote by considering only part of the forthcoming revolution:

> "We are at the beginning of the neuroscientific revolution. At its end, we shall know how the mind works, what governs our nature, and how we know the world. Indeed, what is now going on neuroscience may be looked at as a prelude to the largest possible scientific revolution, one with inevitable and important social consequences."

He saw only part of what is coming. The systemic impact from the combination of AI and neuroscience is far greater than the sum of their individual impacts.

My fifth and final point is indicated by the dotted arrow in Fig. 1.3. It stands for the possibility of the artificial becoming living (or/and the living becoming artificial), thus conflating their distinction. The suggested possibility is not a contradiction in terms, neither does it require a breath of god. We do not have a widely accepted definition of life. Nonetheless, if an AGI society materialised and no other distinction apart from the potentially different types of elementary particles involved in each of the human and robot constitution could be identified, the living and artificial dimensions would become obsolete.

I take the above stated comparative points to constitute adequate basis for naming S the evolutionary continuum of biological and artificial minds.

So far in this chapter I have established the inadequacy of any single paradigm of psychology and AI for the scientific study of mind, the need for unifying at least these two disciplines, the lack of definition of their constitutive (and assumed as constitutive) notions, and the evolutionary continuum of biological and artificial minds. From these results, a methodological question arises: Should the common constitutive notion of 'mind' continue to be used even only as an orienting construct?

Apart from its fundamental inadequacy of not having being defined, the notion of 'mind' and closely related terms like 'mental' and 'mind possessing' are quite often misleading. They are deeply rooted in religion and associated idealist and dualist philosophies and keep alive mistaken belief systems. They are so deeply ingrained in most societies that they creep even into materialist accounts negatively affecting the study of intelligent behaviour and of the systems (e.g., nervous systems) producing it. In the words of Zeman (2008, p. 183):

> "'Mind', 'soul', 'consciousness' are not scientific terms, and lack technical definition. Our understanding of them is powerfully influenced by religious

> and philosophical traditions. So there is an inevitable risk of a disconnection here between scientific enquiry and everyday thought."

Equally unsuitable, for different reasons, are the notions of 'intelligence', and 'cognition'. In summary, all three of these notions, 'intelligence', 'mind, 'cognition' lack characterisation of their nature across their vast literatures and they are all burdened with misleading connotations.

On this factual basis, it becomes highly desirable to have a brand new technical term defining the entities of S. Furthermore, to avoid as far as possible any unintended negative connotations, such a theoretical construct should not be in *current* use in english. To this end I adopt the adjective 'noémon' in conjunction with the notion of system, namely, 'noémon system'.[6] Naturally, to be of any value, this term should be, and is, the constitutive notion of the TNS. In other words, a complete definition of 'noémon system' will constitute a theory of biological and artificial minds. It follows that, methodologically, one may start from an overall conception for a theory of minds in terms of 'noémon system' and proceed with fleshing out such a 'root-conception' until only primitive terms and axioms are used in her description.

My proposed 'root-conception' for a unified theory of psychology and AI is the following:

> **Root-Conception** (equivalently, **Definition-1**): Noémon system (NoS), is a system that consists of at least one individual I of a noémon species, or at least one noémon entity, E, not belonging to a species, or a combination of the above and tools that at least one noémon entity E or individual I can use.

The TNS starts with its root-conception above and fully explicates it in the following chapters of this volume. The theory is extended in the monograph's Consequences volume covering the topics of knowledge, consciousness, emotions, and human nature (Gelepithis 2024b).

[6] It is derived from noûs, -a noun of the Hellenic language- standing, primarily but not exclusively, for 'mind'. Its earliest recorded use was in Iliad (Homer Il. 1. 130). I find it worth mentioning that in Ancient Greek city-states 'Noémon' was used as a personal name. I want to stress that none of the many ancient or modern interpretations of noûs (including materialistic ones like that of Anaxagoras) and noetic (religious, philosophical, or otherwise) are acceptable within a TNS.

TNS is expected to be the first step towards an emerging science of noémon systems. Although it is presently in rudimentary form, its domain of investigation, namely the space of noémon systems, is real and fast expanding. More significantly, both the hybrid and purely artificial subspaces of S expand in an accelerated mode. This expansion not only modifies significantly the characteristics of human societies—it is ultimately bound to shape the evolution of itself.

I have already proposed the study of the space of noémon systems as the domain for a new science initially unifying psychology and AI and eventually all the sciences dealing with *Homo*. In addition, I have called such an endeavour *Homo* science. A significant part of such a science will be anthropology. The reader may object to this thesis. He may claim that anthropology should be identified with the sought human science. I think that anthropology as it is currently conceived and practiced, is inadequate for the task. Consider for instance the following two definitions of the field from the horse's mouth and a world-class university:

> "Anthropology is the study of humans, past and present." Aiming:
> "To understand the full sweep and complexity of cultures across all of human history, anthropology draws and builds upon knowledge from the social and biological sciences as well as the humanities and physical sciences. A central concern of anthropologists is the application of knowledge to the solution of human problems." (American Anthropological Association, 2017).
> "Anthropology is devoted to the study of human beings and human societies as they exist across time and space. It is distinct from other social sciences in encompassing both the full span of human history and the full range of human societies and cultures, including those located in historically marginalized areas of the world. As a result, anthropology is especially attuned to questions of social, cultural, and biological diversity and to issues of power, identity, and inequality." (Stanford, Department of Anthropology, 2017)

Identified in either of the two ways stated above, anthropology lacks three major constitutive elements of *Homo* science: AI, biotechnology, and Earthian ecology. Yes the sought human science is huge. Some may say that it is an infeasible endeavour. Certainly, we need it.

On the other hand certain characteristic phenomena studied by anthropology should play a central (not peripheral as it is currently the case) role in the development of *Homo* science. The most important such phenomenon is culture. Its nature is a bone of contention in anthropology and the social sciences. A fertile ground for unification.

The notion of 'culture', a fundamental, if not defining, notion of anthropology is used in two diametrically opposed senses. One, for social anthropology, 'culture' is something that needs to be explained (an explanandum in philosophy of science terms). Two, and in contrast, cultural anthropology views culture as an explanans, that is, as an independent theoretical construct to be used to explain societal phenomena. For my part, I consider culture as both an explanans (at the level of adequately complex social phenomena like jurisprudence and education) and an explanandum as far as its origin is concerned. In other words, we should distinguish several stages of cultural evolution. From proto-cultures of early eusocial animals (or earlier if sufficient evidence becomes available), to the distinct cultures of the two *Pan* species, and from there to the cultures of *Homo* (not only of the extant and extinct species). Cultures of possible robot societies are clearly beyond *Homo sapiens* and most likely any future *Homo* species. Section 2.3.2 provides a parameterised definition of culture applicable to all types of noémon systems (definition-12).

The fact of the matter is that traditional disciplines like psychology, human biology, anthropology, or AI only study aspects of *Homo sapiens*. In addition, the so called hard and soft sciences cannot be separated in an increasingly technoscientific human society. They only have to learn to talk to each other. Their key objective has to be the same: contribution to the conquest of individual happiness for all human beings. Granted that no existing single discipline can address the immense conceptual and ethical issues we are about to face, we need a new unified approach to address them. Such an approach need to be based on a radically new conception of 'mind' and an equally radical change of humanity's worldview of itself.

The sought new approach should distinguish but not demarcate noémon system (NoS) classes. The latter would remind us of the demarcation that used to be thought to exist between humans and animals. There are colossal differences even within *Homo sapiens* (see Sect. 2.3), let alone between historic humans and the species of other taxa, but such differences do not qualify for classifying noémon systems into fundamentally different categories. Even unique differences (and there are more than plenty in the living world) do not imply fundamental differences. They only support the graded and varied nature of noémon systems, be those biological or artificial, and their intelligent behaviours. Since we cannot demarcate between biological and artificially-intelligent systems we need a science that can study both. Such a science will, of course, change dramatically our views for the nature of human knowledge and of ourselves. The existing disciplines studying human individuality and society should be redefined and become part of the science of *Homo.* I will often use *Homo* instead of humanity in order to capture the past, present, and future of our genus. Humanity usually does not refer to our distant past and definitely not to the future of our genus. Evolution teaches us about our own past and our biological roots and context. But it does not stop with *Homo sapiens.* Our future is both unknown and partially constructable. For the latter point see Gelepithis (2024b).

1.3 Criteria and Tools for Unification

Philosophy of science came to prominence in the late 1920s—starting with the Berlin and Vienna Circles of scientists and philosophers. Conceived as the critical study of the *conceptual* foundations of science, it is and will be a very useful endeavour. The study of animals and robots require scientific criteria for theory development that reflect the particular nature of this field of investigation in addition to established ones required for any mature science. This section briefly:

A. Argues that any mature unified theory of S should fulfil at least four criteria in addition to the standard ones of explanatory and predictive power. They are:

   C-1: Specification of a pivotal system of notions for the unification of S.
   C-2: Consistency with necessary constraints.
   C-3: Specification of minimum vocabularies.
   C-4: Specification of invariant laws.

B. Justifies my choice of language-based axiomatisation as the best tool for constructing a unified theory of noémon systems.

It should be noted that specification of criteria for a mature unified theory of S is radically different from the specification of ad hoc "desirable goals for a unified theory of cognition" (Baars & Franklin 2007, p. 955). I move on with the task of specifying criteria for a unified theory of S.

C-1: Specification of a pivotal system of notions for the unification of **S**
A unified theory of noémon systems covering their whole gamut of phenomena of S is clearly untenable at present. The enormity of the task necessitates, as a starting point, the choosing of a restricted system of such phenomena. This initially restricted system should of course gradually be augmented until it includes the complete range of phenomena under investigation. By necessity therefore, the initially chosen system of phenomena required to be unified is open to discussion.

Taking into account this constraint one proceeds from a minimum appropriate range of phenomena to the ideally complete one. Here we have two contrasting methodologies to choose from:

(i) Initial system of mental phenomena chosen on the basis of the methodological preferences of individual investigators; or
(ii) Initial system of mental phenomena determined by the pivotal notions of S that need to be clarified and unified.

All investigators but the writer of this book have chosen the first approach, the path of subjective preferences. Let us see the kind of problems encountered in choosing the first option by considering Newell's stance on the matter.

He proposed the gradual unification of mental phenomena along the lines of the following open *priority* list (Newell 1990 p. 15):

> "Problem solving, decision-making, routine action. Memory, learning, skill. Perception, motor behavior. Language. Motivation, emotion. Imagining, dreaming, daydreaming, ... "

The key problem with subjectively-determined lists is the near-impossibility of comparing the correspondingly derived theories since by design they reflect individual preferences of investigation. In the particular case of Newell's list no justification was offered for the choice of topics apart from being heavily investigated. Newell's choice of the AI-based perspective as his overall methodology also affected negatively both his priority list and the mono-dimensional treatment of key topics like meaning, memory, and representation.[7] Finally, subjectively-determined lists contribute to the mushrooming of unified theories of cognition and pose difficulties in determining common criteria for comparison. Although Newell's intention was crystal clear, his practice created unintended problems.

The alternative I favour is specification of a *pivotal system* of notions for the unification of S. By *pivotal system* I mean a system that is necessary for the description of *all types of known* noémon system (NoS) that may inhabit or habituate S. Upon agreement of such a system the proposed approach will have two advantages:

A. A1: Any agreed *pivotal system* of notions (PSN) for the unification of S will provide a common basis for any scientist studying or developing noémon systems.
B. A2: A PSN will provide a level field for comparison of at least unification theories (cf, state of physics in C-3 below).

Accordingly, I propose the following:

PSN = {*thinking, emotion, representation, communication, knowledge, consciousness*}.

It should be stressed that building blocks of pivotal notions are not usually included in the PSN (e.g., *meaning, understanding*) despite their fundamental significance and full treatment in subsequent chapters. Obviously, the proposed PSN is open to a community-agreed redefinition. In the meantime, I hold that unified theories of noémon systems should be evaluated along the progress they make on advancing our understanding of the proposed PSN. Figure. 1.4 depicts an explanatory semantic network of key TNS notions within their wider context. It includes all foundational PSN; excludes PSN derived from the foundational ones.

Given the substantial diversity of types of systems populating S, corresponding PSN should be specified. The best starting point is specification of a *minimum* PSN characterising all noémon systems regardless of any additional notions that may characterise their type (i.e., class of noémon system). The *minimum* PSN of the TNS—delineating S—consists of the

[7] For a critical review of Newell's notion of representation see Gelepithis (1995). For the first critical comprehensive survey of the basic tenets of semantics see Gelepithis (1988).

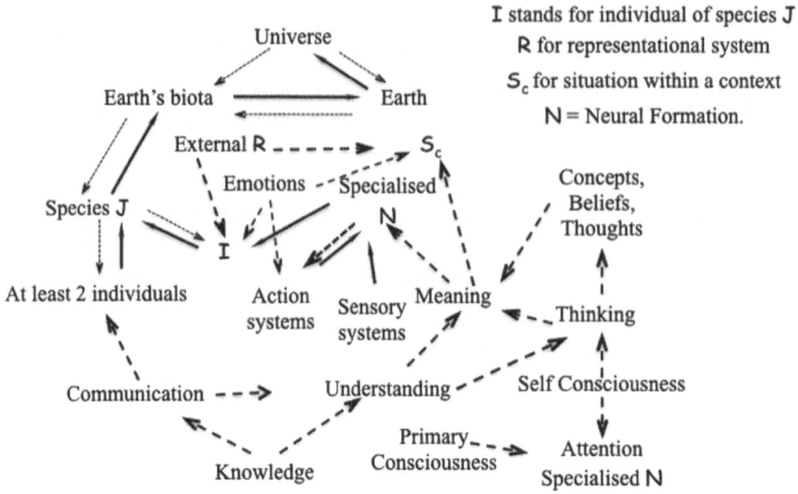

Fig. 1.4 Key TNS notions within their wider context. Dashed arrows stand for 'explained in terms of'; Dotted arrows stand for 'affect'; Black arrows stand for 'part-of'. A few arrows have been omitted for figure simplicity.

following notions: {*representation, thinking, communication*} = *minimum* PSN.

These notions constitute the definiens of noémon system and are discussed, defined and explicated in the following three chapters respectively.

Certain notions like action, development, values, human language, beauty, truth, and morality are quite likely required to be included in a redefined PSN. How such inclusions will affect the relations among the notions of the proposed PSN and the complexity of the correspondingly extended theories is an interesting open research question. Probably, the most suitable candidate for inclusion is the notion of 'action'. For, our theories for action systems (also known as motor or locomotion systems) are not in serious dispute (despite some philosophical discussions in the abstract).[8]

[8] I prefer 'action' as a more inclusive term; 'motor' has engineering connotations and 'locomotion' biological ones.

Finally, it should be noted that the phenomena corresponding to the proposed PSN vary in complexity depending on the particular noémon system that instantiates them. What we are after is understanding their commonalities, similarities and differences. Biological and artificial minds do differ but it is equally true that they have deep common foundations. Consequently, unification of the disciplines studying the space of animals and robots has to be given in non-anthropomorphic terms which at the same time should be extendable to reflect particular noémon systems (e.g., *Homo sapiens*) characteristics. For instance, survival and reproduction have to be taken into account in any theory of biological systems, but written human language is a characteristic of a single Animalia species following a successful major transition in their evolution and, in contradistinction, reproduction does not have to be a characteristic of a *possible* conscious robot society. In a nutshell the notion of noémon system has to be defined in a way that includes the full range of both biological and artificial minds. In other words, the notions of human, non-human living form, 'hybrid', and possibly hyper-intelligent robots should be compatible with each other in a unified theory of noémon systems.

C-2: Consistency with necessary constraints

There is a special class of phenomena that need not only to be explained but also to be taken as constraints in developing theories of biological and artificial minds. Newell (1990) proposed a list of thirteen such constraints that unified theories of mind should *gradually* take into account and on the basis of which UTsC should be evaluated. The subsequent increased interest in unified theories led Anderson & Lebiere (2003) to suggest an alternative list of criteria for the evaluation of unified theories. Their target article along with its associated open peer commentary far from exhausted the debate on the evaluation of unified theories of mind. In particular, they left practically untouched two issues: (i) lack of an appropriate definition of mind; and (ii) the systemic nature of any proposed constraints. I will say a few words on both starting with the latter.

The clearest demonstration of the systemic nature of mental constraints is their inter-dependance. Three examples suffice. One, effective operation of a cognitive system in a real environment presupposes the abilities of operating in real time and behaving flexibly and adaptively in that environment (constraints identified by at least Newell and Anderson & Lebiere). Two, the feedback relation between communication and creativity. Three, the strong interrelations between emotions and consciousness. Neglect of such inter-dependencies have repeatedly led to misleading research programmes. The last two examples are from a list originated with Gelepithis (1999). The three different systems of abilities and external constraints that are assumed to shape the human mind (Gelepithis 2003) reveal disagreement on what constitutes the nature of mind. So far there is agreement only on the fact that the human mind has been evolved in response to numerous challenges. Well before one aims to develop a unified theory of mind, one needs to address a major research problem, namely, to reach an agreement on the formative requirements that have shaped our species. Put in other words, the observed divergence in opinions were caused by a more fundamental problem: lack of a proper definition of 'mind' and, more inclusively and significantly, of *Homo sapiens*. Until a widely agreed definition of the *evolving* human nature is proposed, listing its characteristics will be a minefield. A possible way out of this is to consider constraints that can be shown to be related to fundamental phenomena characterising at least our species.

It should finally be noted that phenomena like emotions can both act as constraints and enablers of thought and action and be affected by either thought or action. Defining the evolving nature of *Homo* and hence of our species requires, at least, identification of the evolving phenomena that constitute it. The PSN proposed in the previous section provide a guide to that end.

C-3: Specification of minimum vocabularies

Despite the importance of minimum vocabularies, discussions of their significance is limited and usually comes under names like theoretical characteristics (Kuhn 1977), or shared standards (Longino 1990). One of Newell's most valuable contribution toward a unified theory of mind is his review of the notions constituting a minimum vocabulary (V) for the foundations of cognitive science.

I hold that a theory of mind cannot be a *unified* theory of mind for as long as it lacks one of the most basic characteristics of a *mature* scientific theory, namely, Vs. Aspects of this viewpoint are not new; they were preceded by Staats in two respects. First:

> "it is important to consider the nature of unified theory and the methods involved in unified theory construction. These are topics our science has thus far not addressed." (Staats 1981, p. 253).

And more specifically:

> "A new theorist in physics would not be allowed to introduce a new term for mass, electron, quark, or other science products; the infrastructure of physics ensures that. There is no such infrastructure to prevent new, redundant terms in psychology or to remove the huge redundancy that already exists and goes unaddressed." (Staats 1999 p. 8).

Physics is characterised by cumulative knowledge; and laws and minimum vocabularies contribute greatly to the creation of such knowledge. In contrast, psychology produces hundreds of unrelated micro-theories that solve minute problems of little significance for the individual or human society. Assuming we want the sought science of mind to become part of the overall human science enterprise, we need Vs to become part of a *mature* unified theory of mind. Sometimes, Staats' viewpoint is seen as surrendering to ontological reductionism. It is not because it does not oppose psychology's special ontological characteristics. It only points to a difficult but necessary objective. Such an objective should, for instance, take into account social and cultural aspects of humanity and the need of being accounted for by Vs that may well be very different from those of physics.

In contrast to ontological reductionism, minimum vocabularies are compatible with the time honoured approach of methodological reductionism, that is, is the scientific attempt to construct theories in terms of the smaller number of notions possible. To be noted that methodological reductionism, does not imply theory reduction between any two or more disciplines. In the ideal case one ends up with a V and an axiomatic system built in terms of the former.

Minimum vocabularies characterise mature disciplines. Probably, its clearest definition is still Russell's (1948 p. 274):

> "in relation to a given body of knowledge, a minimum vocabulary is defined as one having the two properties (1) that every proposition in the given body of knowledge can be expressed by means of words belonging to the minimum vocabulary, (2) that no word in this vocabulary can be defined in terms of other words in it."

It follows that only undefined terms are indispensable. Of course, what terms are to be taken as undefined is partly arbitrary. Equally follows that a V is useful even if it can only be attained for a small part of a scientific field since it reduces the terms used for describing and explaining the various phenomena of that body of knowledge. More significantly, Vs describing a theory can be used to identify gaps and inconsistencies in that theory. In other words, minimum vocabularies are both useful as a stepping-stone toward a more scientifically mature science and theoretically desirable in accordance with the principle of parsimony. Psychology is in particular need of Vs to decrease the bewildering multiplicity of terms used and reduce the number of redundant micro-theories. It is almost needless to stress the close relationship of theoretical constructs to minimum vocabularies.

C-4: Specification of invariant laws

Physics, that is widely considered to be a mature science, is not so much characterised by being dominated by a single paradigm (cf, quantum and gravitation theories) as of fulfilling a second criterion besides minimum vocabularies: invariant laws.

Psychology lacks invariant principles. Some argue that there are no such principles. According to McDowell (1994, 1998) the mind does not fit within the realm of the physical laws because there are two distinct types of intelligibility that govern these two different kinds of phenomena. Therefore, human sciences are methodologically distinct from the natural sciences. More recently Miłkowski (2016, p. 15) has written:

> "[i]t is the lack of laws in psychology and other cognitive science disciplines that justifies the adoption of an alternative account of explanation."

Nevertheless, it has also been argued that psychological laws are substantially different from physical laws like the conservation of mass and energy. Simon (1990) pointingly remarks that in biology

> "even the important general laws (e.g., the laws of photosynthesis) vary in detail from one species to another (and sometimes among different individuals in a single species)."

He goes on to conclude that:

> "[Psychology's] laws are, and will be, limited in range and generality and will be mainly qualitative. Its invariants are and will be of the kinds that are appropriate to adaptive systems. Its success must be measured not by how closely it resembles physics but by how well it describes and explains human behavior." (Simon 1990 p 2).

The discussion about the existence of invariants in psychology is complicated by the lack of any widely accepted definition of psychological law.

In what follows I distinguish three types of laws (invariances) of the space of noémon systems (S) in contrast to the single type of extant psychological laws (corresponding to the micro-theories notion of Allen Newell and Herbert Simon's laws of quantitative structure). One of the additional types proposed is necessary for theoretical discussions concerning S; the other is necessary for more nuanced discussions concerning human invariances.

First, a law that holds true for all noémon systems (i.e., noémon species, noémon entities and possibly extraterrestrial noémon systems). I call such a law an S- wide law.

Second, a law that holds true for all members of a single class of noémon systems (e.g., *H. sapiens*, an animal species, AISs). I call such a law a an $S_{C\text{-wide}}$ law. For instance, human reaction time varies between 10^{-1} and 10^{-2}seconds (from Simon 1990).

Third, a law that holds true for the vast majority of members of a single class of S but not for all of them. I will such a law a *near* $S_{C\text{-wide}}$ law. An unexpected example of such a law is the human STM limit. Although virtually all humans are subject to this invariance, not all of them are (cf, Luria 1965*1968).[9]

In Sect. 4.3 I revisit this topic and propose an S-wide law.

Let me now move to the choice of tool for theory construction. It is another distinctive feature of the TNS approach.

B. Choice of tool for theory construction

Presently, there are three types of tools for theory construction: computational, continuous mathematical systems like differential equations, and written human language.[10]

Speed, precision, completeness, and self-consistency are the key advantages of computational modelling and to a lesser degree of mathematical systems. But, mathematics point more to our ignorance than to deep

[9] With respect to noémon species, it should be noted that their evolution may bring changes in relation to the second and third of the laws identified above.

[10] Although new technological tools including genetically engineered transgenic nonhuman primates (Belmonte et al. 2015) can be extremely important for research and not infrequently their use is a source of inspiration for theoretical development, they are not theory builders and hence are excluded from my consideration here.

knowledge. As Bertrand Russell notes on the relation of mathematics to physics:

> "Physics is mathematical not because we know so much about the physical world, but because we know so little; it is only its mathematical properties that we can discover." (B. Russel 1927, pp. 163–164).

And, of course, physics is much simpler than psychology, let alone, sociology.

Furthermore, a conceptual system described in human language cannot compete in terms of speed and may involve mistakes concerning precision and coherence that are absent from computational systems. Still human language has a unique characteristic that, by design, can never be acquired by a formal system, namely, vagueness (or, as I prefer to call it *derived* or *inherited* imprecision caused by its dependence on the human conceptual system). The vagueness of human language has deep links to our well of knowledge upon which we all draw in creating new scientific theories (cf, Gelepithis 2024b, Sect. 2.2). As Werner Heisenberg (1958*1989, p. 188) wrote:

> "one of the most important features of the development and the analysis of modern physics is the experience that the concepts of natural language, vaguely defined as they are, seem to be more stable in the expansion of knowledge than the precise terms of scientific language, derived as an idealization from only limited groups of phenomena."

This position should not be seen as being against the use of mathematics or computational modelling. It is only against their premature and consequently inappropriate use. An illustration is provided by Grafen's attempt to formalise the theory of evolution. His justification for his attempt is reminiscent of Cardinal Richelieu's presumed provision of an instance of justification that is worse than the act that evokes it to King Louis XIII. In the case of Grafen:

> "Grand theories in physics are usually expressed in mathematics. Newton's mechanics and Einstein's theory of special relativity are essentially equations. Words are needed to interpret the terms, but only for that. Darwin's theory of evolution by natural selection has obstinately remained in words since 1859." (Grafen 2007, p. 1243)

We first need to sort out our concepts and possibly expand our conceptual understanding of the fundamental problems in biology before formalising it. I think we are far away from that. Darwin's theory has been verified in its essence but it has conceptual weaknesses that have not been addressed even by the most recent proposed expansions of the theory (e.g., Pigliussi & Müller 2010; Laland et al. 2015).

Most prominent among those weakness are related to emerging phenomena emerging within S and they need to be addressed by a future unified science that would modify most if not all of our current disciplines including biology, AI and sociology. We do not know how such a *science of humanity* will be described. What we do know is that present day psychology (part of that future *science of humanity*) is characterised by key inadequacies (some of which have been identified above) which cannot possibly be formalised. And, of course, no mathematical theory of the physical world ever sprang up in equations. Any such theory (including Newton's and Einstein's) started in human language and ended up in mathematical terms, only after having sufficiently clarified and understood.

Nevertheless, objections persist. They come up in both biology and even sociology. For instance, Greslehner (2018) claims for the necessity of mathematical models in biology on the basis of the complexity of biological organisms at even the cellular level. But, complexity has first to be understood in order to be, to some extent at least, formalised. Formalisation involves substantial abstraction and the appropriateness of such abstractions can only follow deep understanding. Such understanding we currently lack. More surprising is the implicit call for mathematical models in social science as the following quote illustrates:

> "One of the major drawbacks of social science research is the need to resort to everyday language concepts in both theory and empirical investigation. The inherent fuzziness and the constant evolution of these language categories as well as inter-language, inter-cultural, and inter- individual differences make it difficult to define central working concepts in the universal, invariant, and consensual fashion generally required by a systematic scientific approach." (Scherer 2005, p. 696).

This rather uncritical pursuit of formal models that is implicitly argued for reveals a deep lack of understanding of human society. Nevertheless, alternative voices started appearing. They range from mathematics (e.g.,

Rudolph 2012) to neuroscience (e.g., Roe 2020). Even in economics, sober voices for the excessive and ineffective use of mathematics started appearing. A constructive piece of writing on the "economically unwarranted mathematical assumptions." is presented by Velupillai (2005).

We also need to keep in mind that the human conceptual system is far richer than human language and the latter in turn is far richer than our formal systems. The inherent imprecision of human language is derived from the far greater imprecision of our conceptual system as identified in our nervous system and partially expressed (that is, represented) in human language.

The cause of this fact should be well known to all scientists but usually it is not even acknowledged let alone taken into account. A representation (e.g., a model) is always poorer, by design or definition, from the situation, system, or phenomenon represented. Human language represents aspects of the human conceptual system and human knowledge representation schemes are by definition and design an approximation of both human language and our conceptual apparatus.

So, in short, the complexity of the human nervous system and our current knowledge of it are such that they preclude the development of a unified theory of it in computational or mathematical terms. Of course, the inadequacy of our current mathematics does not imply inadequacy of some future mathematics. At the same time an in-principle mathematical inadequacy for describing the full space of noémon systems should always be entertained by inquisitive individuals. A fourth class of tools for theory construction may be invented by a future noémon species or a noémon society of robots.

Human language is, currently, the only descriptive tool in our disposal for a unified theory of noémon systems. It becomes more powerful when it is combined with the axiomatic approach and, in particular, with the development of a minimum vocabulary. The TNS exemplifies such a language-based axiomatisation. It is rarely used: the only fully grown examples that spring to my brain are *Euclid's Elements*; and Newton's *Philosophiae Naturalis Principia Mathematica*.

This brings me to a foreshadowing of the TNS's major results and issues addressed in terms of invariant laws and its predictive and explanatory power as per Table 1.1.

Table 1.1 Foreshadowing major results of the TNS

Explanatory power:	• Complete definition of Artificial Intelligence (Sect. 2.2, Vol 1). • The gradualist (continuity vs discontinuity) debate (Sect. 2.3.3, Vol 1). • The nature of mathematics (Sect. 2.3, Vol 2). • The place of philosophy within human knowledge (Sect. 2. 3, Vol 2). • The unity of *Homo* knowledge (Sect. 2.3, Vol 2). • Major issues of consciousness studies (Sect. 3.3.3, Vol 2). • Emotion (chapter 4, Vol 2); Individual *H. sapiens* nature (chapter 5, Vol 2).
Predictive power	• Existence of a third type of meaning (Sect. 3.3.1, Vol 1). • The memory-meaning postulate (Sect. 3.3.1, Vol 1). • Limited extent of Human-Ideal (super intelligent) Robot communication (Sect. 4.3, Vol 1). • Limited extent of H-knowledge formalisability (Sect. 2.3.3, Vol 2). • Several predictions of the consciousness theory part of TNS (Sect. 3.3.3, Vol 2).
Invariant Laws	• Communication-understanding principle (Chapter 4, Vol 1).

Volume-2 pointers are included for completeness of section and reader's information.

Chapters' Course The second chapter starts fleshing out the theoretical construct of 'noémon system' introduced in the first one and addresses two of the major debates in the study of human nature. One, the continuity vs discontinuity debate originated with Darwin (1871). Two, the AGI and superintelligence debates originated with Turing (1950). Fleshing out starts with full explication of the notion of representation—one of the definiens of noémon system. Significantly, the chapter proposes the first complete definition of AI and a radical solution to the continuity vs discontinuity debate—based on the argued recognition of a particular transition in human evolution.

The third chapter demonstrates that the building block of both thinking and concepts are the notions of 'meaningful neural formation' and 'meaningful material formation'. The latter is a generalisation of the former. On this basis the chapter outlines a novel, physical theory of thinking—the second definien of 'noémon system'—that includes the following significant notions of both psychology and AI: 'concept', 'idea', 'belief', 'information' and its related notions, and 'reasoning'. It concludes with a few consequences and an evaluation of the theory.

The final chapter of this volume unifies the disciplinary studies of the last definien of 'noémon system', namely, communication. It develops a theory of communication and its building blocks and argues that the processes of communication and understanding are invariances for the space of noémon systems. The ground definien of both of these processes is the notion of primitive term. The chapter concludes with discussion of the limits of communication among noémon systems.

CHAPTER 2

Nature of Noémon Systems: Human and Robot Forms

This chapter starts fleshing out the notion of NoS introduced in the first one and addresses two of the major debates in the study of human nature. One, the continuity vs discontinuity debate originated with Darwin (1871). Two, the AGI and superintelligence debates originated with Turing (1950). In particular:

The first section introduces the principle of noémon systems (PriNS) and discusses the relation between human and artificial minds. It constitutes the backbone of TNS. PriNS specifies the two definiens of the NoS theoretical construct, namely, noémon species and noémon entity. They are defined in terms of parametric conditions that determine necessary and sufficient conditions for biological, artificial, and hybrid minds.

Section two addresses the phenomenon of representation and representational systems (one of the parametric conditions of a NoS), and proposes a complete and most inclusive definition of AI in terms of PriNS. The section concludes with a discussion on the nature of AI, the notion of *own* robot evolution, and develops a novel argument and result on the AGI and superintelligence debates on the relation between humans and robots.

Finally, Sect. 2.3 introduces the current state of evolutionary theory, reviews the gradualist (continuity vs discontinuity) debate, and offers a radical solution to it in terms of *written* human language. The latter is

P. A. M. Gelepithis, *Unification of Artificial Intelligence and Psychology*,
https://doi.org/10.1007/978-3-031-68319-0_2

argued to be the determining tool- factor and a major transition in the evolution of *Homo* artificiality.

2.1 The Principle of Noémon Systems

This section starts with a reminder of the conflict between the individualist and collectivist world views,—related with the introduction and justification of PriNS that follows, and finishes with the fleshing out of its first condition characterising both biological and artificial noémon systems.

Bertrand Russell (1946) in his classic *A History of Western Philosophy* wrote:

> "Philosophers are both effects and causes: effects of their social circumstances and of the politics and institutions of their time; causes (if they are fortunate) of beliefs which mould the politics and institutions of later times." (ibid., p. 7).

Psychology (that is, views of the dominating psychologists of a period), as it is the case in science in general, is not an exception of this potentially feedback relation. William James is an instance of a 'cause'. His conception of psychology as "the science of finite individual minds" (James 1890), has greatly contributed to the individualistic perspective that dominates psychology.

The notion of 'mind' as captured by modern *western* dictionaries stresses its individual aspect:

> "the *part* of a *person* that makes it *possible* for him to, *think*, *feel emotions*, and *understand* things". Italicised words refer to further entries in the dictionary.
>
> (Cambridge English Dictionary).
>
> "the element or complex of elements in an individual that feels, perceives, thinks, wills, and especially reasons".
>
> (Merriam-Webster, 12 March 2017).
>
> "The element of a person that enables them to be aware of the world and their experiences, to think, and to feel; the faculty of consciousness and thought."
>
> (Oxford living Dictionary).

> "Conjunto de actividades y processos psíquicos conscientes e inconscientes, especialmente de carácter cognitivo."
> (Diccionario de la lengua española, Real Academia Española).

This individualistic approach to 'mind' is supported by, indeed most likely derived from, the history of the word. It is derived from the verbal root * men- that means 'to think, to remember'. This verbal root is part of the Proto-Indo-European language assumed by linguists worldwide to have been a single language spoken around 3500 BCE. It is related to the concepts 'manas' (Sanskrit), mens (Latin), μένος (pronounced menos in Greek). For an excellent history of the evolution of the notion of mind (Bennett 2007).

Furthermore, the economic, political, and philosophical versions of individualism (e.g., Wilde 1891*1912; Dewey 1931; Parvini 2020) have provided a fertile matrix for psychological individualism. Of course the latter has also been strengthened by misinterpretations or exaggerations of the modern synthesis theory of evolution (e.g., Williams 1966; Dawkins 1976).

The latest, strong proponent of individualism comes under the guise of neuroscience. Despite the balanced viewpoint of systemic integration characterising an animal, as it is best exemplified by the following quote from Sherrington's classic *The Integrative Action of the Nervous System*:

> "The integration of the animal organism is obviously not the result solely of any single agency at work within it, but of several." (Sherrington 1906, p. 3),

a rampant neuroscientism (cf, Sect. 1.1) that put the brain as the sole integrator system of an individual animal is presently dominant within the neurosciences. Following Sherrington, I hold that advances in the neuroscience have to take into account the importance of other biological systems constituting an individual. Demoting the individual animal in favour of its brain is a gross mistake. Similarly, demoting society in favour of an individual is a gross mistake. The two coexist and influence each other.

Although individualism has come to be seen as the essential feature of human society since the mid 1850s, the debate on whether we move toward increased individualism or a holistic society is open (Macfarlane

1996). The view opposing individualism is communitarianism, namely, the assumption that:

> "individuals are constituted by the institutions and practices of which they are a part, and their rights and obligations derive from those same institutions and practices." (Sterba 1999, p. 719).

And communitarianism in turn brings us naturally to psychological viewpoints that are in several ways related to it, albeit with significant and sometimes fundamental differences to it. Such conceptions, with respect to psychology, were first propounded and documented by Wundt's (1832–1920) pioneering work on cultural psychology. Specifically, in his *Elements of folk-psychology: Outlines of a Psychological History of the Development of Mankind,* he argued for the necessity of bridging together the individual and societal aspects of human mind (Wundt 1912*1916). Unfortunately, his work along with that of Vygotski (1934*1986), Mead (†1934*1962) and Bateson (1972) was mostly ignored and sometimes misinterpreted until at least the mid 1960s. The cultural evolution part of the EES framework provides further support (see 2.3.2). For Marx (1818–1883), humans have neither precise nor fixed nature. Human nature is primarily determined by one's social relations that he enters or finds herself in. Durkheim (1858–1917) is on the same side with Marx. For him society is a reality 'suis generis'. Social facts are external and constraining upon the individual. They constitute a malleable, undifferentiated substratum shaped by the specific characteristics of a particular group and the larger society encompassing the latter. Social life creates individual characteristics. With huge differences but on the same side on the nature-nurture debate are also G. H. Mead (1863–1931), one of the founders of social psychology, who stressed the necessity of cultural dependence and ethological prerequisites for explaining mind and Parsons (1902–79) who aimed to synthesise psychology, politics and economics.

In particular, Mead argued that humans internalise societal values through their social interactions and communication.

> "Until the social sciences are able to state the social individual in terms of social processes, as the physical sciences define their objects in terms of physical change, they will not have risen to the point at which they can force their object upon an introspective psychology." (Mead 1910, p. 176).

Sociologists were not the only ones who stressed the social and cultural aspects of 'mind'. Pioneering philosophers like Aristotle (384–322 BCE) shared similar views. He conceived of humans as social animals with additional distinctive characteristics like reason and speech.

More recently, from around the 1990s, an increasing number of viewpoints started emerging again challenging the individualistic perspective. They collectively come under the umbrella name of situated cognition and include at least the following distinct but related cognitive perspectives: embodied, dynamical, embedded, distributed, extended and enactive (Overmann & Malafouris 2018 for an excellent introduction). Psychology and to a lesser extent AI experience more than any other discipline the increasing amount of research work in situated cognition (Varela et al. 1991; Clark & Chalmers 1998*2008; Wilson 2002; Froese & Ziemke 2009; Di Paolo & De Jaegher 2012; McGann et al. 2013).

Nevertheless, situated cognition currently suffers from an inadequacy that is addressable but far from having even started to be addressed and a strong claim that is, in principle, unsupportable. Its inadequacy stems from the lack of any theory that can compete even remotely with unified theories of mind couched in terms of cognitive architectures (see Sect. 1.3). Its strong claim, namely, extra cranial tools are constitutive of mind, flies to the face of both common sense and any available scientific data. Consider for instance the following claim (stated in a the quarterly scientific journal of the American Psychological Association):

> "neural function is most interestingly situated not within the skull" (McGann et al. 2013, p. 107).

Nearly needless to say that the weak version of situated cognition, namely, our tools and culture influence mind, is simply a reality.

Compatible to communitarianism, perceived to run counter to mainstream western science, there are several other viewpoints and data supporting them. Probably the most general is the interdependent construal of self that characterises both non-western cultures and small parts of western psychology and social sciences (e.g., Markus & Kitayama 1991). Support is also provided by certain findings in social cognition and particularly collective memory (e.g., Fiske 1992; Barnier & Sutton 2008; Wertsch & Roediger III 2008). A rather unexpected ally is to be found in the interesting "social ontology" approach of Gosden (2008) aiming to relate archaeology and neuroscience. A considerably earlier proponent of the society-self interdependence that need to be stressed is clearly expressed in the following excerpt from Piaget's (1978) address at the annual convention of the American Psychological Association in August 1977:

> "Psychology is the science not only of the individual but also of humans in general. For example, mathematics and physics have been created by human beings, and this creation can be understood only in terms of human intelligence in its totality."

A similar philosophy is emerging and gets increasing strength in medicine through psychiatry that hesitantly by steadily come to recognise this fact (e.g., Nour & Barrera 2015).

Of course, individualism and communitarianism do not need to oppose each other. Actually, individuals and communities are inseparably linked. Nature and nurture (environment in general) are characterised by a complex feedback ongoing relationship that characterises each and every species (system in general). This argument and its underlying debate is recently expressed in terms of nature-culture (e.g., Lewens 2017). The strongest, recent support of this viewpoint comes from the extended evolutionary synthesis (ESS) that is steadily replacing the modern synthesis as the backbone theory of the Earthian evolutionary process (e.g., Renfrew 2008; Müller 2017; see also next section).

The above outline can be summarised by the following position on the relations between human brain, mind, society and culture:

> **The EES hypothesis**: The *H. sapiens* brain and a special part of it, called individual human mind, is embodied and situated within human society and its wider physical environment and they all are interdependent.

Identifying mind with part of a nervous system is an advance in comparison with dualist conceptions but it is still both open to criticisms from several quarters including philosophy (e.g., Bennett & Hacker 2003), situated cognition (e.g., Clark 2008), and archaeology (e.g., Renfrew 2008) and being incompatible with the requirements of artificial minds (cf, Sect. 1.2).

In addition, the EES working hypothesis retains the notion of individuality as the defining element of mind. The TNS approach differs in giving priority to the species as the adaptable unit of a variety of traits differentially comprising the 'mind' of its members. This conception give rise to a slightly differently stated, but significantly different, version of the EES working hypothesis, namely:

> **The TNS version of the EES hypothesis**: The *H. sapiens* brain is an integrated system, part of an integrated nervous system, that is part of an integrated system of biological systems comprising an individual of the current *Homo* species that has developed and keeps developing a *H. sapiens* science and technology that may eventually contribute significantly to a unique Earthian culture.

In essence the above version of the EES hypothesis makes system the key unit of the evolutionary process instantiated at the levels of individual, populations, species, and macroevolutionary ecosystem. Of course it does not imply that all work on complex adaptive systems, and even less in general systems theory, is automatically accepted as part of the TNS. It does nevertheless imply that part of that work may well become part of the evolving EES. The TNS is a step to this direction. Let us move on with this task.

The notion of noémon system, stated as the Root-conception of TNS (Sect. 1.2), involves 'noémon species' and 'noémon entity' as its two definiens. Jointly, these two theoretical constructs determine the requirements for a *minimally* noémon system according to the following two definitions and their associated identifications:

'The mind of individual **I**' ≡ 'individual **I** of a noémon species'.[1] *Where*:

Definition-2 Noémon species is a species whose individuals fulfil at least the first two of the following conditions:

(a). Possess *own*-representational systems (e.g., sensory, motor).
(b). Possess the ability of thinking.
(c). Are able to communicate among themselves, and possibly individuals of other species.
(d). Are able to create *permanent* external representations.

I call the above identification-definition system *the principle of noémon species*. The second identification and its associated definition follows:

[1] The symbol '≡' means 'is identified with'.

'The mind of entity E' ≡ noémon entity E (abbreviation E_n). *Where*:

Definition-3 E_n is a system fulfilling at least the first two of the following three conditions:

(a) Possess representational systems (e.g., sensory, motor).
(b) Possess the ability of thinking.
(c) Is able to communicate with other noémon entities.

I call the above identification and its associated definition *the postulate of physical noémon entity*.

The above two principles are foundational pillars of the TNS and in what follows I will refer to both of them by the single abbreviation: PriNS (principle of noémon systems).

Let me come now to a few remarks clarifying certain implicit points. First, I should note a significant difference between definitions 2 and 3. The former involves necessarily the condition of *own*-representational systems whereas noémon entities do not *necessarily* possess such systems. For instance, a E_n may be characterised by *designed* representational systems (e.g., robot; see definition-8), or by *acquired* coding systems as those likely to be developed by lateral gene transfer. The latter may evolve into *own*-representational systems. In other words, noémon entities may also be characterised by *own*-representational systems that are not species-specific and are acquired during a noémon entity's evolution. See Sect. 2.2 for the possibility of *own* representational system evolution.

Second, definitions 2 & 3 delineate classes of noémon systems that are both substantially similar and distinct. For instance, definition-3 delineates classes of systems that not necessarily possess *own*-representational systems neither the ability to create *permanent* external representations. In addition, definition-2 refers to a species and therefore all species characteristics are applicable to it as well. Of course, there are many species concepts proposed and debated (e.g., Queiroz 2005; Mallet 2007; Vaux et al. 2016). For clarity, I state that I adopt the biological species concept (BSC). For a strong argument for BSC and against rival so called species concepts as well as an interesting historical note on BSC and discussion of the species problem see Mayr (2004). Recent work on viruses (Bobay & Ochman 2018) strongly indicates that viruses can be organised into biological species, opening the possibility for a definition of species applicable across cellular and acellular forms of life.

Similarities accrue from sharing condition (b) and partially sharing condition (c). Further similarities (as well as differences) will become more clear as we develop each chapter. For now, it suffices to say that the three conditions of definition-3 delineate classes of noémon systems that identify both artificial minds and biological minds not belonging to a species. Such systems may include coral reefs, termite colonies, and possibly unicellular organisms (e.g., bacteria, archaea, and unicellular eucariotic organisms like an amoeba). Examples of both biological and artificial noémon systems (e.g., organisms, entities, and collective systems) are depicted in Fig. 1.3. Several significant issues that arise in relation to problems of biological classification (most notably the species problem and the issue of individuality) fall beyond the remit of this two-volume monograph.

Third, all the distinct notions coming under the heading of situated cognition hold true for both definitions. For instance, the single system we call 'mind' through its identification with an individual of a species or with a noémon entity is inseparably linked to an appropriate subsystem of an individual organism (e.g., nervous system), or to that of a E_n. Also, the individual of a noémon species is affected by the evolution of that species. The notions of embodiment and situatedness are incorporated in PriNS. The latter actually incorporates the essence of situatedness, as any species has to be situated. Finally, it should be noted that any characteristic of a species is a characteristic of all individuals of the species except for grossly mutated or severely injured individuals. In contrast, a characteristic of an individual of a species or even of a large population within it is not necessarily a characteristic of that species. In other words, there are species-specific and *own* characteristics of individuals. The individual of a noémon species ontogenetically evolves the characteristics of her/his species and s/he may acquire her/his own ones that may in turn be inherited (e.g., Bonduriansky & Day 2009; Penny 2015; Skinner 2015; Sarkies 2020).

Individuality grows within species limits. Its growth potential increases as species complexity increases. Noémon species (replacing the traditional biological notion of minds) like flying species have their own species characteristics. The characteristics of a noémon species are differentially instantiated in, and potentially modified by, individuals of that species. This differential instantiation, and potential modification, is the result of the interactive process between inheritance and the environment (including that species). Naturally, the range of phenomena a noémon species (including the range of 'mental' phenomena) may possess or exhibit depend entirely on that species.

Fourth, the graded (hierarchical) nature of definitions 2 & 3 allow for both broadness and specificity. This graded nature is in full accordance with the single most important characteristic of evolution, namely gradation, as it was repeatedly pointed out by Darwin (1859*2006). He writes, for instance:

> "In the distant future I see open fields for far more important researches. Psychology will be based on a new foundation, that of the necessary acquirement of each mental power and capacity by gradation. Light will be thrown on the origin of man and his history." (Darwin, 1859*2006, p. 759).

Definitions 2 & 3 delineate at least four and three classes of noémon systems within their superordinate classes of noémon species and noémon entities respectively. Two particularly interesting and significant such classes are those delineated by systems fulfilling the first three conditions of both of these definitions. It is worth clarifying here that each additional condition, *at its minimum*, delineates a narrower class of systems (see next point on the parametric nature of each condition). When the third condition is materialised, the class of communicating systems emerges (the cornerstone notion of 'communication' is fully discussed in chapter-4).

Fifth, the parametric nature of definitions 2 & 3 provides the basis for an extremely wide range of classes of noémon species and entities. Essentially, it can be used as a system of criteria for deciding to what *specific* class of physical systems a particular animal species or noémon entity belongs. On this basis, I would say that parrots as exemplified by Alex (Pepperberg 1999) and Griffin (Pepperberg & Nakayama 2016), bonobos as exemplified by Kanzi (Savage-Rumbaugh et al 1998), Cephalopoda as exemplified by the mimic octopus (Norman et al 2001; Godfrey-Smith 2017), and dolphins (e.g., Herman et al. 1984) delineate different and distinct classes of noémon species. These criteria can be enhanced and/or refined by the introduction of animal *primitive* systems (see chapter-4 for discussion) and poly- parametric traits like consciousness and emotion.[2] Much simpler organisms like the individuals of *C. elegans* fulfil the first

[2] These phenomena are discussed in the monograph's Consequences volume.

two conditions of definition-2 and, therefore, are members of a noémon species. As far as we presently know *historic Homo sapiens*

(H) is the only *evolutionary part* of a noémon species fully fulfilling condition (d). By 'fully', I mean the full parametric range of the latter condition. In other words, only *historic* humans are able to use *written* human language whereas behaviourally modern humans seem to fulfil condition (d) only to the extent that it is taken to refer to certain Art work. When applied to *H. sapiens*, the full parametric range of condition (d) delineates distinct phases in its evolution (see, next section for discussion and consequences).

Sixth, in general, a noémon system may be characterised by any system of notions that subsumes the minimum system of notions characterising a *minimally* noémon system as specified by definitions 2 & 3 above. Each *additional* notion is identified with an *additional* parameter that corresponds to an *additional* phenomenon characterising a *different* class of noémon systems. In other words, different *systems of notions* determine *different kinds* of noémon systems. The totality of all possible systems of notions delineate all possible classes of noémon systems populating S. The appropriate specification of their parameters is a major empirical and theoretical undertaking. Chapters 2, 3, and 4 of this volume provide a first cut on the qualitative worth and quantitative extent of these definitions. Chapters 2, 3, and 4 of the monograph's Consequences volume (Gelepithis 2024b) demonstrate further the explanatory power of these definitions by applying them to the phenomena of 'knowledge', 'consciousness' and 'emotions'.

My final remark concerns the similarities and differences between the PSSH and PriNS principles. Both principles provide necessary and sufficient conditions for delineating the space of noémon species. Their primary differences are two. First, the PSSH delineates a flat space whose members cannot be differentiated. In sharp contrast the PriNS delineates a highly structured space whose members are differentiated by the number of conditions they fulfil. The first two conditions of PriNS delineate as many types of noémon systems as the PSSH does with a significant difference. PriNS allows existence of the human constructability constraint whereas the PSSH supports either human omnipotence or biological degradation by ignoring basic neuroscientific findings. In addition, the third condition of PriNS introduces a major constraint in the space of noémon systems, namely, the ability to communicate. Finally, the fourth condition of noémon species (definition-2) partitions the space of systems capable of understanding into two qualitatively different subspaces.

The second difference between PSSH and PriNS stems from the different overall theories supporting them. Namely, the information processing approach and TNS. They, in turn, are based on different minimum vocabularies. TNS's vocabulary is smaller than that of the computational approach and explains a wider class of noémon systems phenomena.

The above remarks provide a first cut justification of definitions 2 & 3. Their full justification rests with the full explication of all parametric conditions of PriNS in this volume in terms of the foundational development of TNS. The latter's full strength becomes clear with the second volume of my monograph (Gelepihtis 2024b). Let us start with the first condition of definitions 2 & 3: representational systems.

2.2 Representational Systems and the Nature of AI

> "Twentieth century bacteriology was a prime example of a science not seeking to define itself, letting itself instead be defined by external influences."
>
> (Woese 2004, p. 177).

AI is in a similar state. Like bacteriology (Stanier & Van Niel 1962; Woese 2004), AI has failed to define its constitutive notion. Unlike bacteriology many 'definitions' of AI have been proposed. All of them are inadequate. Appendix-1 demonstrates their inadequacies.

Representational systems and the nature of AI are not usually related. Of course, knowledge representation and reasoning (KRR) systems in tandem with machine learning are the two pillars of AI. Still, work on these two key components of AI systems is mainly limited to their technical, not conceptual foundations. This section breaks away with this state of affairs demonstrating the close relation between representational systems, the nature of AI, and human nature. In particular, it reviews and defines representation, proposes a complete and most inclusive definition of AI in terms of PriNS, and concludes with a novel stance on the relation between the feasibility of the AGI hypothesis and the evolving nature of *Homo sapiens*. Let me proceed with my review.

The literature on the nature of 'representation' is daunting and controversial. Even the existence of 'representation' has been debated (e.g., Rorty 1979; Brooks 1991, Kelso 1995 against; Bechtel 1998, Clark & Toribio 1994). Stufflebeam (1998) sits on the fence with a leaning towards the against side.

Taking for granted that 'representation' does exist, there are only three points of general agreement. First, our ignorance of the nature and mechanisms of representation is stunning and clearly expressed. For instance, Dietriech (2007, p. 1) remarks that "no scientist knows how mental representations represent". What is worse though is, that it is still the case that what counts as representation is still unclear. In addition, the literature on representation conflates human thinking and mental representations with KRR schemes in AI (Rich and Knight 1991; Winston 1992; Luger 2002). The result is stalled progress on both.

The second point of agreement is that all approaches to the nature of representation draw upon or combine, in varying degrees, two ideas: (i) aspects of Peircian semiotics; and (ii) the mathematical notion of isomorphism (e.g., Gallistel 1990; Edelman 1998).

So, Newell (1990 p. 59; and 1992 p. 426) identified the notion of mathematical isomorphism with what he calls "the representation law". In a nutshell, his proposed law of representation reads:

> "decode[encode(T)(encode(X))] = T(X) where X is the original external situation and T is the external transformation."

This proposal is assumed, without argumentation, to capture the essence of representation (Newell 1990 p. 59; and 1992 p. 426). This is a pretty simple and useful picture but not the whole one. It is a conception avoiding Peircian complexities and it is biased towards KRR schemes and tool-based reasoning.

There is a large number of scientists whose view of 'representation' is based on the assumption that if a structure is regularly and reliably activated by a distal condition then that is adequate reason to believe that structure as representing the distal condition. This assumption of "receptor representation" has been effectively criticised by Ramsey (2003).

Von Eckardt (1992) made explicit the common view of the nature of representation adopted by the majority of cognitive scientists. That view is a simplification of Peirce's (1877) theory essentially identifying his notion of "interpretant" to a "thought or series of thoughts in the mind of the interpreter" (ibid). Computational formalisms, whether logic- or graph-based, try to explicitly describe the "interpretant".

Within this broad framework theories on the nature of representation abound. For instance: Representations as enduring states and by implication in terms of memory (Broadbent 1989); dynamical approaches viewing the brain and mental representations as systems of differential equations (e.g., Van Gelder 1998); Connectionist approaches in terms of the artificial neural network notions of activation and weights and their mathematical idealisation in terms of vector spaces (e.g., Churchland, Patricia S. & Sejnowski 1992); representation in terms of stimuli (Hurford 2003); second order resemblance theory of mental representation (O'Brien & Opie 2004). The latter is in broad agreement with von Eckardt's approach. Resemblance is one of the three modern names (the others being conventional and causal) used instead of Peirce's original expressions of iconic, symbolic and indexical to refer to the three ways in which signs represent (modern parlance: grounded).

The third point of general agreement is that there are two basic types of representation: internal (or mental), and external. This point is actually so obvious that no-one has been really interested in comparing these two types. I decided to differ. In what follows I identify both important similarities and *the* key difference between mental and external representations. The identified key difference, namely, permanent external representations is partly responsible for the uniqueness of—what used to be called and still is—human mind within the spectrum of biological and artificial evolution (see next section). According to TNS, the traditional notion of 'human mind' may only have meaning as part of an individual of the *Homo* genus.

I start with the most familiar case, external human representations, and continue with AI representations.[3]

Consider the following ubiquitous examples of *external* human representations and try to think of the *processes* that created them:

(1) Designs of all sorts and small scale models like those used to represent a major urban development, a spacecraft or a teddy bear.

[3] A very small part of the following discussion on representation draws upon Gelepithis (1995).

(2) Logic expressions, geometrical diagrams, computer programs, equations.
(3) Camera images, (further processed or not), and miscellaneous forms in theatre, painting, sculpture, or cinema to name the most obvious ones.
(4) Certain patterns or behavioural acts like those involved in speech, sign or written language.

In all these cases, representations are characterised by the following properties: (i) they are simplifications of some situation B; (ii) they aim to preserve the essential characteristics of B; (iii) they can be processed by humans; and (iv) they are part of a physical material. Therefore:

Definition-4 For a human H, an external representation of a situation B *is* an artificial construction C_a of her characterised by the properties:

(a) C_a is a simplification of B; and
(b) C_a preserves, at least some of, the essential characteristics of B.

Interestingly, this definition is in accordance with both Aristotle's (4th c. BCE*1984b) views on poetry and drama as human endeavours to mimic (i.e., re-present) *the essence* of human actions and the standard cognitive science view stated earlier.

We are now faced with two questions:

What are the essential characteristics of B?
What is the system of human processes creating C_a?

The received answer to the first question is straightforward: what counts as 'essential' depends on the objectives of the representation set by H. Specifically, by the following two parameters:

(i). The aspects of B that H has decided to represent (technically known as the scope of a representation); and
(ii). The amount of their detail (technically known as the grain size).

This standard analysis clarifies definition-4 and adequately addresses Van Fraassen's (2008, p. 15) query:

"We confront here the general question of how an item such as a picture can correctly represent, misrepresent, caricature, flatter, or revile its subject."

Notice for instance that "correctly represent", "misrepresent" etc.are all types of representations (as defined above) differentiated by the parameters of scope and grain. The second question (Q2) falls outside the standard analysis and leads one to distinguish between human thinking (definition-24, Sect. 3.2.1) and tool-based reasoning. The latter, although ultimately depends on human thinking and constructability, is characterised by a system of rules which –after having been specified by H—enable anyone to draw conclusions mechanically. Naturally, such tool-based reasoning whether it is carried out by grammars, graph theories, or in general, mathematics- either is based on abstract characteristics of human mechanisms of thinking or implements mechanisms of tool-based reasoning (i.e., of KRR schemes) unrelated to actual human mechanisms of thinking. Some early work on semantic networks attempted to address some of the psychological mechanisms of thinking but it was soon forgotten and abandoned. Of course, both approaches can be and have been combined.

External representations have evolved from static constructions (like initial forms of say teddy bears or, earlier, by African wooden figurines) to dynamic systems able to draw conclusions themselves (e.g., AI systems). To refer to any type or instance of *external* representations I will use the symbol ${}^{ext}R_H$. Finding out even some of the mechanisms for the creation of ${}^{ext}R_H$ would be a major breakthrough. I am tempted to suggest that an investigation of the mechanisms for the creation of ${}^{ext}R_H$ through the process of understanding and its associated systems of primitives may be worth pursuing (cf, Chapter 4).

The next step in the study of human representations is even more demanding. It stems from the existence of a fifth category of representations that need to be added to the previous four (1)–(4) we specified earlier. It may be described as follows:

(5) Visual images or other representational formations of the human nervous system.

A third question should now be added to our previous system of two questions, namely:

> What is the system of human processes creating internal (e.g., *nervous system*) human representations (${}^{int}R_H$)?

The added difficulty may easily be seen when one realises that creation of ${}^{int}R_H$ may well involve unconscious processes and in addition ${}^{int}R_H$ they usually lack the permanence of ${}^{ext}R_H$ (whether Cycladic figurines or KRR schemes). It should be noted that the previous sentence does not imply that ${}^{ext}R_H$ may not involve unconscious processes. I only wanted to point out the possibility that ${}^{int}R_H$ may be more affected than ${}^{ext}R_H$ by unconscious processes.

Similarly to ${}^{ext}R_H$, specification of the mechanisms for the creation of ${}^{int}R_H$ (in contrast to mere identification of its end result) is a significant open question in the study of mind. As with ${}^{ext}R_H$, it appears that ${}^{int}R_H$ may well be related to understanding. In contrast to ${}^{ext}R_H$, such understanding, if indeed related, may, more often than not, be unconscious and hence hardly accessible with the current state of technology. Whether they do, and if yes exactly how they are related, is another important question.

Although theories of brain representation along with comparison models and studies based on brain imaging techniques abound: Research on spatial representational system (e.g., Moser et al. 2008); numerical representation (e.g., Nieder & Dehaene 2009); representational distance matrices (e.g., Kriegeskorte & Kievit 2013); models reconstructing a person's specific visual experience by measuring brain activity (e.g., Kay et al. 2008; Carlson et al. 2013; Güçlütürk et al. 2017), no theory on the mechanisms of brain representations has been proposed.

These problems not withstanding, since we assume the continuity of the *Homo* genus (and therefore of some relation between neural and external representations) and take into account the notion of perceptual image, we find it reasonable to adopt the following working:

Definition-5 For a human H, a NS representation of a situation B *is* a 'meaningful' structure of 'neural formations', C_n, such that:

(a) C_n is a simplification of B; and
(b) C_n tends to preserve the essential characteristics of B.

The notions of 'neural formations' and 'meaningful' are defined in Sect. 3.2.1, definitions -14a and -14b).

The above definition is both in agreement with neurobiological requirements of internal representations (e.g., Blakemore et al. 2002, Moser et al. 2008) and avoids Ramsey's (2003) criticisms of receptor representation. It is also straightforwardly generalisable to hold for a good number of animal species in full agreement with Bickerton's (1990) argument that a primary representational system, developed in various forms, exists in all higher animals and Hurford's (2003) argument of powerful neural representational systems. Finally, it is compatible with the classical ethological finding of relative uniqueness of nearly every species through their species-specific representational capabilities.

It is worth noting that neuroimaging experiments, incorporating the notions of scope and grain size of a representation, may just be possible to indicate potential neural structures that preserve certain characteristics of Kurto & Itskov's (2008) work on group cells and their relationship to the Kantian concept of space may be seen as an example of such work. It should be stressed though that the issue of neural representations, even in the special case of spatial representation with its nearly forty years history (e.g., O'Keefe & Dostrovsky 1971), has far too many open questions (e.g., Moser et al 2008) for definitive conclusions concerning its nature to be drawn.

In any case, we are now in position to provide a working definition of the crucial notion of representation in its generality (i.e., independent of human characteristics):

Definition-6 A representation of a situation, say, B, *is* a construction, C, characterised by the properties:

(a) C simplifies B; and
(b) C preserves the essential characteristics of B. (revised from Gelepithis 2001f, p. 251).

Now let us consider again the representation examples that were given in (1)–(5). First, (1) *are not* in human language or any other form of notational convention. Representations in (2) are in coded form (known or even unknown to some of us). Those in (3) may employ cultural and/or linguistic conventions as well as expressions of feelings, therefore, they may *be* in both linguistic and non-linguistic materials. Representations in (4) *are* in the behavioural material (e.g., speech). Those in (5) are nervous system representations.

In summary, human representations are of two different kinds: $^{int}R_H$ (category-5 examples) and $^{ext}R_H$ ones (categories 1–4 examples). Within the latter class, all but one type differ only in the degree of their formalisability and interpretability. The outstanding type are computer programs. Their key differentiating characteristic is their *relative* autonomy and *derived* thinking capabilities. To be precise all work in AI has, and continues to be, concentrated on developing theories and techniques that enable *humans* to build machines with cognitive, perceptual or motor capabilities to carry out jobs *humans assign* to them. All such developments are characterised by representing aspects of *human* knowledge, problems, reasoning processes, sensory information, etc. They require from us humans to represent everything in a way that is computer-processable. Systems of AI employ *computer-based representations* that are *human-dependent* and, subsequently, so are the *current* robots.

So far, I have used the abbreviation 'AI' and the word 'robot' in a common sense way. Aiming to unify psychology and AI, one need to have a clear understanding of the nature of AI and of its constitutive notions. Jointly, the following three definitions define AI.

Definition-7 AI is the study, design, and development of artificially-intelligent systems (AISs) and robots. *Where*:

Definition-8 An AIS is a system that fulfils the following conditions:

(a) Possess representational systems of human knowledge.
(b) Possess the ability of thinking.
(c) (a) and (b) are designed and built by humans.

Definition-9 Robot, *R*, is an AIS possessing, in addition, a motor system that enables it to move in and affect its environment.

NB: An AIS with movable parts that is not moving is of course not a robot.

How do my definitions fare in relation to the two perennial issues of the field: The definition of AI and the feasibility of AGI? In the rest of this section I consider them in turn.

All but one of the numerous definitions of AI suffer either from being circular or being obscurantist (i.e., stated in terms of obscure definiens). Appendix-1 provides a panorama of these numerous unsuccessful attempts to define AI along with brief critical remarks.[4] In addition to my definition of AI, the only other non circular or obscurantist one is by Newell (1990). The following few paragraphs compare Newell's definition with the TNS one.

Newell offered the first non-circular and non-obscurantist definition of AI in terms of his unified theory of cognition that I briefly introduced in Sect. 1.3. Specifically, he wrote:

> "AI is the study of the mechanisms of intelligence and all supporting technologies, extending to perception and motion, namely robotics." (Newell 1990 p. 40).

Where,

> "A system is *intelligent* to the degree that it approximates a knowledge-level system." (ibid. p. 90).

The notion of knowledge level system and Newell's conception of knowledge have been dealt with in Sect. 1.3.

On the positive side of Newell's definition is clarity and the wide range of intensional specification. In addition, it is cast in terms of the primitives notions of his unified theory of cognition that makes it the first theory-based definition of AI. Finally, it is free of circularity and obscure definiens. On the negative side it faces two insuperable problems. One, it is based on a conception of knowledge that is exclusively goal-oriented. Two, it is restricted to *syntactic* AI. In contrast to Newell's definition, the TNS one does not suffer from any of the said problems.

Newell chose not to comment on the feasibility of AGI or superintelligence. Let me start commenting on them. I start with a provisional classification. By comparing definitions 3 and 8, one deduces that any AIS is a noémon entity; the inverse is, of course, not true. The class of noémon entities is broader than that of AISs. It should be noted that the notion of noémon entity is not necessarily restricted to artificial systems.

[4] Of course, the Appendix does not include legalist definitions of AI like the one developed by OECD for administrative uses—and accepted by many countries for the same reasons. Such definitions avoid the essence of the problem and eventually I expect them to turn out to become obsolete if not progress- hindering ones.

Biological systems that do not fulfil the requirements of a species (a major open issue in biology) may well belong to the class of noémon entities. An example of such a biological system is Archaea (cf, discussion following definition-3). Our current knowledge of the living world on our planet is quite limited and does not allow us to classify Archaea. Figure 2.1 compares classes of noémon systems delineated by the minimum number of conditions characterising them.[5]

A sixth one is lurking in the bush of possibilities: a robot with its *own* representational system. Although, the possibility of an AIS with *own* representational system is probably equally likely, for convenience I will focus the following discussion to robots. So far we have discussed external and internal representations and saw that humans and non-human animals possess their *own* nervous systems representations that differ remarkably among themselves. In sharp contrast to this category of internal representations, *Homo sapiens* has developed an incredible rich range of external representations (cf, definition-4).

In general, there are two fundamentally different classes of representational systems: those ***materialised by*** nervous systems; and those ***based on***

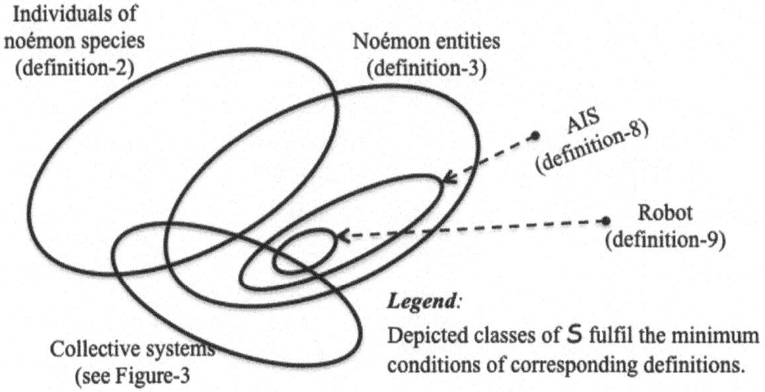

Fig. 2.1 Comparison of five classes of noémon systems

[5] It should be noted that definiens like 'thinking' that are constitutive conditions of definitions 2, 3, 8, and 9 are differentially materialised in classes of noémon systems more specialised than those delineated by these definitions.

non-nervous systems. In particular, within the human external representations a further fundamental distinction exists: the class of computational representations materialised within AISs (definition-8). Figure 2.2 illustrates our analysis so far and points out to the intriguing possibility of a robot with its *own* representational system.

The reader may well think that Fig. 2.2 is partly mistaken in allowing the possibility arrow depicted in it to originate from the non-nervous systems node. If at all possible it would appear reasonable to originate from the AIS branch of the Computational node or to actually define the 'other' branch of the latter node. Nevertheless, that would contradict a key result concerning the foundations of AI. Let me explicate.

The strong AI objective has been shown to be untenable *by humans*, because of limits of human constructability (Gelepithis 1984).[6] In the same work, I indicated the possibility of a genuine, hyper-human, 'artificial intelligence' not constructed by *Homo sapiens*. Jointly, the foundational result and the possibility of robots with hyper-human intelligence justify the selected origin of the possibility arrow of Fig. 2.2.

In that early work such a possibility was envisaged on the basis of the nature of evolution and logic. In later work, Gelepithis (2001f) introduced a specific condition under which such a possibility could be

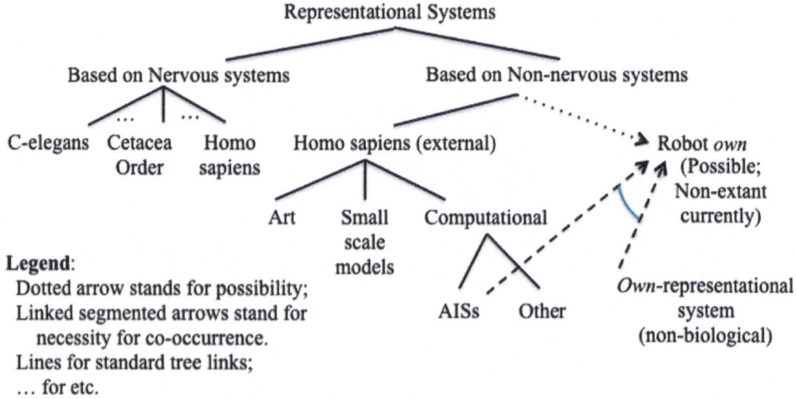

Fig. 2.2 Classes of representational systems. See text for explanations

[6] For summary of the argument see Gelepithis (1991).

realised without contravening the limits of human constructability. The required condition is the development of *own*- representational system that would be independent of both human constructability and of any human characteristics or features, which might have been limiting its functions or development over time. In other words the sought requirement should leave open the possibility of human-independent noémon entity evolution. What sort of representational system would fulfil the above requirements?

The following definition does fulfil the sought requirements.

Definition-10 An E_n possesses its *own* representational system, R_o, if and only if, R_o is independent of the language of another kind of noémon entity E_n^*.

(Adapted from Gelepithis 2001f).

Noémon systems materialising the notion of *own* representational system are ubiquitous. Virtually each and every noémon *species* possess a different one. Definition-10 reveals a possible way that does not violate Gelepithis' conclusion. Such a way requires the combination of two elements: (a) traditional AISs; and (b) own-robot evolution. Is the latter kind of evolution possible?

The possibility of machine evolution has been argued by Buttler (1872) in his classic science fiction *Erewhon, or Over the Range*. Nevertheless, Butler's notion of machine evolution was based on the evolution of human constructability which we now know to be subject to intrinsic limits.

The idea of *own*-robot evolution is fundamentally distinct. In the rest of this section, I take the idea of own representational system a step further down the road by introducing the idea of an autonomous robot entity and briefly remark on the idea of *own*-robot evolution.

Definition-11 An autonomous robot entity, (ARE) is a noémon entity that may *only* partly be designed and built by humans that fulfils the following conditions:

(a) Possess R_o (e.g., sensory, motor, knowledge); and
(b) Possess the ability of thinking.

NB: Materialisation of conditions (a) and (b) will lead to *own*-thinking. *Own*-robot *evolution* does not necessarily follow though.

To avoid any potential misunderstanding, I should haste to stress that an ARE is still just a theoretical notion within TNS. It is an elaboration of the theoretical construct of 'ideal robot' that I introduced in my doctorate (Gelepithis 1984). It is possible that it may never get to be materialised. The key difference between the two theoretical constructs boils down to the following point. The 'ideal robot' was an ad hoc hypothetical construct, whereas ARE is an integral theoretical construct of TNS. To avoid any potential ambiguity and maintain the link to my early work, I will alternatively call an ARE an own-robot. The latter, of course, is an instantiation of the notion of *own*-AI. For the human, animal, and robot kinds of thinking see Sect. 3.2.2. For the limits of communication between ARE and humans see Sect. 4.3.

The possible emergence of AREs would bring with it major consequences. Only very few of them I could envisage. For instance, AREs would initially possess a hybrid nature involving a minimum of human design and *formal* human knowledge. This initial 'endowment' could of course be discarded by them at any point sufficient further down on their evolutionary path and disassociate them from their human origin. The split in the hominini lineage may come to one's mind.

It should be noted that AREs, would develop *own*-knowledge, *own*-problems, and most likely *own*-ethics. In such a case, it is nearly certain that, human science would be overtaken by *own*-AI science. The relation of ARE ethics to *H. sapiens* ethics would be a major open issue –if humans had a say. It would not be the only one. The speciation problem would acquire an extra dimension for us, but it might have an obvious solution to an ARE society. The principles of evolution would have to be modified more radically than ever.

Could or should we impose constraints on the design principles used to construct AI systems so that the probability of ARE materialisation is decreased to the minimum possible? This is a very difficult issue because AI increases exponentially the impact on and possibilities of both *Homo sapiens* and its members. It has three fundamentally different types of impact on human society. First, on human employment and decision making. Second, on human knowledge that is now partly derived by AI systems. Although, such knowledge is still based on human primitives, we are unable to derive it on our own. AI-based science is bound to influence our *future* evolution (barring destruction of human technoscientific civilisation). Third, on the increasing modification of the anatomical and physiological characteristics of humans. All of these three types of impact may turn out to have positive or negative results. We cannot know in advance. We can only try to think what is best for human society as a whole and try to achieve it.

How could an $\mathsf{R_o}$ of an ARE be developed? Obviously, I could not know for otherwise I would have been arguing against myself on the limits of human constructability. Still the possibility exists and actually reaching our thinking and design limits is also a must. My own attempt follows. The start of such a process is both obvious and necessary. It must begin with some human 'seeding'. Specifically:

> *Seeding*: At least one robot *R* (designed and built by humans) with as many formalised aspects of human knowledge as possible. To avoid any potential misunderstandings, I should add that *R*'s body of knowledge includes as one of its subsystems a human-based representational system.

NB: All AI work can play the role of seeding. Some work explicitly aims at building robots exhibiting *aspects* of one or more fundamental or high-order human features like emotions. Please note that I stressed *aspects* above. For, certain *aspects* of emotions, (e.g., conscious awareness of them), cannot be possessed by an *R*.[7] Such work incorporates useful seeding work but it will keep failing to capture the non- formal aspects of any human trait.[8]

What steps might be required for an *R* to to develop *own* representational system, $\mathsf{R_o}$, of its/her/his environment?

At least two pathways exist (and of course their possible combination). The first involves mere chance, the second initiative on behalf of *R* (both independent of human action). I say a few words for each one of them in turn. In the first case, a chance event in *R*'s X-ware could lead to new *own* systems of representation and thereafter to *own*-robot evolution. The second case appears to be possible via *R*'s development of a *new* machine learning process. Specifically, a system seeded with a multiplicity of all distinct types of learning may well increase the likelihood of *R* deducing

[7] Knowledge, consciousness and emotions are huge topics. They are addressed in their own chapters in the Consequences volume of this monograph (Gelepithis 2024b). Specifically, the points raised here are addressed in Sects. 2.2.3 (AIS-derived knowledge); 3.3.2 (possibility of robot *own*- consciousness); and 4.3.2 (limits of robot emotionality).

[8] Due to limits of human constructability (Gelepithis 1984, 1991) and more recently Gelepithis (2021).

a *new* learning process instead of simply deducing pattern combinations unknown to and undeducible by humans. Of course, a chance or deduced combination of the two pathways increases the likelihood of an R_0 development.

Finally, it may be worth mentioning that were an R_0 to be developed, the question of its relation to *R*'s body of human-based knowledge is raised. Again two pathways would be possible. First, *R* would develop its *own* systems and ignore its human-based body of knowledge. The end result of such a process would be an ARE with the minimum formal communication with humans. Alternatively, *R* may (decide to) relate the compatible elements of the knowledge systems of itself and *R*. In this case, either the developed ARE would subsume the compatible parts of the original *R*'s human-based knowledge system as a subsystem of itself, or it would keep the compatible knowledge parts of itself and *R* available to be used by itself as per situation.

The next section introduces the evolutionary component of noémon systems focusing on Hominin evolution, reviews the continuity vs discontinuity (or gradualist) debate, and takes a closer look at one unique type of evolving representational system: human language. As a preamble, it should be noted that the written form of human language has played a singular role in the evolution of *Homo sapiens* and along with its consequences are increasingly transforming human nature, our society, and our perceived relations to both other primate species and robots.

2.3 *Homo Sapiens* Evolution: The Written Language Transition

> "There can be no doubt that the difference between the mind of the lowest man and that of the highest animal is immense."
>
> (Darwin 1871*2006, pp. 836–7).
>
> "Any ape can reach for a banana, but only humans can reach for the stars. ... Especially awe inspiring is the fact that any single brain, including yours, is made up of atoms that were forged in the hearts of countless, far-flung stars billions of years ago."
>
> (Ramachandran, 2012, p. 4).

Darwin (1809–1882), in *The Descent of Man, and Selection in Relation to Sex* (1871*2006), considered all the key mental traits and behavioural aspects that were then assumed to be unique (i.e., to differ ***in kind***) to humans, and argued that the differences between humans and animals, on all of them, were really differences *in degree*. All examined traits and behavioural aspects, he concluded, had precursors in lower animals. Darwin's argument for continuity (DAC) was exhibiting, for the first time, an unbroken continuity between humans and lower animals. His list comprised the following:

> D_L = {Brain size and gross anatomy; Emotions; Curiosity; Imitation; Attention; Memory; Imagination; Reason; Progressive improvement; Tools and weapons; Language; Self-consciousness; Developmental issues; Sociability; Sense of beauty; Belief in God, spiritual agencies, superstitions; The moral sense}.

That book, synthesis of new evidence and a logical consequence of his *On the Origin of Species*, explained human mind and behaviour in terms of his theory of natural selection and the "numerous, successive, slight modifications" that nature takes advantage of and can be inherited by subsequent generations of biological systems (Darwin 1859*2006).

At the end of the third quarter of the nineteenth century, Darwin's list was perceived to be comprehensive and his coverage of the available data comprehensive. In such a state of affairs Darwin's conclusion was unassailable for all non-dogmatic thinkers. Since then, the spectacular expansion and deepening of human science and technology brought to the fore a wealth of new data that led evolutionary biologists to modify, in some cases substantially, certain aspect of his theory.[9] Presently, Darwin's theories of evolution (DaTE) along with a number of modifications have come to be known as the EES (extended evolutionary synthesis) approach. Within the emerging EES approach the debate on human nature plays a significant contributing role.

Historic *Homo sapiens* (H) evolution is characterised both by an exponential acceleration of its scientific knowledge (i.e., both science—in its widest sense—and its associated technologies and techniques) and an

[9] Mayr (2004, p. 97, 98) in a "[G]reatly revised version of Mayr (1985)" argued for five logically distinct theories of evolution developed by Darwin and that "Darwin's blindness to recognise this became one of the main reasons for the never-ending controversies on evolutionary biology after 1859.".

exponential impact of its use on planet Earth and its biosphere. The planetary impact of H has been relatively recently recognised in the increasing use of the term 'Anthropocene' epoch and the debate for marking its origin and formal acceptance by the International Union of Geological Sciences.

Clarification of the notion of modern humans requires an unambiguous answer to the following question: What does *H. sapiens* mean? In other words, what is *Homo* nature? We still do not know (e.g., Wood & Collard 1999; Collard & Wood 2015). The Anthropocene cannot be fully explained either by the modern synthesis (MS) theory of evolution or the currently emerging cultural evolution and the wider EES approach (some call it framework). What is the source or driving force of the Anthropocene? This lacuna in evolutionary theory is exacerbated by considering questions like: How does *H. sapiens* evolution fare in comparison with major evolutionary transitions? Are there features shared by all major evolutionary transitions? (Szathmáry & Maynard Smith 1995; Maynard Smith & Szathmáry 1997; Szathmáry 2015). To this cluster of evolutionary issues I would add the following unusual, but closely related, question: What is the applicability time span of DAC? For instance, could DAC be extended to explain the observable differences in the behavioural outcomes of historic *Homo sapiens* between 1871 (H_{1871}) and 2021 (H_{2021}), or, more plausibly, H_{2424}?

This section provides a preliminary answer to these questions. In particular, it:

(a) briefly introduces the major modifications of DaTE (2.3.1);
(b) reviews the major recent developments on the continuity vs discontinuity (or gradualist) debate and the issue of the driving force of human cultural evolution (2.3.2); and
(c) identifies a new, major transition in *H. sapiens* evolution (2.3.3).

As an intellectual hors-d'oeuvre, I would like to notice in advance that the identified transition is caused by *written* human language (WHuLa). It determines the uniqueness of H and provides the necessary, evolving framework for a new inevitable transition stemming from it. The argument for the WHuLa transition involves an unexpected solution to the gradualist debate, and leads me to express my preliminary viewpoint on the emerging debate on the future of humanity.

2.3.1 *From Darwin's to The Extended Evolutionary Synthesis Theories*

Earthian evolution is still a largely unknown system of material processes. Its study permeates all of the life sciences. Seeds of the the Earthian evolutionary theory are to be found in Anaximander's work arguing for the descent of humans from fish and going through a good number of proponents and pioneers of evolutionary theory like Georges-Louis Leclerc (most widely known as Buffon 1707–1788) and Lamarck (1744–1829).[10] Darwin, in three books (1859, 1871, 1872) established the first materialist (exclusively natural) theory of evolution drawing upon an astonishing variety of sources including the fact of the extinction of species established by the key proponent of the fixity of species (Cuvier 1769–1832). DaTE was first extended and consolidated into the MS theory of evolution in the first half of the twentieth century. Subsequently, MS, a very sophisticated growth version of DaTE, was found to be wanting on the basis of evidence from a host of new branches of human knowledge and was proclaimed to be "effectively dead" by Gould (1980).

The ongoing development of the EES framework involves substantial modifications of the MS derived from advances in several fields including: molecular biology and especially genomics, systems biology, and the evo-devo approach. Of the large variety of new theoretical concepts, one can indicatively refer to: inclusive inheritance, phenotypic plasticity, niche construction, multilevel selection and a suite of concepts (e.g., emergent properties, bistable changes) and approaches like systems biology (see Müller 2017 for an excellent introduction and an argument for the necessity of the EES). So far, although Müller's necessity argument is being accepted, a unified theory of evolution integrating all the characteristic new elements of the EES framework lies considerably far in the future. To avoid the generation of an endless number of micro-theories obstructing such a unification objective, we need to develop theories of systems of related major issues that are compatible with the EES framework. The TNS provides an instance of such a theory addressing the foundational

[10] Buffon influenced both Lamarck and Cuvier and has been greatly praised by both Darwin and Ernst Mayr.

notions of noémon systems (including the traditional notion of human nature).[11]

The great amount of new data incompatible with the MS theory and the associated conceptual modifications had unexpected consequences. For instance, evolution was not required to be exclusively gradual while discontinuities between species were not any more taken to invalidate the principle of selection introduced in DaTE. The interesting consequence is an enrichment of the Darwinian principle of selection.

With respect to the cluster of issues investigated under 'human nature', the key difference between MS and the EES framework is the addition of the cultural form of evolution to the original organismic form. The former is widespread in Animalia and features in exceptional ways in humans. As Whiten et al. (2017, p. 7777) note:

> "the scope and penetration of culture is exceptional in humans [four references cited], and because of this, human culture extends biology in many additional and extraordinary ways." (Whiten et al. 2017, p. 7777).

Unfortunately, at least as far as Earthian ecosystems are concerned most of the effects of the *currently* dominant human culture are detrimental to their well being and even existence (e.g., Alberti et al. 2017; Boivin et al. 2016).

A closely related issue is the significance of human evolution within the overall evolutionary process of our planet and its effect on the EES. This was introduced by Szathmáry & Maynard Smith (1995) in explicitly discussing the overall issue of "[T]he major evolutionary transitions". Although they did not define the notion of 'major transition', they stated three features "that occur in many of the transitions" and provided a list. Their three features were: (i) reproductive complexity; (ii) division of labour; and (iii) information. Their list of 8 major transitions started off with the move from "replicating molecules to populations of molecules in compartments", through the move from prokaryotes to eukaryotes, to the latest transition from "primate societies to human societies". For the latter, language is taken as the driving force Maynard Smith & Szathmáry (1997).

[11] The topic of human nature and its evolution is addressed in Gelepithis (2024b, chapter-5).

More recently Szathmáry (2015) revised the original proposal of major transitions and reduced their number to seven. For our purposes, it suffices to remark that the transition to human societies remains and Szathmáry eventually concludes that human societies are on the road to become a major transition. His argument is essentially based on the fact that it includes elements highlighted in other transitions recognised as major. These elements are identified to be: cooperation, a form of eusociality, a powerful novel inheritance system, and living in groups (ibid, p. 10,110). This revised theory of major transitions brings to the fore from a different perspective the significance of ingredients of human culture for human evolution. I will return to human culture as an important contributor to the development of EES. For the time being let me introduce a second element differentiating MS and EES. It is more a perspective but it is important. It concerns the issue of transitions in biological and in particular human evolution. In essence it is an alternative to the origins approach that used to characterise evolutionary theory and introduces the notion of levels of complexity in material organisation.

Probably, the clearest exposition is by Foley (2016). He sees evolution as consisting of two elements. The first, called normal evolution, is common to all evolutionary changes and is an updated version of DaTE, pretty close to the MS theory. Its basic mechanisms are selection, variation, mutation, isolation, gene flow and drift. The second element termed transitional evolution consists of three additional fundamental types of evolutionary change. These four types of evolutionary change are identified or defined as follows:

(i) Normal (or baseline) evolution (as defined above).
(ii) Novel taxa, that is, occurrence of new lineages out of one ("usually through cladogenesis and speciation". Additional mechanisms like allopatry or genetic incompatibility may be required.
(iii) New adaptive zones, that is, "significant new adaptations which open up new ecological structures and opportunities" (ibid, p. 3). Examples range from echolocation, to homeothermy (c. 250 Ma), and amphibian colonisation of land (c. 370 Ma).
(iv) Major transitions. They are characterised by the emergence of "new biological processes", "or new units of selection, and there is increased complexity" (ibid.).

Can 'human' evolution count as a major transition? A suggestion, following an argument for a new *H. sapiens* transition, is made in the next section. Section 2.3.3 takes a closer look at this issue.

In addition to the ambiguity of the term 'human', 'major transition' is differentially used by Foley and Maynard Smith & Szathmáry.[12] As a result they reach different conclusions. First, MS&S identify 'language' as the driving force where Foley prefers an ambiguous answer:

> "There are several obvious candidates that could lead to such a transformation—technological dependence, language, cumulative culture, high levels of reproductive cooperation, and cooperation beyond kin- related individuals. To some extent they are all inter-related, such that it is probably impossible to untangle which is the key element." (Foley 2016, p. 11).

Second, Szathmáry (2015) argues, or rather believes, that human societies are on the road to a major transition, Foley (2016) envisages the possibility the currently tiny twig of human evolution to evolve into a branch in the tree (or coral) of life by persistence of *Homo sapiens* and extinction of closely related species.

Foley et al. (2016) take a different stance on both the issue of whether human societies constitute a major transition and the mechanism for reaching their current state. With respect to the former they write: "the major transitions of human evolution are comprised of multiple smaller ones." Regarding the latter they note that on the basis of suggestive evidence:

> "hominin evolution is neither a simple punctuated process, nor a constant gradual one, but a complex interaction between variable rates of change, environmental dynamics and the competitive interactions of the hominins and their sympatric fellow-travellers in evolution." (ibid. p. 3).

I agree with their point on the mechanisms but I cannot help noting that this viewpoint is essentially the same with Darwin's views on the rate and types of evolutionary change (Darwin 1859*2006). A different viewpoint, part of the TNS, is developed in subsect. 2.3.3 below.

[12] In this two-volume monograph, I use 'transition' in relation to a taxon (e.g., species) to be an evolutionary process that eventually leads all members of that taxon (species) to possess a particular characteristic or capacity.

I want to finish this subsection with two comparative remarks concerning DaTE and Newton's gravitational theory. First, a point of *apparent* dissimilarity. Newton (1643–1727) approximately described one of the fundamental mechanisms of Universal motion. Darwin (1809–1882) discovered one of the fundamental mechanisms of variation (type of change) of Earthian living systems. I wrote apparent because some have already argued (e.g., Dawkins 1982*2017) that DaTE is much more than a local theory concerning life on a little planet of an average star system. It can be seen as an adequate account of phenomena we associate with life in general. The second is a point of similarity. With respect to *Homo* knowledge, both theories will always be only approximately true. Newton's has already been subsumed within the general theory of relativity, Darwin's is undergoing a similar transformation in the form of the developing EES framework.

In overall summary, DaTE is an integrated, unified theory of Earthian life evolution and possibly of universal life with several inadequacies. The new emerging EES-based theory is expected to become a preferable cumulative theory of Earthian evolution of living forms.

2.3.2 Brief Review of the Gradualist Debate

Following an introductory note on points of agreement and debate issues on the wider issue of Hominin evolution, this section provides a brief review of the continuity vs discontinuity debate on the relation between humans and animals.

Points of agreement are very few and mostly expressed in ways revealing explicit or implicit sources of controversy. Let me illustrate with three examples of diminishing agreement. First, it has been estimated and widely accepted that Hominins split from the *Pan* genus at approximately 7 Ma. The second point of agreement is that the history and evolution of our closest relatives is far from being settled and the 'origin of *Homo sapiens* remains a matter of debate.' (e.g., Mounier & Lahr 2019). The third and last point of agreement is the range of mental traits and behavioural factors considered for uniqueness. It is recognised to be almost identical with D_L with the addition of a further single item, namely, the recognition of the significance of climatic changes for (Hominin) evolution. In relation to my last point it should be noted that there is considerable work on certain characteristics (e.g., symbols, numerosity) that sound new but they actually follow from, or depend upon, a combination of traits or behavioural factors of D_L.

The *Homo* clade of Hominin evolution is full of debates. Veldhuis et al. (2014) state at least twenty four key debating questions and since then more controversies have been added (e.g., the hunting-scavenging debate Pobiner 2020), and old ones have flared up (Moonier & Lahr 2019; Schlebusch et al. 2017; Stringer 2016). One rather major debate in paleoanthropology concerns the time-lag between the appearances of anatomically and behaviourally modern humans. The said transition, assumed to have taken at least 100 ka, is usually explained in terms of their intrinsic cognitive competences (e.g., McBrearty & Brooks 2000) and their associated archaeological signatures like technical innovations. Sterelny (2011) proposed a different account in terms of reliable transmission of accumulated information and the subsequent development of suitable learning environments. In this case the key archaeological markers of behaviourally modern humans are taken to be the following: broad-range foraging; environmental management; technical innovations; and symbolic culture (ibid., and references cited there). It is worth stressing that debates outside strict human evolution boundaries like the value of inclusive fitness (Birch 2017; Woodford 2019) provide interesting and in some cases illuminating perspectives (Bertolaso & Dieli 2017; FitzPatrick 2017). Finally, I want to note a point of disagreement that it is hardly ever directly recognised to exist. It concerns the notions of 'culture' and 'language' which are used either vaguely or defined in such a general way that cease to be of any substantial help. More on this below (Sect. 2.3.3).

Let me now move to my brief review of the continuity vs discontinuity debate (i.e., is there a unique human trait not shared in a precursor form by animals?) It may be worth reminding us that the sought uniqueness may be either a single trait or a unique system of traits. I would also like to clarify here that uniqueness refers to qualitative not quantitative human uniqueness. The latter is indeed obviously the case for several features shared by both humans and other animals. For instance displacement exhibited by bees, symbolic thinking exhibited by several species.

We saw that, within DaTE, DAC was irrefutable. Understandably, with respect to the middle of nineteenth century, DAC only addressed the observable behavioural differences between the "highest animal" and the "lowest man". Presently, the DL plus the climatic change range of characters should be considered at two levels:

(a) Individual phenotypic repertoire; and
(b) Non-phenotypic individual human system (e.g., genotype, nervous system). Wide-ranging research in the many disciplines contributing to a better understanding of our nature has produced a tremendous amount of data interpreted either as strengthening or refuting DAC and modifying DaTE while retaining its foundational principles.

In the last quarter of the twentieth century arguments supporting DAC used to be made mainly by comparative psychologists and primatologists (e.g., Savage- Rumbaugh 1986; Savage-Rumbaugh et al. 1998). At the turn of the century McBrearty & Brooks (2000) argued that human behaviour is characterised by the following four capabilities: abstract thinking; planning depth; behavioural, economic and technological innovativeness; and symbolic behaviour. In this context, they noted that examples of behavioural innovations of the Middle stone age in Africa include: Images, beads, fishing, long distance exchanges, pigment processing with LADs ranging from 45 to 280 Ka respectively.

Much more interesting, in my mind, is their claim (supported by considerable evidence) that.

> "the main behavioural shift leading to modernity lies at the Acheulian-MSA [Middle stone age] boundary about 250–300 Ka, not at the MSA-LSA [Lower stone age] boundary at 50–40 Ka as many assume." (ibid. p. 529).

This claim has by now been widely accepted. More recent work has confirmed (Marwick 2003; Sahle et al. 2013) and expanded the time horizon of the behavioural modernity of *H. sapiens* to > 300 Ka (Brooks et al. 2018). Nevertheless, claiming the above identified behavioural repertoire as a "major transition in human social and cognitive behavior" (ibid.) is plainly a mistake. I will return to this point in the next subsection.

Additional support for DAC is provided by work in several quarters. For instance, Greenspan & Shanker (2004), Pepperberg (2020). In line with DAC, Premack (2007) examined eight cognitive abilities and found that in all cases the "similarities between animal and human abilities are small, dissimilarities large." Heim et al.'s (2012) experiments fortified the homology of numerical estimation and numerical comparison between humans and monkeys. Kimbel & Villmoare's (2016) argument is based on "brain size, hand morphology and earliest technology". Some interesting, mostly indirect support, for DAC I am aware of is a target article by Chapman & Huffman (2018); The associated commentary includes dissenting voices. A selected couple of the latest data points that can be convincingly interpreted to support DAC is the demonstration of self-control by cuttlefish (Schnell et al. 2021), the orphan adoption of infants from a different social group by wild bonobos (Tokuyama et al. 2021), and the work on cetaceans (e.g., Rendel & Whitehead 2001).

The discontinuity claims cover most of the human specialisations considered by Darwin as well as new domains like numerosity, causality, transitivity, grammar, symbolic thinking, and brain-reading (i.e., ability of an animal, usually human, to draw inferences concerning the mental states of another one). To be noted that the latter domain is also known under the names of brain-coding, and theory of mind. The TNS that has been developed in this book and its companion (Gelepithis 2024b) supports the term brain-data understanding in preference to the previous ones. The reasons will be clear as the reader proceeds with her reading. In some cases, special instances of consciousness like death awareness are brought to one's attention (Avise & Ayala 2010), but consider Anderson James R. (2018). Equally exotic suggestions include "the emergence of mental time travel in evolution" as a crucial step in *H. sapiens* evolution (Suddendorf & Corballis 1997).

Despite Darwins's discussion of moral sense, an argument against DAC can be made on the basis of distinguishing between capacity for moral sense and the expression of moral norms (Ayala 2010). The former, like the Chomskyan language faculty is assumed to be unique to humans. The key problem with this view is twofold. One, 'moral sense' and 'moral norms' are not very likely possible to be separated as they both presuppose a society for their very existence. The second, and more devastating, point is Darwin's (1871*2006) remarks concerning the moral sense of animals.

A very different argument was presented in a relatively recent target article (Penn et al. 2008) in the *Behavioral and Brain Sciences*. They argued for a 'profound functional discontinuity between the human and nonhuman mind' and attempted to explain it on the basis of Newell's physical symbol system hypothesis (e.g., Newell 1990; See also Sect. 1.3). Their work was useful in reviewing, rather selectively, most of the evidence for unique human traits as well as the three major discontinuity theories, namely, the massive modularity hypothesis, the mind-reading hypothesis, and the language-only hypothesis. However, their overall argument was rather weak as they themselves changed their views on their response to the Peer Commentary. Specifically, they contradict themselves by arguing both for discontinuity and claiming that human and nonhuman minds differ in the *degree* they approximate a physical symbol system!

Interesting arguments favouring human uniqueness come from within neuroscience. Of course, the similarity of the nervous system of humans and other primates was a well established fact and it was well described by Darwin (1871*2006). What were inadequately documented were the differences between human and animal brains (see Passingham (2008) for an excellent documentation of human brain specialisations). Subsequent work provided further evidence. For instance, Sousa et al. (2017) view "the brain as the core component of human identity"; and Raghanti et al. (2018) have posited the unique neurochemical profile of the striatum as the root cause of human uniqueness. Comparative connectome studies provide findings on interesting and some times significant differences between humans and our closest living primate relatives (e.g., Ardesch et al. 2019, chimpanzees).

Partly surprisingly, partly expectedly, neurologically-based theories of human uniqueness derive their maximum strength when combined with evolutionary explanations of language. Barring divine intervention, there are four types of theories of language evolution. According to the first one, language is a highly specialised organ that grows similarly to the way other human organs do. Its first appearance is claimed to have occurred by one or more nutations. In this sense language is compatible with the principle of emergence. Chomsky proposed this theory back in the 1970s and is under development since then.

The second theory, introduced by Pinker (1994) is closely related to, but distinct from, the first one. Pinker's proposal differs from Chomsky's in claiming language to have evolved by the natural selection mechanisms of DaTE.

The third theory is indeed different from the previous two. Gould proposed that language developed from the earlier mechanism of thinking. The latter in turn assumed to have provided our ancestors with significant representational capacities. In this view language is based on exaptation (a type of adaptation).

Actually, it is quite useful and precise if one sees exaptation as a second or higher order adaptation. Two interesting versions of the exaptationist theory of language are those of Fitch (2011) and Ramachandran (2012).

I will present a less incomplete picture of the latter as it addresses the more interesting issue of language acquisition which also holds central position in the nature-nurture debate.

Fitch's (2011) theory is based upon research on spoken human language that he claims to be testable. Specifically, he proposes three hypotheses for the evolution of syntax each positing a modification of functionality in a precursor brain region. For instance, Fitch proposes that an expanded and elaborated human arcuate fasciculus serves human syntactic comprehension and the former comes from a precursor arcuate fasciculus that was subserving vocal imitation. It should be noted that work on the arcuate fasciculus as the neural basis of at least some linguistic function has attracted wider interest. For instance, Rilling et al. (2008) noted that the urcuate fasciculus is "much smaller or absent from nonhuman primates" and Rilling et al. (2012) proposed it as the key region in human brain responsible for syntactic and some semantic aspects of language.

In one of the best examples of the brain-based claims to human uniqueness, Ramachandran (2012) argues that a few functionally unique human brain regions like Wernicke's area and the left temporal lobe are responsible for the uniqueness of human nature. A strong point of his theory is the recognition of the compatibility between functional uniqueness and anatomical continuity, namely, "every part of our brain has a direct analog in the brains of the great apes." (ibid. p. 22). His argument is based on what Ramachandran calls "*mental* phase transition", which is a classy name for the old adage the whole is more than the sum of its part. It is of course explained in neuroscientific terms and specifically in terms of mirror neurons. Although the subtitle (*Unlocking the Mystery of Human Nature*) of Ramachandran's book may be at least slightly inaccurate, his in-depth explorations of puzzling brain phenomena reveal functional NS relations that should, eventually, be taken into account by any theory of human mind. A good illustration of his overall approach is the way he accounts for a basic feature of human language: competence.

Ramachandran's explanation for language competence evolution is called by him "synesthetic bootstrapping theory". He has identified three types of map-to-map resonance that are assumed they were in action in the early Homo (and possibly Hominin) brain: visual-auditory; auditory/ visual-motor (in Broca's area); and resonance between "Broca's area and motor areas controlling manual gestures." (ibid. p. 175). The interesting element of Ramachandran's proposal is the linking of several brain areas as a possibility "that may have accelerated the evolution of protolanguage." Apart from the standard Broca and Wernicke areas, he identified interactions between the hand and face areas of the motor cortex (HF), the auditory and inferotemporal cortices (IA), and the angular gyrus, and he assumed to be responsible for cross-modal abstraction. The connections between the broader Broka and Wernicke areas (i.e., the arcuate fasciculus; see above Fitch's theory) "are involved in cross-domain mapping between sound contours and motor maps". The other two types of connections may be more important. The HF interactions mediate the bouba-kiki effect, and the IA interactions mediate synkinesia effects.

Finally, and very significantly, Ramachandran reminds us of a neglected clinical observation; the possibility of an interesting connection between language and thought; and key unresolved issues that only very recently started being recognised by neuroscience. The first concerns observational data according to which the independence of Broca's area from that of Wernicke collapses. Specifically, it has been clinically documented that Wernicke aphasics produce speech that is partially abnormal in its syntactic structure too. The second concerns the possibility that thought and language share the same rules of transitivity. The third refers to central issues in the philosophy of mind and for some of them in linguistics and cognitive psychology. Ramachandran specifically recognised the near ignorance of neuroscientists of phenomena like 'meaning', 'think', and 'understanding' that he characterised as "complete mysteries" (ibid. p. 184). Chapters 3 and 4 make a small step in addressing such biological, and for *H. sapiens*, sociological phenomena.

Overall, I think that exaptationist explanations suffer from what I call 'moving the neuroscientific goalposts' syndrome, and 'complexity neglect'. The former consists in identifying a more elaborate brain region (in relation to earlier assumed structures in Hominins) as the explanation mechanism of a linguistic function without providing even an indication of the actual mechanisms involved. The latter refers to forward and backward extrapolations in evolutionary explanations without taking into account the extreme variations in complexity organisation between phenomena separated by millions or even hundreds of thousands of years. Actually, personally I would argue that even extrapolations concerning hundreds of years should be carried out with extreme caution—if at all. Nearly needless to add that complexity organisation hardly ever affects a single phenomenon.

Overall objections to the exclusively neuroscientific account of human mind have been raised in Sect. 1.1. Here I point out a few further objections from the perspective of human evolution. Let us consider the following questions:

> Q1: Do all of the systems of an individual of a species evolve through the same evolutionary mechanisms? In particular:
> Q2: Does the Hominin brain evolve through the same selection processes as other hominin systems?
> Q3: Do the Hominin and 'modern' human brains evolve under the same selection processes and use the same evolutionary and developmental mechanisms?

Although answers to these questions fall well outside the remit of this monograph, they contribute to the development of alternative ways of viewing phenomena addressed in this book. For instance, Christiansen & Chater (2008), in a target article in *Behavioral and Brain Sciences*, raised the following two opposing views on the relation between brain and language:

> Q1: "why is the brain so well suited to learning language?"
> Q2: "why is language so well suited to being learned by the brain?" (ibid. p.490).

Within an EES framework, both questions are ill-posed. A better question would be:

> Q3: How do the development*s* of the brain and language interact within the overall development of the individual in her particular ecosystem?

Interestingly, all commentary views on Christiansen & Chater's (2008) target article were either for (the majority) or against C&C's thesis.

Finally, a different source of support for the uniqueness of human language comes from biology at large. For instance, Woese (2004, p. 180) remarks:

> "Human language is a development that has set *Homo sapiens* worlds apart from its otherwise very close primate relatives, adding new dimensions to the phase space within which human evolution occurs."

This is definitely the case but not for the reason correctly assumed by Woese to be the case, namely, the communication element that shares with multicellularity (ibid.).

Overall, we reach two conclusions. First, human language is a social phenomenon and therefore the exclusively neuroscientific approach, and in general any individualist one, is inadequate. Second, the debate on the uniqueness of human language (i.e., whether there are precursors of human language in animal societies) is still ongoing. As I will argue in the next section the cause for the continuation of this debate is due to lack of properly defining 'human language'.

An apparently more suitable phenomenon considered to be responsible for human uniqueness is 'human culture'. Darwin had discussed moral sense and sociality and had clearly pointed out their precursors in lower animals. Since sociality is the basis and source of any culture and the traits in his D_L are prerequisites for any 'human culture', he probably thought it superfluous to discuss the latter notion. Be that as it may, let me briefly review the current situation.

Whether the definition of 'culture' becomes the source or terminal point of a theory of 'culture', its necessity is indisputable. In our case, we further need an unambiguous specification of the meaning of the qualificative adjectives 'human' and 'animal'. Let me start historically.

The notion of 'human culture' has been defined in a multiplicity of ways. In all cases Patterson's (2014, p. 3) remark is still true: "[there] is a persistent lack of consensus or rigour in defining culture". Actually, the situation is much worse. There is an intellectual chasm between the humanities (including social sciences) and the cultural evolutionist approaches to human culture (see Sect. 1.2). The following two quotes illustrate their variance. The former may be best exemplified by Geertz:

> "I take culture to be those webs [i.e., webs of significance that the human animal has spun and is suspended in], and the analysis of it to be therefore not an experimental science in search of law but an interpretive one in search of meaning." (Geertz 1973, p. 5).

The latter is probably best exemplified by a widely circulated definition of culture as:

> "information capable of affecting individuals' behaviour that they acquire from other members of their species through teaching, imitation and other forms of social learning". (Richerson & Boyd 2005, p. 3).

It is worth noting the use of two different words 'meaning' and 'information' used by these two approaches respectively. Although, they are both extremely varied in the range of senses they are used, they are usually employed by the so called soft and hard sciences respectively (see chapter-3 for a comprehensive discussion of meaning and information).

Furthermore, cultural evolutionists employ a suite of traditional scientific methods and techniques like,

> "formal and mathematical modeling, quantification and statistical analysis of numerical data, hypothesis testing, and systematic experimentation [seven references cited]." (Whiten et al. 2017, p. 7777).

and more or less directly look down at the humanities approach:

> "there is still an epistemological gulf between the scientific, evolutionary approach outlined here and much of the social sciences and humanities". (Mesoudi 2017, p. 7858).

Aspects of this approach is evidenced by the increasing number of micro-theories of cultural products (e.g., Bentley et al. 2004; Rogers & Ehrlich 2008; Claidière et al. 2014) and of attempts of outlining a unified science of cultural evolution (e.g., Mesoudi et al.; 2006; Henrich et al. 2008). In accordance with this approach, cultural evolutionists define 'culture' in very general terms to include any type of 'animal culture'. Specifically, they explicitly or implicitly define 'culture' in terms of social learning, and the social transmission of information (e.g., Richerson & Boyd 2005; Whiten & van Schaik 2007; Plotkin 2011). As Avise & Ayala (2010, p. 8900) remark, culture "defined as the deployment of socially learned information" has a duration of at least two million years, and is considered to be "the proximate reason for our remarkable success as a species" (ibid.). This way of approaching 'culture' allows for continuity between human and animal 'cultures' but it fails to capture the special and possibly unique features of human culture. As Byrne et al. (2004) remark one may define 'culture' in a way that is compatible with her belief in continuity or discontinuity.

Within this understanding, let me summarise the major views of the two sides on the debate of the origin of, or transition conditions to, 'modern human culture'. Continuity is based on theories supporting the view that innovations indicative of modern cognition have appeared and *eventually* consolidated in Africa *approximately* between 40 and 200 ka (e.g., Kolodny et al. 2018).

The opposing discontinuity theories split between those favouring one or more genetic mutation, and those favouring a gradual evolution of a "uniquely cumulative" human culture. The former type vary in relation to the time of occurrence: from ~ 50 ka (d'Errico & Stringer 2011) to at least 170 ka (Lind et al. 2013). The latter type varies on the time span of such a culture (e.g., Stout 2011; Whiten & Erdal 2012; Mesoudi 2017); what makes human cognition unique (e.g., Dean et al. 2012; MacLean 2016); and comparative work on human and animal 'cumulative' culture (e.g., Dean et al. 2013).

Proponents of the uniqueness of human culture face the difficult task of developing a theory compatible with the organismic evolution that is itself being modified as part of the EES. For instance, Mesoudi et al. (2006), in their target BBS article, suggested that human culture exhibits key Darwinian evolutionary properties and argued for a "science of cultural evolution that should share fundamental features" with the science of biological evolution. In their response to the associated commentary they become bolder by:

> "reiterat[ing] that using evolutionary biology as a model for unifying the social sciences within a single synthetic framework can stimulate a more progressive and rigorous science of culture." (ibid., p. 366).

Nevertheless, their preliminary evolutionary framework faces many issues some of which are reflected in the open peer commentary. I take the following five to stand out (see commentary and authors response for details and additional issues):

1. What are the mechanisms of cultural transmission?

This is a huge topic that cannot be explained in terms of Dawkins' 'meme' neologism (e.g., Dawkins 1989), or by restricting redefinitions of this term (e.g., Mesoudi et al. 2006).

2. Could the blind, non-cultural evolutionary process be synthesised with conscious cultural biology?

Sopher (2006) raises several issues and processes that at least justify this question.

3. Are there fundamentally different types of cultural traits?
4. To what extent exclusively MS-based models could be used in cultural biology?
5. Are there conscious factors affecting the development of natural human languages?

Dennett & McKay (2006, p. 353) answer the last question in the negative. They consider language to be one of the:

> "undeniable cases of cultural features that evolve by Darwinian processes without any need to invoke authors, designers, or other intelligent creators." And a bit further: "languages … evolve without any need for grammarians, deliberate coiners, or other foresighted guardians of these cultural items."

I think their claim is grossly mistaken. Science, for one thing, is full of concepts, principles and theories that have been consciously developed (without barring unconscious influences).

The majority of scientists working on extending MS to include human culture adopt the following two theses. First, it is taken for granted that "[c]ulture normally evolves more rapidly than genes" Richerson et al. (2010, p. 8985). In a report composed of both jointly agreed statements and individual position papers Dyer et al. (2005) made the same point from the general systems perspective of temporal change of biological, cultural, technological (especially AI) and physical systems. This assumption was recently confirmed by Perreault (2012) who showed that cultural evolution is faster than organic evolution. It is worth noting that WHuLa-based cultural evolution is faster than pre-WHuLa cultural evolution (Sect. 2.3.3 for discussion of the WHuLa transition). Second, they use 'social learning' as the process for defining culture. For instance, Richerson et al. (2010, p. 8985) define culture as "[t]the use of socially learned information". Because I consider this definition as obviously too broad, I will confine my attention to a couple of general points related to learning and teaching.

I start by reminding us that all learning is eventually memory-based and goes back at least to the emergence of the first animals (c. 600 Ma). On this understanding, it is subject to three types of constraint each corresponding to mechanisms at a different level of spatial or temporal organisation of the individual concerned. The organisational levels of these mechanisms are: (i) genetic; (ii) nervous systems; and (iii) developmental. But, what is more important for our purposes is the source of learning.

There are two types of learning differentiated by the nature of two fundamentally different sources. The first source is identified with the learning individual: she learns on her own. I call this type of learning: own-learning. The second source involves at least one more individual from whom the learner learns either by imitation or by teaching (I take apprenticeship to be a hybrid of the above). Learning related to culture can be of either type. Lack of culture diminishes learning severely. Of course these two types of learning can co-occur according to the requirements of the situation in hand and the preferences of the learner.

This brings us naturally to teaching and its relation to the evolution of our species. Teaching is rather easily defined as cooperative behaviour aiming to improve learning in conspecifics. Nevertheless, standard evolutionary conceptions of teaching have been stretched to fit inadequate MS-based models of evolutionary theory. For instance, Thornton & Raihani (2008) take a cost–benefit perspective that may be plausible for some period of the Hominin evolution but fails, at least, in our age. The same perspective is adopted by Fogarty et al. (2011) and leads them to claim either the obvious or the 'defeating-the-purpose'. In their words:

> "We find that teaching is not favored where the pupil can easily acquire the information on its own, or through copying others, or for difficult to learn traits, where teachers typically do not possess the information to pass on to relatives." (ibid. p. 2760).

All cultural evolution theories suffer from a common significant problem: lack of clarity of their object of investigation. This problem gets worse by a proliferation of new names for well known aspects of cultural evolution like artificiality.

Most accounts of the origins of our cumulative technological culture (CTC) are given in terms of socially derived cognitive mechanisms like those already stated and alternatives like mind-reading, and metacognition. Osiurak & Reynaud (2019) proposed that CTC originates in "technical-reasoning skills". A compromising position was more recently argued by Lucas et al. (2020). They proposed that social learning "coevolved with an increasing reliance on complex tools." The weak side of their argument is double extrapolation. That is, they extrapolate backward for at least 2.5 Ma with respect to recursion and they also extrapolate forward from that age to our times with respect to teaching. In a nutshell, it is increasingly forgotten that the primary characteristic of a mature science is the cumulative nature of our understanding of science's fundamental notions (see Sect. 1.4). A mature science adds new concepts to its vocabulary only when such additions are demonstrated to be necessary from new evidence. In this respect a more cautionary approach to cultural evolution is welcome. For instance d'Errico & Stringer (2011) argue for:

> "the need for further inquiry into the relationship between climate and demographic/cultural change" (ibid. p. 1060).

Their reasoning is based on the further need of understanding the interactions between *H. neandertalensis* and *H. sapiens*.

The above brief comments are indicative of the problems faced by cultural evolutionists. In addition, Foley et al. (2016, p. 5) notes two central problems universally agreed as such. First, "[w]e are a long way from understanding the nature of the various transitions in human evolution"; and second, there is no single cause for it. Finally, an internal critique of cultural change as fundamentally Darwinian is provided by Nettle (2020).

Our brief review of the gradualist debate essentially questioned some aspects of the neuroscientific and evolutionary theories. A comprehensive, rigorous and fare critique of the excesses of both the *exclusively* neuroscientific approach and of a *distorted* account of DaTE is provided by Tallis (2011). He makes a scathing, and as I see it fully justified, attack on "Neuromania" and "Darwinitis", namely, the exaggerated claims of a large number, if not the majority, of neuroscientists and evolutionary biologists. In a nutshell, Tallis argues against the twin ideas that brains on one hand and animality on the other are adequate descriptions of ourselves. His arguments are convincing—if conviction were indeed needed for the obvious. In addition, although he does not provide a theory of human nature, his book contributes to the development of such a theory by exposing clearly the many false assumptions of Neuromania and Darwinitis. An excellent précis of a critique of biological determinism and "Ultra Darwinism" combined with a constructive perspective transcending genetic determinism is provided by Rose (1999). The associated Open Peer Commentary and Rose's response constitute a very worthy reading.

Overall, I think that work on the gradualist debate and, more generally, human evolution lacks definition of its most fundamental term, namely, 'human evolution'. In addition, the study of 'human culture' and its definition is pursued in two very different approaches by cultural evolutionists and scientists in sociology and the humanities.

The following TNS-based definition of culture aims to provide a bridge between these two sides. The next Sect. (2.3.3) describes the major transition in *Homo sapiens* evolution.

Definition-12 Culture Y of a multi-member noémon system Z is:

(a) the system of socially learned and inheritable behaviours between generations that Y has evolved to become;
(b) Y is being developed by members or groups of Z; and
(c) Y may affect the development of any member or group of Z.

NB: The range and complexity of behaviours are open-ended. Indicatively, they include: cooperation, beliefs, arts, customs, laws, science, technology, and associated activities. Their development may be reflective or not.

Probably, the major advantage of this definition is bridging the gap between humanities and cultural evolutionist approaches in two crucial respects. First, it allows differences between societies in space and time. Second, it incorporates the continuity between *Homo* sapiens and other primates while allowing for the uniqueness of historic humans. Third, the definition allows human culture to be used as both an explanandum and an explanans. Fourth, and most importantly, all its definiens are completely defined in the following chapters. To be noted here in advance that all the definiens are graded. This allows for a large family of both human and other animal cultures to be specified.

Within the family of cultures delineated by definition-12, rudiments of the cultures of anatomically modern *H. sapiens* have been documented in many animal species in addition to primates. This fact corroborates Darwin's continuity hypothesis for anatomically modern humans until the advent of behaviourally modern humans. The latter—until the advent of H—are characterised by some further features that are difficult but not impossible to be seen as differences in degree between the mind of those humans and of other animals. Nevertheless, the culture of H is characterised by unique features derived from a unique human development, namely *written* human language. This demarcates a gap between ourselves and our closest behaviourally modern humans that cannot be explained as a gap in degree. The next section fleshes out the previous two sentences.

2.3.3 *The WHuLa Transition: The Mental Gap is* **within** *H. Sapiens*

As we saw in the previous section human uniqueness is still debated. This section proposes a major transition characterising H, namely, the emergence of *written* human language (WHuLa) as a key aspect of the artificiality component of *Homo* evolution.[13] To start with, let us be clear of what we are talking about. The following *couple* of definitions make clear the meaning of artificiality both for humans and noémon systems in general.

Definition-13a Homo artificiality at time t, is the degree to which *Homo*-at-t has incorporated the tools constructed by it by time t. Where:

[13] The wider issue of human transitions during the Holocene period (11.7 Ka—Present) is discussed in Gelepithis (2024b, Sect. 5.2).

1 *Homo*-at-t refers to all members and institutions of all of its societies at time t. Obviously, distinct societies can interact and even communicate (Chapter-4).
2 Incorporation refers to the relations developed among tools and their users. Users refer to both individual and institutions of any kind.
3 Within TNS, 'human tool' is anything that is human-made. This definition is in contrast to the much narrower definition of tool as an object that extends an individual's ability to modify her environment. Therefore, by following the wider definition of tool, 'art', 'agriculture' and 'language', are special kinds of tools.

The notion of *Homo* artificiality can easily be extended to any noémon system according to the following coupled-definition:

Definition-13b Artificiality of a noémon system is the degree to which it constructs and incorporates tools in its development or evolution.

NB: The integral comments of definition-13a apply to this one too—with the obvious generalisations. For instance, a NoS tool is anything that is NoS-made.

The following six points focus on *Homo* artificiality and its relations to the notions of cumulative culture and evolutionary transitions.

First, let us be clear that as defined, *Homo* artificiality both includes and differentiates all past and possible future species of our genus and constitutes a subclass of NoS-artificiality. However, it is not applicable to a new lineage that may stem from a possible future species of *Homo.*[14] It should be noted that a particular kind of *Homo* artificiality, H-artificiality can be claimed to have started to affect the overall evolutionary path of our genus (Gelepithis 2024b, chapter-5).

Second, in discussing human cultures the notion of 'tool construction' should be preferred to that of 'tool use'. For: (i) its rarity in the animal kingdom makes it consistent with its appearance in some of the *Homo* species; (ii) it does not suffer from definitional problems like the notion of 'tool use' (e.g., Beck 1980; St Amant & Horton 2008; Hunt et al.

[14] Human artificiality has started with the construction of the first stone tools by the *Homo* genus (estimated origin ~ 2.6 Ma). It should be noted that this date is different from the one of the earliest tools yet found (~ 3.3 Ma). Whether it was *H. habilis* or another species of *Homo* that initiated tool construction is irrelevant for our discussion.

2013); and (iii) tool construction has been less involved with the biology of our species and more with our social nature.

Third, the notion of *Homo* artificiality is stronger than the notion of cumulative culture (Boyd & Richerson 1996). This point is consistent with reason (iii) above, that is, it provides a more balanced basis for the explanation of human nature. Although a critical review of the models, concepts and hypotheses introduced to explain cumulative culture is beyond the scope of this book, a few examples will illuminate my previous points. One, Boyd & Richerson (ibid.) used the notion of 'observational learning'. Two, Dean et al. (2012) experimentally investigated all eight hypotheses that have been proposed as necessary conditions for cumulative culture. Their experiment included three groups: humans, chimpanzees (*Pan troglodytes*), and capuchin monkeys (*Cebus apella*). Their findings strongly support the view that "teaching through verbal instruction, imitation, and prosocial tendencies" are required for cumulative culture, and that such processes "are absent or impoverished in chimpanzees and capuchins." (ibid., p. 6). Three, Stout & Hecht (2017) developed the notion of "a uniquely human technological niche". This sounds promising until it is revealed that it is "rooted in a shared primate heritage of visuomotor coordination and dexterous manipulation." (ibid, p. 7861). Four, Birch & Heyes (2021) advocated their "self-assembly hypothesis", namely, "cultural evolution evolved culturally". Finally, for an interesting review of definitions, uses, and tests of cumulative culture and its evolution (Mesoudi & Thornton 2018).

Fourth, the notion of *Homo* artificiality accommodates the results of Muthukrishna et al. (2014) supporting the view that sociality influences positively cultural complexity and is of course supported by proponents of the view that human language is primarily a social, (i.e., human-made) tool. However, the artificiality notion and in particular the WHuLa transition proposed below are quite likely that it will be opposed by those doubting the cumulative complexity of technological traits (e.g., Vaesen & Houkes 2017).

The fifth point concerns the notion of transition and its relation to WHuLa. Although transitions are processes, not points in time, sometimes it is useful, if at all possible, to identify points in time acting as strongholds of a transition or pointers to the full establishment of one. With respect to the WHuLa transition we are able to specify an approximate time for both its first stronghold and its nearly full establishment.

The first stronghold of WHuLa can be reasonably safely placed at approximately 2600 BCE. This is a reasonable estimate of the then state of linguistic affairs on the basis of currently available evidence. Specifically, it is taken to be the date by which written human language was 'securely established' within the top urban classes in Mesopotamia and Egypt. By 'securely established' it is meant that already coherent texts had appeared. For, the earliest known true writing systems appeared around 3200 BCE. And, the earliest literary authors known by name, Phahhotep who wrote in Egyptian and Enheduanna who wrote in Sumerian, lived in the period 2400–2240 BCE.

The sixth and final point concerns a distinction between geological transitions and biological ones. Speaking in formal geological time terms we live in the Holocene epoch consisting of three sub-epochs: Greenlandian (11,700 yr b2k); Northgrippian (8,236 yr b2k); and Meghalayan (4,250 yr b2k).[15] Informally, we have entered the Anthropocene epoch that, pending approval by the appropriate international geological associations, is most likely to be specified to have started at 50 yr b2K. In contrast, human evolutionary transitions lack the refinement of geological ones. This is particularly annoying with respect to the anatomically modern humans transition (200 ka). The period starting with the WHuLa transition is characterised by a unique behavioural repertoire ranging from marvellous achievements (e.g., historic art, science) to catastrophic and even atrocious large-scale acts (e.g., genocides, WW II, destruction of other species' habitats, climate change). In accordance with my earlier notation I will refer to this period as the H-period. In addition to its intrinsic significance, the H-period couples nicely with the Meghalayan sub-epoch. Of course it should be noted that the H-period has not been identified as a distinct age within *H. sapiens* evolution let alone as a ***unique*** one by any of the disciplines studying it. Furthermore, although the proposed major transitions in evolution (Maynard Smith & Szathmáry 1997; Szathmáry 2015) have included human evolution along with several others in their list, consideration of major transitions within *H. sapiens* evolution have not been identified (Foley 2016). Recognition of the WHuLa transition is long overdue. The rest of this section argues for it.

[15] B2k = before AD 2000. According to Phil Gibbard, Secretary General ICS, Cambridge 26.6.18. See https://en.wikipedia.org/wiki/Holocene (Wikepedia note 8, 14/04/2021).

The *very* recent evolution of *H. sapiens* introduced a new element of artificiality, WHuLa, that is fundamentally different from all forms of artificiality that had appeared so far in their evolution. WHuLa is identified as the key transition in the evolution of '*Homo* artificiality'.

The roots of *Homo* artificiality are hardly distinguishable from those of non- human animals species: simple tool use and later simple constructions (e.g., Jones & Kamil 1973; Mulcahy et al. 2005; Emery 2006; Foerder et al. 2011; Shumaker et al. 2011; Biro et al. 2013; Krützen et al. 2014; Jacobs et al. 2016; Rutz et al. 2016; Klump 2019). Nevertheless, it has evolved to become remarkably different in *H. sapiens* and it is actually both unique and orders of magnitude greater than any other type of artificiality exhibited among Earthian Animalia. Furthermore, its rate of increase is steadily increasing. What is the engine of *H. sapiens* artificiality? How such an 'engine' is related to the range of cognitive traits exhibited and shared by humans and other animals?

Let me start with an estimated timeline of the major stepping stones of *Homo*, and quite possibly Hominin, artificiality (Fig. 2.3). The construction of the first stone tools made by the genus *Homo* used to be dated back approximately 2.3 million years.

The discovery of stone-tool-assisted removal of animal tissue at $\geq$ 3.39 Ma by McPherron et al. (2010) suggested a much earlier date. Further evidence of tool production found at the much earlier date of 3.3 Ma by Harmand et al. (2015) provide strong evidence for a much earlier time of tool manufacture. This may imply either that the origins of our genus have to be moved still further back, or that Hominins not belonging to the *Homo* genus were able to construct tools assumed so far to be only constructable by our genus (see Fig. 2.3). The problem of defining *Homo* appears to become identical with defining the past and future of 'human' nature, or equivalently, the evolving nature of our species.

The following remarks identify two major prerequisites and one major consequence of the use of 'tools'. They demonstrate the dependence of our interpretations on the type of tool and the physical, mental and social capabilities of our ancestors. Many traps are wide-open, still mostly neglected.

Even the simplest tool construction (not simply tool use though) presupposes certain *conceptual representations* in the mind of the toolmaker concerning the shape, size, and future (even near immediate) use of a tool. Therefore, 'design capability' should have been a feature of even

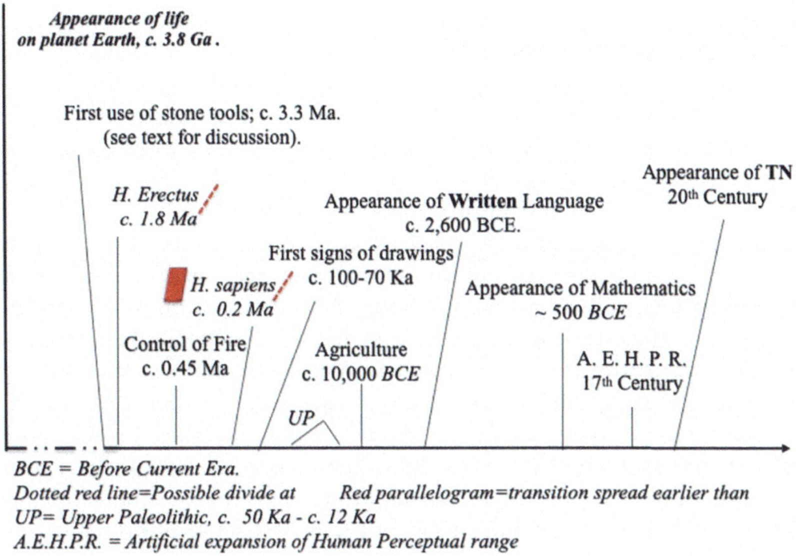

Fig. 2.3 Major stepping stones in the evolution of *Homo* artificiality (Pleiocene, Pleistocene, Holocene, and Anthropocene epochs)

the earliest tool-makers (most likely Hominins and therefore not only *Homo*) at least around 3.3 Ma. The linking together of such representations, when consolidated, may be seen as steps of a recipe for achieving a goal. Qualitatively, one may think, not very far away from what we nowadays call an algorithm in computer science. Is such a thought justifiable? Not really. Design capability is both graded and comes in different kinds.

Similarly, controlling fire ca. 500–400 ka (cf., James 1989) could be thought to have provided some of the rudiments of our sophisticated notion of control exemplified throughout its evolution from early design concepts, to the invention of centrifugal governors by the great Dutch scientist Christiaan Huygens (1629–1695), to Cybernetic devices and complex AISs. Nevertheless, the temporal gap between these two events seems to suggest no connection. Continuity seems unlikely to exist. Why? Are there qualitative *conceptual* differences between controlling fire and the controlling of room temperature by a thermostat? Invoking meta-cognition as a conceptual difference is not strong enough because it does not alter the basic principle of control. It only reapplies it. Nevertheless, such a comparison would be misleading as it compares fundamentally different control systems. Specifically, in the thermostat case the human has been excluded from the control system. More significantly, the control of fire although unique to humans does not enable them to construct the edifice that WHuLa has enabled them to do. Controlling fire is an ability that helps subsistence; it cannot modify human nature.

A major consequence may well have been organisation. The changes that took place in the minds of our ancestors by the construction of new tools were followed of course by changes in their communities and, in particular, in the relations among their members. In general, the introduction of a new entity, simple or complex, artificial or not, in a community changes the existing relations until a new equilibrium state is reached. Of course, the more complex or novel the new entity introduced is the more difficult becomes predicting the individual, group or overall behaviour of the community. Although organisation seems to be impossible to follow from tool construction, tools in the widest sense of human-made employed here, and their use may well have done so.

Art (that is depiction of environmental situations or externalisation of internally originated representations) may well have contributed to societal organisation. But, if art did not contribute to group organisation, human agriculture certainly did. The latter along with use of wheels (ca. 4000 BCE), and the move from neolithic villages to cities did require considerable organisation skills and behavioural changes at both the individual and social levels.

Nevertheless, agriculture is not a uniquely human capacity. As Mueller et al. (2005) remark:

> "Agriculture has evolved independently in three insect orders: once in ants, once in termites, and seven times in ambrosia beetles They [insect farmers] (*a*) sequester their gardens from the environment; (*b*) monitor gardens intensively, controlling pathogens early in disease outbreaks; (*c*) occasionally access population-level reservoirs of genetically variable cultivars, even while propagating clonal monocultures across many farmer generations; and (*d*) manage, in addition to the primary cultivars, an array of "auxiliary" microbes providing disease suppression and other services."

Indeed the 50-million year old agricultural practice of insects is a fact that is required to be taken into account in considering transition events in *H. sapiens*.

Rather unexpectedly, recent research has shown sophisticated behaviour by micro-organisms and Brock et al. (2011) has shown that a type of social amoeba.

> "has a primitive farming symbiosis that includes dispersal and prudent harvesting of the crop."

Bacterial husbandry by amoebas and fungus farming by insects do not only demonstrate convergent evolution, they also show the deep evolutionary roots of presumably unique human behaviours.

Overall, mental changes, whether due to the use of tools or not, are material changes of the organisms concerned. As such, they should cause, (if adequately effective) at least one type of biological change at one organismic level. The least impermanent will be shown at the gene level; the most modifiable at the acquired neurophysiological level. A good example of the former includes the "cultural evolution of agricultural subsistence" (Richerson et al. 2010, p. 8990). Examples at the neurophysiological level are given in chapter-3. All the above events and transitional phenomena have produced identifiable material changes. Most importantly, all of them and their associated individual and social changes are quantitative—however great they are. Let me now move to the core of *Homo* artificiality: WHuLa.

All theories of *H. sapiens* evolution recognise 'language' as the primary, if not the only unique, feature of human nature (e.g., Sapir 1929; Deacon 2010). Nevertheless, the notion of 'language' used in such theories is taken to be equated with that of speech. Although this viewpoint, as we shall see below, is not justifiable, it prevailed for at least the following reasons. First, speech develops naturally in children whereas writing has to be taught. Furthermore, the established historical, functional, and biological priority of speech over written language (Lyons 1981), has led both layperson and linguists until very recently to consider the former, implicitly or explicitly, the defining characteristic of our species. Although by the end of the twentieth century, speech was recognised as one of the modalities of human language it is still considered as the key modality by many.

WHuLa had never before been considered as a major transition in the evolution of our species. This, I will argue, is a gross mistake.[16] Earlier, such a claim would have invoked the wrath of eminent linguists like Bloomfield (1933) who insisted that writing is mere recording of language and most likely Hall (1959) who was writing in favour of the importance of speech over writing. Presently, a more balanced view is promoted as it becomes evident from the following quote from David Crystal's (1997, p. 180) *The Cambridge Encyclopedia of Language*:

> "From a scientific viewpoint, we know far less about the written language than we do about the spoken, largely because of the 20th-century bias in linguistic studies towards the analysis of speech- a bias which is only nowadays beginning to be corrected."

In addition to WHuLa's part in the evolution of *H. sapiens* nature, it has never before being considered to be a fundamental transition in our evolution. The following paragraphs will justify this viewpoint. Putting aside both the obvious but neglected fact that WHuLa is unique among the Animalia taxon, I will proceed by demonstrating the following points:

(i) WHuLa is substantially different from speech;
(ii) it is much more powerful than oral language; and
(iii) it provides the necessary foundation for *H. sapiens* science.

As I stated in the opening paragraph of this section, *H. sapiens* science may evolve to become sooner rather than later (in evolutionary time scale terms) a transition of its own in the evolution of historic humans.[17]

WHuLa involves elements of artificiality that speech lacks and make WHuLa *the* key transition in the evolution of *Homo* artificiality in the sense that it is *the* prerequisite for two further unique and evolving social structures of our species: science and AI. Jointly, these three evolving social structures contribute more to the continuing evolution of H than its organic part. What are these unique elements of WHuLa artificiality?

[16] To avoid confusion and stress my point, I will only use the expression 'human language' in case I want to refer to both speech and WHuLa. In all other cases I will use either speech or WHuLa as the situation demands.

[17] Examples of transitions and an argument for the need for a *designed* transition within H-evolution are discussed by Gelepithis (2024b, chapter-2 and Sect. 5.2.2 respectively).

The distinction between WHuLa and early writing systems will take us naturally to these unique characteristics.

I start with a point made by (Goody & Watt 1963, p. 311):

> "cave paintings, rock engravings and wood carvings are morphologically, and presumably sequentially, the forerunners of writing."

The implicit point here is that such graphs might well reflected necessities of cave dwellers at least as much as being expressions of art. This point seems to be strengthened by the use of clay tokens that it was possible to be used for, several thousand years before writing, the recording of transactions like barter. In addition, such markings are substantially different from even the elements of a writing system from the perspective of lacking any sequencing or hint of narrative. They are static and self-contained. In contrast, of course, rock engravings and clay tokens lack even the most basic characteristic of the earliest writing systems, namely, combination of recurring symbols with accepted values.

This is relatively close to the notion of a human communication system that uses conventional visible marks, which in turn is essentially Gelb's (1963) definition of writing and is substantially different from Diringer's (1968 p. 8) definition: [w]riting is the graphic counterpart of spoken language." (see earlier comment for the priority of speech over WHuLa). The first link of visible marks to the original Sumerian cuneiform writing system has come with the work of Schmandt-Besserat 1980). Such marks (in the form of tokens) are dated back to ~ 10 ka and they are still far way from WHuLa and even further away from speech. Nonetheless, they do share with the former a feature than the latter does not possess: permanence.

Let us now consider in relative detail all the unique differences and characteristic similarities between oral language and WHuLa. Specifically, there are three characteristic similarities that define oral language and are inherited by WHuLa. All three of them have by now shown to be exhibited, in some degree, by certain lower animals corroborating Darwin's continuity thesis (with respect to speech).[18] Specifically, precursors of

[18] Actually, Darwin claimed that language evolved from music, whereas Pinker (1994) argued for animal cognition and Tomasello (2008) that evolved as a type of socially learned communication system. In sharp contrast to all three, Chomsky (2000) has argued for the discontinuity of human language.

both syntax and semantics, thought to be unique to humans, have been discovered in both birds and mammals (e.g., Savage-Rumbaugh et al. 1998; Zuberbühler 2019). Compositionality seems to exist in at least rudimentary form in certain species (e.g., Suzuki et al. 2019). For a carefully worded cautionary view (Rendall 2021). In sharp contrast, and in addition to permanence, WHuLa has unique characteristics not shared by either oral language or any animal communication system. To these characteristics I turn next.

Thoughts can be expressed in oral, sign, or written form. In their first two versions, they are either lost in the air or, at most, they may affect the state of a close- by listener or recipient. Their third version has three unique characteristics: adequate permanence (already mentioned), exact reproducibility, and nearly unlimited distributability. *Written thoughts are a kind of neural fossils*. They may well outlive the person who expressed them and they can be exactly reproduced and, more or less, easily distributed. A particular important aspect of the relation of WHuLa to thought is discussed in Sect. 3.3.1.

Before the discovery and establishment of WHuLA, memorisation could and did support traditions but no substantial philosophy, science, literature, technology or history. The creation of WHuLa resolves both the ephemeral and extremely limited range of short-term memory and the restricted and potentially distorted permanence of long-term memory. Consider, for instance how oral tradition while extending ontogenetic durability at the same time eventually distorts the transmitted information (for better or worse). Of course, distorting a written text is also possible, but such distortion has to be intentional and much more easily detectable within the overall text. Although the oral and written forms of human language differ only in terms of the differences identified above, the consequences of these differences are cataclysmic for the development of both human mental phenomena and behavioural repertoire.

WHuLA enables deeper understanding of a phenomenon, claim, or description by enabling one to juxtapose and scrutinise ideas independently of the time and place of their production. Such a technology allows the transition from speech (a capability enabling the transfer of 'useful' traditional knowledge among generations) to the stage of knowledge accumulation and, as a prerequisite, of deeper and broader conceptual synthesis. Without WHuLa, conceptual evolution would be minimal and definitely would not have reached the stage of elaborate scientific theories. Figure 2.4 illustrates with examples distinct classes of concepts corresponding to the pre-linguistic, oral and WHuLa stages of *Homo* evolution. A couple of additional examples from each of the three classes of concepts will drive safely my point home. Instances from the pre-linguistic class of concepts include: food and joy. From the 'speech class of concepts' examples include: expressed experience and giving information. Finally, from the WHuLa stage of *Homo* evolution examples include: molecule, superego, and the SARS-CoV-2 virus.

The consequences of these fundamental differences between oral human language and WHuLa have not been identified or, at least, adequately appreciated. They actually constitute the sunk part of the iceberg of the nature of WHuLa. In a nutshell, the latter is transforming human mind, society, and culture in ways that speech is, *in principle*, unable to do. Let us now see the relation between speech and WHuLa from a different perspective.

During the several hundreds million years of animal evolution, at least some internal organismic processes have evolved probably as much, if not more, than behavioural animal traits. Among such processes mental processes are most likely the more complex both in the 'variations' they have evolved to in modern humans and in their evolutionary pathways. In humans mental evolution has been further augmented by the numerous successive artificial modifications in the ways they were pursuing their lives. Most of them were differences in the degree of their artificiality. A few like the control of fire were qualitative. None of them can be compared with the combined effect of speech and writing system, i.e.,

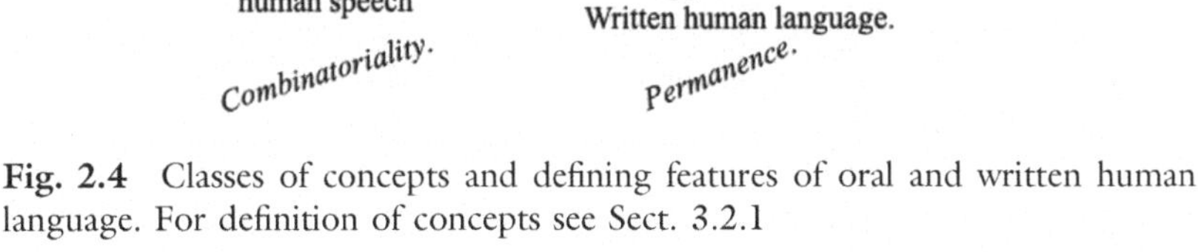

Fig. 2.4 Classes of concepts and defining features of oral and written human language. For definition of concepts see Sect. 3.2.1

WHuLa. It has to be realised that speech, WHuLa, sign-language are different language systems within 'language'.

The transition from oral to written human language marks a new age within the Holocene epoch. Mental phenomena that have appeared millions of years ago across a wide number of very different species have undergone unprecedented transformations in *very* modern humans by being interacting with WHuLa. Its invention and development is, in essence, the engine of the *current* evolutionary path of *Homo*. Furthermore, it was and still is the necessary ingredient of a series of several further breakthroughs in historic *H. sapiens* artificiality. They include: Mathematics, the artificial expansion of the human perceptual range, science and science-based advanced technologies like biotechnology and AI (see Fig. 2.3 again).

WHuLa is demonstrably the first social structure that is unique to historic humans. It follows that H is uniquely different not only from the Pan genus but also from prehistoric *H. sapiens*. Put it differently, a few tens of thousand years ago, when all three *H. sapiens, H. neanderthalensis*, and *H. floresiensis* were around the presumed range of traits available for comparisons would be narrower than today and the differences between any of these species and then extant species of the Pan or Gorilla genera would be narrower. In addition and contrast, a few tens of thousand years in the future from now aspects/traits of the then *H. sapiens* or *H.x* will differ substantially from the aspects/traits characterising today's representatives of *Homo*—if our species does not become extinct in the meantime.

This unusual thesis on the mental gap (Fig. 2.5) can be further supported by the relationship between WHuLa and thought. Although it is a well established fact that animals do have concepts and therefore concepts predate the emergence of human language, it is equally true that there are human concepts (e.g., electron, quark, gene expression, globalisation) that are only possible as part of advanced scientific knowledge and societal organisation. It is a trivial consequence that the latter phenomena and associated concepts can only exist because of WHuLa. The mental gap is within *Homo sapiens* and indeed within the very narrow time interval of the H- period.

The Anthropocene could not have existed without the WHuLa-based artificiality of our species. Put it slightly differently, the mental gap is within our species and not between *H. sapiens* and any other of the extinct

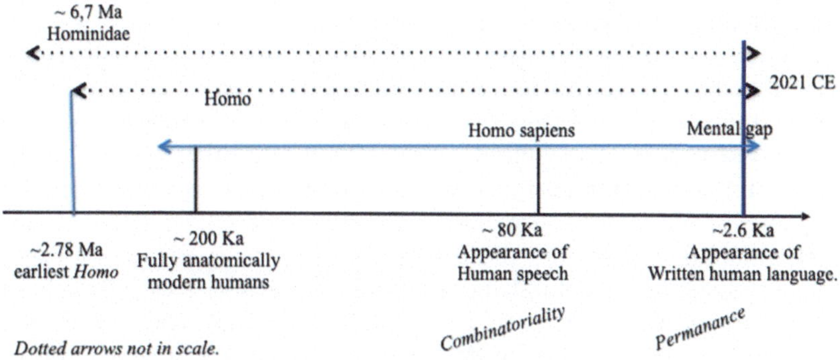

Fig. 2.5 The mental gap is within *Homo sapiens*

species of our genus, nor, of course, between *Homo* and our closest relatives, the genera Pan and Gorilla. Specifically, it has been caused by the development of WHuLa that propelled out of proportion the development of the artificial component of the human mind. *The discontinuity* that does exist *is within* our species: *historic* humans are fundamentally different from *pre- historic* humans.

Anatomically modern *H. sapiens* appeared c. 200 ka. For more than 97.7% of that time WHuLa did not exist; neither existed a mental gap between *Homo sapiens* and all other then-extant *Homo* species. Put it differently: *H. sapiens* traits have undergone 2 major types of modifications: (i) on the basis of the anatomical, neurophysiological, and cultural adaptations before WHuLa; and (ii) adaptations, exaptations, and the non-linear development of the cumulatively artificial on the basis of WHuLa. The first one was primarily gradual and eventually resulted in human characteristics that were significantly different in degree from those of other animals. During this transition DAC holds true.

The second transition has already resulted into the Anthropocene. Of course, our species still retains the same anatomical and neurophysiological features. Nevertheless, it is more likely than not that these features will be modified by advances in AI and biotechnology. For once, anatomy and physiology will follow the *wisdom* or *folly* of a single biological species instead of blind evolution. The topic of designed evolution is discussed in the Consequences volume of this monograph (Gelepithis 2024b).

WHuLa is the necessary foundation for the development of high abstraction, scientific knowledge, enhanced and devious morality, and our transformative artificiality of both our planet and our own-species. Let me slightly expand on the latter trait of historic humans. Although *Homo* artificiality has common roots with tool use and construction by non-human animals, the transformative subsystem of H- artificiality is both unique and orders of magnitude greater than any other type of artificiality exhibited among Earthian Animalia. Its uniqueness stems from the uniqueness of human science among Earthian species. And, the science of H is WHuLa-based. On the basis of science our species has created a huge, increasing, and fundamentally different artificial world in sharp contrast to the rudimentary and very limited artificial world *before* the invention and development of WHuLa. Science, in the widest sense of the word encompassing both physical and social sciences, has also changed significantly our overall culture. The fundamentally distinct nature of *H. sapiens* transformative artificiality is evidentially supported by the fact that it falls outside the pyramidal classification of animal and prehistoric cultures (Whiten & van Schaik 2007).

Developments within the Anthropocene that I take it to have started in 1950 have already created AISs and robots that outperform ourselves in an increasing number of mental phenomena, extend our behavioural repertoire, and started enhancing aspects of the anatomy and physiology of individual humans (cf, Fig. 1.2 in Sect. 1.2).[19] It affects significantly Earthian evolution and, it might end up influencing extraterrestrial evolution. The artificial change of *Homo sapiens* itself is underway under the combined effect of biotechnology and AI. Our uniqueness is of our own construction. The mental gap is within *Homo sapiens*. The processes involved are extremely complex. Some of them operate in ontogenetic time, some in phylogenetic time.

Finally, it is worth noting that the recent, extremely welcome albeit belated, push for literacy by most world organisations (e.g., UNESCO, World Bank, European Union, OECD) provides direct recognition of the fundamental significance of WHuLa. It is recognised as the de facto prerequisite for all learning (cf, Valtin et al. 2016) and therefore for culture (see discussion on the uniqueness of human culture in previous section). It is of still greater importance of course the way literacy is

[19] The Anthropocene Working Group voted (May 2019) to submit a formal proposal to the International Commission on Stratigraphy by 2021 locating stratigraphic markers around the middle of the twentieth century CE.

perceived. Far from defining literacy as ability to read and write (the way perceived before 1950), UNESCO's definition of literacy, reads:

> "Literacy is the ability to identify, understand, interpret, create, communicate and compute, using printed and written materials associated with varying contexts." (Montoya 2018).

Of equal importance is the fact that the above definition is increasingly used by powerful world organisations.

Specifically with respect to culture, the continuous development of WHuLa, science, associated technologies and related species actions, eventually led to the era of the *non-linearly artificial* (i.e., the period of a non-linear accumulation of human- made systems). Figure 2.6 depicts both the ultimate causes of WHuLa and the key relations among the requisite abilities and tools that contributed to the dawn of the era of the cumulatively artificial. Certain arrows like the one linking $^{\mathbf{ext}}\mathbf{RH}$ to speech should not be taken to refer to a single causal relation. They stand for the system of factors characterising such a causal relation. For instance, the discovery of using external representations and its relation to the required 'amount' of $^{\mathbf{int}}\mathbf{RH}$ in order for the discovery to occur is an interesting open question. In the case of speech the sought system of factors that led to human speech is still under debate (e.g., Hockett 1960; Lieberman 2007; Perreault & Mathew 2012). For clarity, a number of important events in human evolution are not depicted in Fig. 2.6. Such events include the control of fire, and agriculture. Research to unearth further direct and indirect contributions to the emergence and evolution of CAC (cumulatively artificial culture) would be most welcome.

To be kept in mind that CAC and CTC (cumulatively technological culture) differ substantially. First, the former subsumes the latter (see related comment at the beginning of this section). For instance, unique behavioural systems like dance, theatre, music constitute an integral part of CAC but are excluded in CTC studies. Second, they differ in terms of the 'engine' propelling or generating them. Osiurak & Reynaud (2020) define CTC in a very broad way including a multitude of tools and claim "technical reasoning" as being the engine of CTC. The 'engine' of CAC is WHuLa. Reasoning, and in particular technical reasoning, is a special type of thinking (see chapter-3).

Vaesen & Houkes (2017) provide a very interesting and balanced critique of the five major versions of the "technological complexity

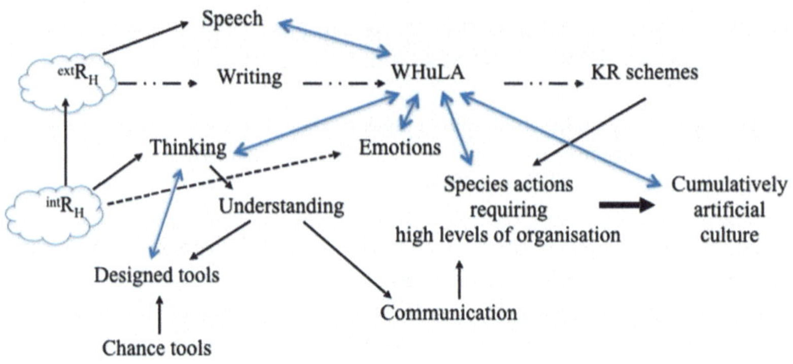

Legend:

$^{int}R_H$ = internal human representations.

$^{ext}R_H$ = external human representations, e.g., gestures, vocalisations.

KR schemes = Knowledge representation schemes.

For diagram simplicity, most arrows to Emotions and Designed tools are omitted.

Fig. 2.6 The becoming of historic humans. Symbols are explained in text

thesis". They conclude that there is "insufficient credible evidence" either for or against this thesis. They also highlight nine different definitions of technological complexity employed to illustrate the issue of adequacy criteria for a test of that thesis.

WHuLa enabled tool-based reasoning in the form of mathematics and eventually KRR schemes like those employed in AI. The latter are less general than WHuLa but at the same time much more powerful in their predictive and design capabilities for certain classes of problems. Language-based axiomatic theories cover the space between formal systems and non-axiomatic systems of WHuLa. The development of such tools and their further creative use by historic humans significantly contributed to the creation of CAC but they are far from being its engine. The era of AISs, electron microscopes, implants, world-wide web, and "robot scientists" is unique, but their extreme significance and novel consequences should not disguise the fact that, on their own, they are useless. Currently, the human is still required to be included in the *eventual* decision taking system. This point is related to the extended mind hypothesis. Their common thread is their lack of meaning. Let me explicate.

When thoughts are written, they can act as stimuli to any person who may read them at any point in time. In particular, of course, they act as a stimulus to their creator. Therefore, a feedback-based modification can be originated that becomes a *system* of feedback loops if related thoughts and their written expressions are further created, or if the person has 'second thoughts' on the precision of her translation. I call this type of thought modification: written-based thought enhancement (WriTE).

A remark concerning WriTE systems should be made here. Clark (2008 p. xxviii), building on Clark & Chalmers (1998), claims that such systems "are not all in the head". He is partly right and partly wrong. He is obviously right when he claims that human technology is enhancing human thinking. This is indeed the case and happens through WriTEs—among many others. This is a rather well known view (e.g., Ong 1982). He is wrong nevertheless, in claiming that thinking itself is literally realised externally in the form of symbolic or material re- arrangements.[20] For, the external parts of WriTEs are *fossilised* 'skepseis' (kind of fundamental nervous formations; defined in Sect. 3.3.1). Without an appropriate person to interpret and think about them, they will forever remain inert and meaningless. Clark & Chalmers (1998*2008 p. 222) write that: "If we remove the external component the system's behavioural competence will drop, just as it would if we removed part of its brain." This is true but beside the issue in hand. The question is what does happen when there is no brain at all. And the answer is nothing at all. In WriTE, persons are necessary for the loop to be meaningfully operational; The external parts of WriTEs, on their own, do not realise any thinking at all. They exclusively record some *formal* aspects of the skepseis of an individual.

In summary, the WHuLa transition and the social structures and advanced technologies built on the basis of WHuLa have implied unexpected consequences and open up promising opportunities, and great challenges. First, they have made us realise that the immense gap between humans and any other animal cannot be caused by structural or/and functional differences of nervous systems. Not because the human mind is immaterial –which is not. Nor because part of human thinking is realised outside an individual's brain –which as we saw it is not. But, because, the H-period is causally shaped by the development of WHuLa as well as the derived developments of science, technology, and our overall cumulative

[20] And so is Chalmers to the extent he accepts their active externalism thesis (Clark & Chalmers 1998*2008).

culture.[21] They provide the artificial component of *H. sapiens* evolution and jointly have caused the mental gap within the H-period. The differences between the minds of pre-historic humans and nonhuman animals are differences in degree. The differences between the minds of pre-historic and historic humans differ in kind—allowing for the establishment of the WHuLa transition (see fourth point below for clarification).

Second, WHuLa, science and AI open up, for the first time for a biological species, unprecedented opportunities and determining challenges including fundamental changes of the nature of our species and possible colonisation of space by a future hybrid *Homo* species or a conscious robot society. How shall we proceed it will modify, more or less, the evolution of our species and of other life forms.

Third, I suggest that the EES should be extended to include notions and associated theories derived from data and phenomena characterising our species in the Holocene (ca. 12 ka -1949) and Anthropocene epochs (1950—present). In particular, the WHuLa, science and AI transitions should be studied as an integral part of the evolution of *H. sapiens*.

Fourth, historic humans cannot be separated from non-historic humans by the start date of the WHuLa transition. As individuals, they can only be distinguished by possession or not of the full dynamic capacity of WHuLa. On the other hand, H is characterised by the WHuLa transition. The latter should be seen to be extended from the earliest writing systems to at least the second H-generation whose *all* members are characterised by literacy as defined by UNESCO above. The individual and the species are different selection units. The decision of how our species will proceed, most likely, will not be taken by either. It is likely to be taken by a minority of our species members. Do conscious decisions affecting our species have to be taken by a minority? This is a question of huge importance. My answer to it is that such decisions must be taken by a majority of at least 70% of H-membership.

The evolution of Earthian life implies either extinction or further evolution of *Homo sapiens*. So far, our evolution has been shaped by a succession of minor and major transitions. In this section, I have proposed and argued for a new transition (WHuLa) that, within *Homo* evolution,

[21] The unfortunate existence of illiterate people does not affect the strength of the argument.

can be safely accorded the status of a major transition. It may turn out that the superstructure of an advancing H-science and associated technologies like biotechnology and AI may eventually become a super transition of Earthian evolution.

CHAPTER 3

Thinking and Meaning: Biological and Artificial

"It is indeed true that only the individual is capable of thinking. There is no such metaphysical entity as a group mind which thinks over and above the heads of individuals, or whose ideas the individual merely reproduces. Nevertheless it would be false to deduce from this that all the ideas and sentiments which motivate an individual have their origin in him alone, and can be adequately explained solely on the basis of his own life-experience."

(Mannheim, 1929/31/54*1954, p. 2).

"An important problem neglected by neuroscientists is the problem of meaning."

(Crick & Koch 1998, p. 104).

"It is deeply regrettable that we are still a long way from knowing how to integrate explanation and understanding, information and meaning, science and the humanities."

(Heyes 2019b, p. 43)

Thinking is widely agreed to be the most basic mental phenomenon that permeates all others across animals and machines. Its building blocks are unanimously taken to be 'concepts' (cf, Margolis & Lawrence 2019). This chapter demonstrates that the latter viewpoint is mistaken. The building blocks of both thinking and concepts are the notions of 'meaningful neural formation' for biological systems, and its generalisation of 'meaningful material formation' for all types of noémon systems. This view implies a clear stance on the more or less explicit war raging between

P. A. M. Gelepithis, *Unification of Artificial Intelligence and Psychology*,
https://doi.org/10.1007/978-3-031-68319-0_3

opponents and proponents of a meaning-based approach to mind (e.g., Whiten 2019; Heyes 2020).

A complete physical theory of thinking should fulfil as many of the following requirements as possible:

(a) Described in naturalistic terms.
(b) Broad enough to encompass all types of noémon systems.
(c) Rich enough to be able to account for the full range of human thinking.
(d) In accordance with observable behaviour, biological evidence, and physical principles.
(e) An integral part of a much larger theory of mind.

A procedural point of exposition. Fulfilment of conditions (b) and (c) require addressing a vast range of phenomena and a corresponding huge area of diverse studies. To make the work manageable I discuss the human case and provide definitions for the robot and animal cases. That will result in three definitions sharing a serial number and differentiated by a subscript. In all *such* cases, definitions without subscripts refer to the initial definition concerning humans. Comments illustrating the differences will follow the definitions wherever they are required.

The next section critically reminds us of the three main approaches to the study of thinking, and provides a succinct review of the major theories of meaning summarising their main advantages and disadvantages in tabular form. Section 3.2 outlines a novel physical theory of thinking and meaning that is extended to include the following significant notions of both psychology and AI: 'concept', 'idea', 'belief', 'information' and its related notions, and 'reasoning'. Finally, Sect. 3.3:

(i) introduces two of the theory's key consequences: one, concerning the language- thought issue and two, the relation between memory and meaning.
(ii) proposes a qualitative topological model for the representation (or construction) of concepts.
(iii) evaluates our theory of thinking and meaning against the major theories of meaning reviewed in Sect. 3.1 and Hebb's pioneering theory of thinking.

In summary preview, the proposed theory fully addresses conditions (a), (b), and (e) and partly addresses aspects of conditions (c), and (d).

3.1 Review of Theories of Thinking and Meaning

There are three major approaches to the study of 'thinking': philosophical (the oldest), computational (the currently dominant but declining), and biological (emerging). Each has contributed its own requirements for a theory of 'thinking'. Specifically, philosophy always assumed that, implicitly or explicitly, cracking the problem of meaning is the real issue that needs to be accounted for. This is the key, fundamental requirement for a theory of thinking derived from numerous philosophical analyses through the ages. It is worth noting that this requirement was tacitly assumed to be the case within the Artificial Intelligence field since its inception, and presently has been nearly universally accepted in biology too. Consequently, all theories of thinking end up as one or another of a large number of theories of meaning (e.g., Davidson, 2001; Lurtz 2007; Millikan 1998; Newen & Bartels 2007). More recent studies of thought use the predictive processing and probabilistic reasoning approach to thought (Christoff & Fox 2018; Mills et al. 2021). Computational approaches are split between those adopting the strong AI view (thinking is computation) shared by a large number of investigators from Turing (1950) through Newell and Simon (1976) to Dietrich (2007) and Smolenski (2012), and a softer perspective shaped by the need to incorporate the substantial expansion of research into areas like implicit thinking (e.g., Litman & Reber 2005), motivated thinking (e.g., Molden & Higgins 2005), emotional effects (e.g., Ashby et al. 1999; Thagard 2002*2006), animal thinking (e.g., Taylor et al. 2007). The latter perspective is probably best exemplified by Holyoak and Morrison's (2005a) reader. In remarking on the difficulty of providing scientific definitions of mental terms, they illustrate that difficulty with their own preliminary definition of thinking:

> "*Thinking is the systematic transformation of mental representations of knowledge to characterize actual or possible states of the world, often in service of goals.*" (Holyoak and Morrison 2005b, p. 2, their emphasis).

As they self-critically remark, their definition introduces "a plethora of terms with meanings that beg to be unpacked, but which we can only hint." (ibid). Here therefore, the implicit requirement is for a theory of thinking within a wider context. Probably, the most general proposal, so far, is mental models (Johnson-Laird 1983; 2005).

Biologically, the most elaborate treatment of the nature and basic mechanisms of thought and mind as the activity of the brain is still Hebb (1949, 1968, 1976, 1980a, 1980b). Subsequent work in this tradition either tried to expand on some of his ideas (e.g., Freeman 1999; Edelman & Mountcastle 1978; Changeux 1983*1985; Edelman 1987; Buzsáki 2010; Li et al. 2016); provided useful discussion of and further evidence for Hebb's theory (e.g., Pulvermüller 1999) or moved into the fascinating area of animal thinking (e.g., Köhler 1925; Premack 1985; Shetlleworth 1998; Norman et al. 2001; Sulkowski & Hauser 2001; Bates et al. 2007; Taylor et al. 2007). More recently, as part of the cultural evolution part of the EES, some of the cultural aspects of thinking have been pointed out (Heyes 2019a). An early advocate of the effect of culture and more generally society on thinking and mind, whose work is increasingly recognised, is Vygotski (1934*1986). In all cases no contribution to the nature or basic mechanisms of thought has been made.

The philosophical and biological (including psychological) approaches to thinking are reduced to a multitude of corresponding theories of meaning; the computational approach is reduced to a single type of AI theory of meaning. Cultural evolution theories have not produced a theory of meaning, despite the emphasis on the semantic significance of culture by proponents of evolutionary cultural anthropology (e.g., Hewlett 2016). Table 3.2 summarises the key advantages and disadvantages of the main theories of meaning along with a succinct presentation of their views on its nature.

In Gelepithis (1988), a full review of semantics covering the philosophical, linguistic, formal, and biological theories of meaning is provided. Table 3.1 does not include recent theories that are essentially the same with earlier theories (i.e., such more recent theories have not modified the nature of earlier ones). For instance, experience-grounded semantics, conceptual role semantics or model-theoretic semantics for the TTM; functional role semantics for essentially the use theory of meaning; or informational semantics for essentially Grice's theory of natural meaning. For a recent technical survey the reader may consult Wang (2005) and the third part (nature of meaning pp. 151–389) of Lepore & Smith (2006). For a recent exchange of views on meaning normativity (Hattiangadi 2006; Ginsborg 2012; Glüer & Wikforss 2015).

Table 3.1 Summary of key advantages and disadvantages of the main theories of meaning (updated version of Gelepithis 1988)

Name and key proponents	*Nature of meaning*	*Main advantage*	*Main disadvantage*
RTM. 1919. Russell 1905,	The language-world link	Pinpointed the relation of language to the world	Too narrow. It cannot account for e.g., indexicals.
ITM. Grice, 1957, 1968, 1969.	Intended effect on audience.	Distinguishes between linguistic and non-linguistic	Inability to combine personal with public meanings.
UTM. Wittgenstein, †1953.	Use.	Recognises the effect of context on meaning.	Ignores underlying mechanisms.
LTM Katz & Fodor 1963; Chomsky 1965.	Purely linguistic.	Inclusion of syntax to account for meaning.	Excludes context and the world.
TTM. Tarski 1944 ; Davidson, 1967, 1973, 1974.	Knowledge of truth conditions.	(a) Pinpoints the relation of thought to the world. (b) Succinct representations.	Cannot account for non-truth conditions.
AITM. 1977. Jonhson–Laird	Procedure.	As with UTM. As with TTM (b)	Cannot account for non-executable expressions.
Id.TM. Locke 1690; Saussure †1974; Ogden and Richards 1923.	Encoding.	Considers the close relation of language to thought.	Cannot account for the abstraction problem.

(continued)

Table 3.1 (continued)

Name and key proponents	*Nature of meaning*	*Main advantage*	*Main disadvantage*
BTM. a) Osgood, 1971, Osgood & McGuigan 1973. b) Dretske 1981. c) Millikan 1984, Macdonald & Papineau 2006.	a) Function of response. b) The condition that typically causes an intentional state. c) Truth conditions of intentional states in terms of the biological functions of these states.	Brings in our relation to things.	Does not recognise perceptual effects on meaning.
STM, Mead †1934*1962.	Resides in social collectivities.	Takes into account the sociocultural dimension of meaning.	Ignores the biological dimension.

TM Theory of Meaning; *RTM* Referential TM; *TTM* Truth TM; *STM* Social TM *ITM* Intentional TM; *AITM* AI TM; *UTM* Use TM; *Id.TM* Ideational TM; *LTM* Linguistic TM; *BTM* Behavioural TM

NB. See text for recent literature and justification for not included in this Table.

Table 3.2 Types of conditionals and illustrative examples (adapted from Gelepithis 1993a, p. 8)

Types of Conditional	*Illustrative examples*
Indicative	If John beats Jack then John is a good player.
Subjunctive	If John were to beat Jack then John would be a good player.
Counterfactual	If John had beaten Jack then John would have been a good player.
Definitional	If Mary is a spinster then she is unmarried.
Decisional	If McEnroe looses, John promised to eat his glove.
Hypothetico-deductive (see text).	If all humans are mortals and I am a human then I am mortal.
Causal	If the grass is green then the grass has chlorophyll.
Material	If $x < 5$ then $x < 9$, for all $x \in R$.

Since the beginning of the twenty-first century, the interest in the relation between meaning/mind and brain has been exponentially increased. The latter interest may well be due to Crick & Koch's remark quoted at the start of this chapter. This is in accordance with Hebb's thesis (Hebb 1949, 1980)—the study of mind can be advanced if only we develop biologically constrained *theories*. Nevertheless, current work is fragmented. For instance: brain supported differentiation between meaningful and meaningless pictures (e.g., Mensen 2017); the implementability of complex semantic structures in animals and AISs (e.g., Martin & Baggio 2019; Philips 2019); work on "detecting the actual activity of cell assemblies" (e.g., Sakurai et al. 2018). In sharp contrast to these fragmented theories and rather dissociated data, Hebb's theory is still the most well integrated. The theory outlined in the next section expands Hebb's theory of thinking and bases it in a neuroscientifically-grounded theory of meaning lacking in all theories of thinking. Foundational seeds of this theory were introduced in Gelepithis (1984; 2009).

3.2 A Materialist, Evolutionary, Theory of Thinking and Meaning

In the introduction to this chapter, we noted five requirements that a complete, scientific and physicalist, theory of meaning and thought should fulfil. Accordingly, this section demonstrates that the notions of 'meaningful neural formation' and its generalisation of 'meaningful material formation' are necessary and sufficient for a full theory of noémon systems thinking. Expectedly, such a theory encompasses a full physicalist theory of meaning. We start with the physical theory of meaning for all member of **S** and close with my theory of thinking for biological, artificial and hybrid noémon systems.

Because of its extreme importance, I must repeat here a point I made earlier. *All definitions are time dependent*. It is exclusively for presentation simplicity reasons that in most cases in this book I do not explicitly include the time variable.

3.2.1 Physical Theory of Meaning

The mind-brain identity hypothesis is presumed for any neurophysiological theory meaning.[1] In addition, I use the 'mental-material identification postulate'. Namely, any mental state, process, or phenomenon is identified with a material state, process, or phenomenon. This allows for an extension of my biological theory of meaning to the artificial domain (AISs, robots and autonomous robot entities). Therefore, we have to account for the following two fundamental problems respectively. First, delineation of a class of *meaningful* 'neural formations'. Second, delineation of a class of *meaningful* 'material formations'.

Because we are most familiar with human meanings and they are the most evolved ones, I start with the human case and proceed with the animal and artificial ones.

Fullford et al. (2006, p. 428) have expressed the human case of the meanings problem by the following question: "In what sense, precisely,

[1] It should be noticed that the mind-brain identity hypothesis does not imply membership to the individualist tradition (e.g., Chomsky 1995, Fodor 1980, Stich 1978). Equally important is to keep clearly distinct the notions of identification and coding. The latter has been proposed by Bolton & Hill (2004). See also the final of the remarks following definition-16.

do [human] mental states carry meaning?" The following two definitions *jointly* provide the basis for the description of the huge space of human meanings.

Definition-14a For an human H, I call 'neural formation' (symbol N), a structure of *interacting* sub-cellular components across a region of H's nervous system (NS).

A clear example of N is a synapse; any type of neuronal synapse. A second example is the type of structure developed by the *interaction* among astrocytes, pre- synaptic and post-synaptic terminals. I italicised 'interacting' to emphasise the fact that processes are part and parcel of neural formations (NFs). As is well known such interactions involve extremely complex reentrants. The reader will also have noticed that I used the word 'structure' rather than system in the above definition. The reason is that I wanted to avoid drawing any connotations of *necessary* completeness and, on the contrary, I wanted to indicate the sense of *potential* fleeting existence. In other words, NFs may be either short-term or long-term. Naturally, in accordance with standard functional biology, the cardinality, size, shape, composition and interconnections of NFs change over time. These characteristics are aspects of what I mean by the term 'functional complexity' or ontogenetic development of N. To be kept in mind that in biology there is no such thing as pure anatomy or pure function; they co-exist and are in constant interactions. The relations of ontogenetic development to phylogenetic change and multiple inheritance will not be discussed here (see Feldman & Ramachandran 2018 for discussion of models of the genetic contribution to human phenotypes incorporating cultural inheritance).

Three more points should be noted. First, the proposed theoretical construct draws heavily upon Hebb's (1949, 1980) notion of cell assemblies. Their key difference boils down to the fact that the proposed notion is more inclusive in two respects. One, it allows the possibility of non-synaptic plasticity (Kandel & Pittinger 1999; Bollmann & Engert 2009) and non-neuronal correlates of mental abilities (e.g., Bennett 2007a). Two, it encompasses the increasing recognition of the importance of the interaction between the glia and neuronal networks. For discussion of the nature of cell assemblies (Buzsáki 2010; Li et al. 2016) and alternative theoretical proposals (e.g., Li et al. 2016). Finally, I would like to stress that NFs are not, *necessarily,* mental representations.

The next coupled-definition delineates the class of meaningful N (completing the neurophysiological definition of meaning), and provides the basis for both redefining the two traditional senses of meaning (definitions 15 and 16), and extending its sense to cover a significant but neglected fact (relation 2 in definition-26).

Definition-14b For an human H, a specific neural formation N is meaningful, (symbol N_m), iff N is able to influence the survival or reproduction of H.

Two remarks should be made here concerning: (i) an implicit feature of this definition; and (ii) the verifiability of N_m.

First, the implicit feature concerns motor activity. Both survival and reproduction necessitate action activity as part of their existence. The ability of a NF to influence either survival or reproduction presupposes the existence of motor capability. It is in this sense very close to Sherrington's notion of reflex-arc and its associated nervous systems functional structures.

With respect to the second remark concerning verifiability, given the inadequate current resolution of fMRI scanning there seems to be a problem in actually linking N_m to the conditions stated in the previous definition. This is a real problem to which, presently, I may only suggest two routes to a possible solution. One route may be via exploitation of the bridge between neural formations and homeostasis that glia cells provide.[2] The second route is linking the reproduction or survival of extremely simple animals like sponges to genes in their proto-post-synaptic scaffold. Such a link would seem to provide further justification for the proposed definition through advances in our understanding of the evolutionary transition from sponges who lack neurons with clearly recognisable synapses to earliest nerve systems (Sakarya et al. 2007). In this respect calls for the development of new tools for analysing the functioning of neural circuits are very welcome (e.g., Belmonte et al. 2015). In particular, as far as fMRIs are concerned, they must be improved significantly, in particular their currently grossly inadequate resolution, in order to address the often fleeting and distributed characteristics of Ns.

We are ready now to redefine the traditional senses of human meaning in accordance with definition-14b. First, I need the following:

[2] For a recent survey of their roles see Barres (2008), Allen and Barres (2009).

Abbreviation: I will use the symbol S_c to stand for a stimulus within its context.

With respect to a human H, an S_c may be perceptual, linguistic or a combination of the two. Both types of S_c can be extremely complex. A perceptual one is characterised by four parameters: location, modality, duration, and intensity. The discovery of "place cells" provides significant neurophysiological support to this notion (O'keefe & Dostrovsky 1971). Linguistic complexity brings with it the generative capacity of natural language. Furthermore, S_c may be novel (i.e., not previously encountered) or not. If novel, two sub-cases can be distinguished: (i) for whatever reason, no meaning is assigned to S_c (a N may be created though); and (ii) a meaning is assigned to S_c. The following two definitions address the case of a novel S_c and previously encountered S_c in turn. They do not differentiate an S_c in terms of its complexity.

Definition-15 The meaning of a novel S_c, for the human H at time t, is whatever N_m is created by the interaction of S_c and H at time t.

Definition-16 The meaning of a previously encountered S_c, for the human H, at time t, is the *prevailed* N_p of $\mathbf{N_p}$. Where:

$\mathbf{N_p}$ is that subsystem of M (i.e., the dynamic system of all meaningful neural formations) that has been relatively permanently developed by the time t. Of course, $\mathbf{N_p}$ is a proper subsystem of M.[3] 'Prevailed' means the particular neural formation, N_p, that is eventually selected among its family members that constitute $\mathbf{N_p}$. Selection may involve several processes.

The following remarks aim to clarify the above definitions and point out their significance.

First, given that all subsequent building blocks of thinking as well as the phenomena of understanding, communication, knowledge, consciousness, emotions, and human nature are defined, ***at a minimum***, in terms of N_m structures, the complexity of M is demonstrably vast. It should be explicitly stated that M is a subsystem of an individual human's internal space of phenomena. The specific relations between the two

[3] Definitions 15 and 16 are based on an undifferentiated definition of meaning in Gelepithis (1984) where the extremely important role of context was also briefly discussed (cf, chapter 4).

spaces is a very difficult open question. The fact that M is part of an individual human's nervous system is of significant help but the mapping of M remains a huge task. Advances on this front will bring advances in psychiatry—at least.

Second, I want to stress the rather obvious point that although definitions 15 & 16 do not specify any mechanisms, mechanisms are involved in the *creation* (definition-15) and *prevailing* (definition-16) processes determining the formation of novel and previously encountered S_C respectively. A particular, necessary, class of such mechanisms constitute learning (e.g., Pavlovian or operant conditioning). Understanding the meaning of an S_C, let alone of sentences and texts, delineates a second class of semantic mechanisms. The next chapter-4 will go to some length with respect to the complex process of understanding. The identified classes of complicating processes do not exhaust the complexity of definitions 15 & 16. The most prominent of such additional complicating processes involved in the *creation* and *prevailing* processes of the two phenomena identified by definitions 15 & 16 is the class delineated by 'emotions'. Chapter-4 of the Consequences Volume of this monograph is dedicated to emotions (Gelepithis 2024b).

Third, with respect to the general case of selection processes, we do not know how they occur. In simple organisms like aplysia (Kandel 2006) selection processes have been identified with the mechanisms of Pavlovian and operant conditioning. My hypothesis is that selection is the eventual result of an extremely complex *system* of neurophysiological processes occurring because of unconscious processes or consciously aiming to achieve a goal or objective (cf, understanding in chapter-4). Of course, the strength of N_p associated to S_C does play a role but it does not necessarily determine whether a neural formation will eventually prevail or not. Put in other words, the term 'prevailed' is used to indicate the potential complexity involved in the struggle for selection (e.g., unconscious vs. conscious processes).

Fourth, with respect to definition-16, it is not required of H to be aware of the previous occurrence of S_C. In other words, it allows the possibility of subliminal stimuli recording.

Fifth, it is only natural to identify $\mathbf{N_p}$ with H's long-term memory. Section 3.3.1 introduces my memory-meaning postulate.

My sixth point concerns the more general case of animal meanings and opens up the possibility for some interesting comparative research. Specifically, it should be the case that partial neural re-presentations of aspects of the environment (some of them useful for survival and reproduction) formed as the end result of processes starting with the sensory systems of the animalia taxon. As such these early meanings, (and possibly, concepts and thoughts), differ widely in tandem with the variety of sensory systems available in the animal kingdom. Figure 3.1 relates several classes of animal meanings to both internal and external representations (Sect. 2. 2), as well as to a particular evolutionary pathway of meanings, namely, that of *Homo.*

Actually, animal meanings can be formally based on the following definition (analogous to definition-14b. I use A for a particular animal species, and *A* for the animalia taxon.

Definition-14b **ᴵA** For an individual member I of a particular animal species A (ᴵA), a neural formation N is meaningful (symbol N_m), if and only if N is able to influence the survival or reproduction of ᴵA.

Despite their formal similarity, definitions -14b and -14b ᴵA differ significantly. In accordance with the TNS outlined so far, exclusively human meanings only appear when *H. sapiens* enters the WHuLa transition (see sections 2.2 and 2.3). In that respect, all *exclusively* WHuLa-based meanings are out of reach for any animal taxon. In contrast, humans as an extant biological species share a good number of nervous systems traits

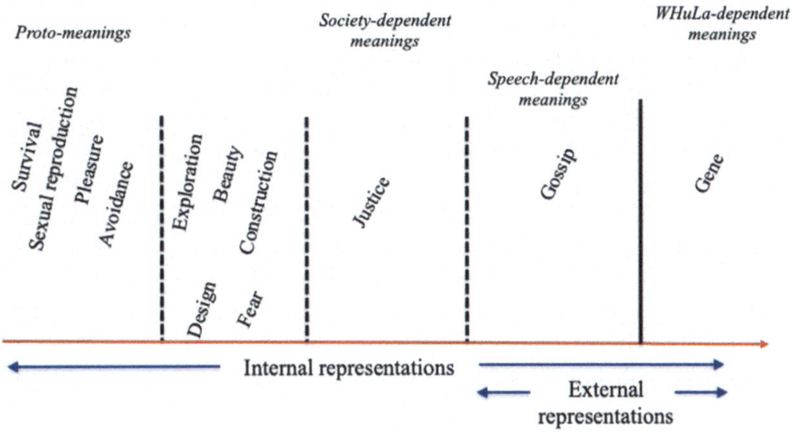

Fig. 3.1 Evolution of *animal* meanings: From proto-meanings to WHuLa-dependent meanings

with animal taxa—chemically our affinities with out evolutionary past go back to a much earlier time. On the other hand, human and animal N_m have to differ at least to the extent of different representational systems evolved in Animalia (e.g., bats, dolphins, birds, and even certain primates) in accordance with the requirements of their distinct environments.

Finally, in case of ARE (autonomous robot entity) emergence, any current human comments should be considered with a lot of scepticism (see Sect. 2.2). For, since AREs would possess *own*-representational systems (R_o), *and* they would very likely be 'immortal', their fundamental value systems would be considerable different.[4] However, for completeness reasons, I want to state that the fundamental notion of 'meaningful *material* formation' would be defined in a way reminiscent of definition-14b (meaningful neural formation). Simply reminiscent because the characteristic prerequisites of the latter definition—namely, survival and reproduction—might even be irrelevant for an ARE. At the very least, they would be different. For instance, possession of an R_o implies at least a minimum of consciousness (chapter-3 of the Consequences Volume of this monograph—Gelepithis 2024b).

3.2.2 *Physical Theory of Thinking*

The physicalist theory of meaning introduced in the previous section provides a sound starting point. It also revealed the great complexity of such a theory. It follows that a *complete* physical theory of thinking has an even greater complexity to address. Namely, the inherent complexity of thinking as a biological and artificial phenomenon of the space of noémon systems, as well as the interactions between the physical phenomena of meaning and thinking. A further complication is introduced by the evolution of thinking. There should be a difference between pre-WHuLa thinking and the thinking of modern H. Such differences invite both challenging and interesting research work. Figure 3.2 provides a glimpse of the subspace of thinking systems. In relation to this subspace of S, one should note that in case an ARE is materialised, it might have 'thoughts' and thinking patterns the nature of which any human theory of meaning and thinking will not be able to explain—let alone predict. In addition

[4] I did not consider robots because the meanings they can process, and may express, are those that some humans have chosen to include in their representational systems along with possible consequences not envisaged by humans (section 2.2).

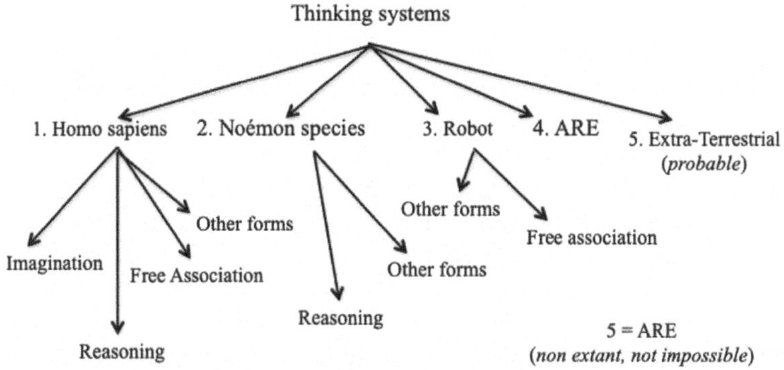

Fig. 3.2 Extant and potential types and specialised processes of thinking systems

to the discussion on AREs made in Sect. 2.2, the reader is invited to consider the corresponding sections in Chapter-4 of this volume and in chapters 2–4 of the Consequences Volume (Gelepithis 2024b).

The thinking process involves several distinct elements. I take the following to be indispensable: 'concept', 'thought' (as a single result of thinking), 'belief', 'information' and its-related notions. Before starting with the notion of concept, I should stress the point that, in general, these elements are identified with different levels of neural organisation. Please note that the latter notion subsumes Buzsáki's (2010) notion of neural syntax. The extent, architectural modifications and dynamic existence of the structures and associated mechanisms identified with each of the semantic biological phenomena depend on the individual, the species and their environment (physical, cultural, and social).

A recent theme issue in the *Philosophical Transactions B* addressed the topic of abstract concepts. Interestingly, one of its major preliminary conclusions (Borghi et al 2018) is discarding the old distinction between concrete and abstract concepts in favour of a multidimensional space that distinguishes concepts by grounding them along several axes. Although the dimensions of such a space were not specified (although suggestions were made), I would expect such a space to include at least the following axes: abstractness, perception, action, language, culture, and personal development.

Overall, the papers of this theme issue lacked substantial integration. There were of course cross-references and references to some related literature, but there was no integration in terms of the key underlying issues, namely, representation, meaning, memory, information, and belief. In addition, suggestions for grounding concepts were at a very general level except in cases of knowledge representation models which nevertheless lacked comprehensive coverage. Finally, the two most important issues concerning concepts, namely, their nature and representation, received rather limited treatment; exceptions were the work of Cuccio & Gallese (2018), and Borghi et al (2018b).

With respect to the nature of concepts, most workers in cognitive science view them as mental representations. For a brief discussion and references of the two alternative views (concepts as abilities or abstract objects) see Margolis & Lawrence (2019). The TNS provides a *fourth* perspective and addresses the issues of the ontology and structure of concepts. Additional significant issues like nativism are seen to be resolved as consequences of my TNS.

The following definition captures the essence of my views on the ontology and structure of concepts. Fodor (1998) provides a critical review of the major theories of concepts.

Definition-17 Let ${}^{1}N_m$ be the first neural formation *created* by the specific triad (S_{c1}, H, t_1). Then the *system* of all ${}^{j}N_m$ (j a natural number) of human H that have been created by time t later than t1 I call it a concept of H up to t and symbolise it by ε(H, t).

For simplicity we may use the letter ε to refer to an ε(H, t) but it has to be understood that ε is identical with ε(H, t). Naturally, an ε(H, t) is a very tiny subsystem of M.

Below I succinctly summarise eight basic consequences of the above definition. First, definition-17 implies a range of factors (identified with corresponding contexts) contributing to the overall meaning of a *human* concept. Such factors include perception, language use, emotional experiences, and scientific knowledge. The various contexts may be seen as dimensions of the space of context (cf, Borghi et al 2018). Since definition-17 determines a space of concepts along several contexts over time and individual human, the traditional distinction between abstract and concrete concepts ceases to exist. This conclusion has also been reached by Barsalou et al. (2018) although previously Barsalou & Wiemer-Hastings (2005, p. 155) have claimed that "a concept generates a multitude of situational representations". This mental representations view of concepts is remnant of a dualist ontology. It also places the cart (concept) before the horse (situational stimuli).

A second major consequence concerns the grounding of abstract concepts (Pecher & Zeelenberg 2018; Zdrazilova et al. 2018 and related articles in the theme issue of *The Royal Society*). Within the TNS developed so far, abstract concepts necessarily involve language and in most cases they are WHuLa-depended (Sect. 2.3.3). Depending on whether an abstract concept is purely linguistic or not, the grounding is purely linguistic or hybrid (see chapter-4 for discussion). For a dissenting viewpoint arguing for relinquishing the notion of grounding (Leshinskaya & Caramazza 2016).

The third consequence, related to the second, concerns the debate between nativism and empiricism. Like nativism, definition-17 implies amodality of concepts; contra nativism, concepts are systems of meaningful neural formations (not abstract symbols).

Fourth, definition-17 implies a physicalist and internalist perspective of concepts. A key aspect of this dual consequence, in the form of an outline of a topological model of the token-type distinction, is discussed in Sect. 3.3.1.

Fifth, my notion of concept implies that the semantic aspects of the activity patterns of neuronal populations, (a special case of meaningful neural formations), are more important than those of individual neurons. This implication is supported by recent work (e.g., Yuste 2015; Driscoll et al. 2017).

Sixth, the proposed theory is in sharp contrast to both the standard psychological view of concepts (e.g., initially Fodor 1975; recently Margolis & Lawrence 2007) and the propositional (equivalently, Fregean or semantic) view (e.g., Peacocke 1992). The key characteristic of the rudimentary theory of concepts sketched here is that it depends on both an organism's physiology and its cultural environment (whenever applicable). Although a reasonably incomplete theory of concepts is considerably far in the future, recent work (some of which was cited above) contributes to that objective and qualitative models may contribute the elucidation of difficult problems (see Sect. 3.3.1 below).

Seventh, the proposed theory can easily be extended to the Animalia taxon. Such an extension implies existence of a vast number of classes of non-human animal concepts, each class corresponding to a particular taxon down to the species level. Since the relevant literature is huge, I only provide a few indicative examples: Herman et al. (2008) provide evidence for non-primate mammals understanding concepts; and Krichbaum et al. (2020) for a very informative review of behavioural studies of animal cognition with an emphasis on concept learning and canine cognition. Some of these concepts or classes of concepts may for ever remain outside the bounds of *Homo sapiens* knowledge and a fortiori experience. Of course, this fact has to be counterbalanced by the fact that WHuLA, via scientific knowledge, has created human concepts well beyond those of any Earthian non-human animal.

Finally, an extension of the notion of human concept to an ARE-concept can be made along the line suggested in the last paragraph of the previous section. The case of animal concepts is a straightforward extension of the human case (see also subsection below on animal thinking and reasoning).

Let me move to the notion of 'thought' in the sense of a single idea, that is, as the product of the process of thinking (covered by definition-24 below and the discussion following it).

Definition-18 σ is a thought (equivalent idea) of human H if and only if σ is a flexible, not necessarily permanent structure of concepts and/or N_m (definition-14b), that encompasses the possibility of action by H.

The above definition of idea is in full agreement with the widely accepted view that ideas are conceptual combinations (e.g., Marupaka et al. 2012). Although the notion of 'thought' in the above sense of a single idea is not really an established area of research, it is useful to have a neurophysiological based definition for it. At the very least it has the advantage of both referring to a structure that is substantially different than that of a concept and to possible action. Thought may also be involved in larger semantic structures (definition-26) that reveal a third type of meaning distinct from those of definitions 15 and 16. This is dealt in Sect. 3.3.1.

I want to add that it may be worthy differentiating between thought and idea; nevertheless so far I had been unable to specify differentiating conditions corresponding to sufficiently different biological phenomena. There may be an interesting project lurking underneath this inability of mine.

The next definition reveals both the similarity and considerable differences between 'idea' and 'belief'. This does not make much easier their identification with compound meaningful neural formations but indicates possible routes of investigation.

Definition-19 Belief of H =def A structure of NFs and meaningful NFs of H on the basis of which H is prepared to act, argue, or live by.

I should note that this definition brings in behavioral constraints while at the same time is the widest possible in terms of its neurophysiology. It is a key definition in view of the central position that 'beliefs' play in human life (cf, Davies 2010). More than any other notion so far, the empirical identification of beliefs requires novel neurophysiological tools and techniques. This is primarily due to the complexity and diversity of the neurophysiological structures involved in most beliefs. Belief, as defined, may well include any combination of concepts, thoughts and elements of the space of semantic structures of a human.

The complexity and diversity of an individual human's belief systems becomes evident when one considers the motivational and emotional aspects of such systems. In addition, emotions and motivations are interrelated. The net result makes the anatomy and neurophysiology of belief systems extremely difficult to be investigated with our current tools. One of the difficulties is that such systems span several levels of the physical organisation of a human.

A major additional issue is revealed by accepting the physiological aspects of beliefs. I put it starkly by juxtaposing the following pair of statements:

S-1: If a person commits a crime because of a brain tumour is not considered responsible.

S-2: If a a person commits a crime because of a belief is considered responsible.

How can we deal with this ethical and legal issue? A hugely important and complicated issue on a par with ethical and legal issues in AI. Unavoidably, the issue of free will, their common thread, requires an answer (Elstob 2018).

My penultimate point has to do with partially shared belief systems like those developed in human populations by means of education or propaganda (often subtly related to each other) and theories that can be affected by belief systems. Theories, as social commodities, undergo two types of changes. The first, scientific modification, is necessitated by the discovery of new evidence, gradual improvements, and the introduction of conceptual or technological breakthroughs. The second, societal modification, is motivated by ignorance, negligence, dogmatic beliefs, or benefit. In all cases, such societally-originated theory change invariably plays into the hands of the status quo. They may be turned into established pseudosciences like astrology, or they may be fossilised into their original mistaken form like the flat earth delusion. In both cases pseudo problems are maintained to the detriment of human society.

Pseudo-problems usually stem from confusing a genuine problem with a fake description of it. For instance:

> "Various writers confuse the genuine question Does the physical universe have a temporal *origin*, and--if so--what does physical cosmology tell us about it? with the quite different pseudo-problem Was there a *creation* of the universe, and -if so- what light can science throw on it, if any?" (Grünbaum 1989, p. 373).

Sometimes, genuine and important problems like the relations among human behaviour, nervous system, culture and society are clouded by prejudices and attachments to old cherished but mistaken belief systems. Belief systems that were built on assumptions derived from fear and vested interests like idealist or dualist ontologies. The precise form of this issue appeared with Descartes. Its origins lie with Plato. Its negative aspects are maintained for the benefit of dogmatic or populistic organisations. Within a naturalistic *H. sapiens* science, the mind-body problem is a pseudo-problem. Of course the relation of mind to the rest of the brain is a genuine and difficult cluster of problems.

Scientists should take a stance on pseudosciences and mistaken viewpoints with negative repercussions to society (e.g., fake news). There are too many genuine and urgent problems requiring solutions. We do not need to retain useless labels of any sort. Edward O. Wilson, 2014, pp. 177–178) stated it far more generally, eloquently, and to the point:

> "Our leaders, religious, political, and business, mostly accept supernatural explanations of the human existence. Even if privately sceptical, they have little interest in opposing religious leaders and unnecessarily stirring up the populace, from whom they draw power and privilege. Scientists who might contribute to a more realistic worldview are especially disappointing. Largely yeomen, they are intellectual dwarves content to stay within the narrow specialties for which they were trained and are paid."

The notion of 'mind' as an immaterial entity plays pivotal role to such belief systems. The same applies to the notion of 'culture'. Both culture and mind are exclusively material as a human body or a poem are.

I want to finish my discussion on belief systems with a topic that is raised by a diminishing number of scientists but still haunts the wider public. One of the most notable scientists commenting on it was Sir John Eccles. He wrote:

> "Is not the theme [the mind-body problem] under consideration the most important for man, reaching to his fundamental nature? If Feigl is right, then man is no more than a superior animal, entirely a product of the chance and necessity of evolution. His conscious experiences, even those of the most transcendent creative and artistic character, are NOTHING BUT the products of special states of the neural machinery of his brain, itself a product of evolution. If Polten is right, man has in addition a supernatural component, his conscious self that is cantered on his pure ego. Thus with his spiritual nature he transcends the evolutionary origin of his body and brain, and in so far could participate in immortality." (Eccles 1973 p xii).

Eccles, despite his eminence in neurobiology, does not base his reasoning on it. He focuses on the worthiness of human life. This view is highly commendable and I totally and utterly support it. But then he, along with most opponents of materialism, makes a baseless claim concerning the proponents of materialism. He ascribes to them the view that humans are "no more than a superior animal" (ibid.). But, this ascription can easily mislead people with its mistaken connotations of what is an animal. Characterising materialism in any such way is both mistaken and possibly purposefully misleading.

I am an evolutionary, non-reductive materialist and I consider historic humans (i.e., *H. sapiens* with WHuLa) to be the conscious link in the awesome evolutionary process that started billions of years ago and is leading to the next *Homo* species and eventually to a happy human society. I cannot specify the constitution of such a society in terms of the proportion of biological and artificial noémon systems neither in terms of the future nature of humans. What I can ascertain is that it will be partly based on the preceding evolutionary process of *Homo* and partly on our increasing scientific knowledge and free-thinking approach to the wonders of the universe. There is nothing diminishing healthy human self-respect, balanced self-esteem, and fairness to all fellow humans in this materialist viewpoint. On the contrary, I can see a lot of human folly in the origination and pursuance of economic, religious, and ideological wars. Also, I can only see hubris in the claimed crown-position of humans over the rest of the animals in view of the current state of humanity and our environment. Folly and hubris are not shared by any other animal. Cheating for survival purposes can be easily found among animals, but then we have excelled; Human hypocrisy and lies prove it. Ethics and even theories (e.g., the political distortion of Darwin's theory) can be strongly affected by belief systems. We need a better education system. One that develops critical thinking, cultivates fair behaviour for all, and explores unusual ideas.

Finally, as with the biological phenomenon of thought, the notion of human belief can easily be extended to nonhuman animals. Robots can only have human- derived beliefs (see Sect. 2.2 and brief comment—the animal and robot case). In case of ARE emergence and a fortiori in case of an ARE-society it is unlikely that their *own*-beliefs will be human compatible. Such a discussion may be useful but it is definitely beyond the scope of this book.

The next important notion I consider is 'information' and the closely related notions of 'symbol', 'sign', 'signal', and 'data'. Unfortunately, 'information' has been used misleadingly or superficially both in key issues like consciousness and in disciplinary assumptions and major associated approaches like information- processing (Sect. 1.1). It is also the central common notion of both Information Science and Information Systems.[5] Yet and despite the fact that the need for foundational and interdisciplinary work has been well established (see, for example, Machlup and Mansfield 1983; Gitt 1989; Checkland 1992; Marijuan 1996) no physical, unified theory of information has been developed so far.

A summary presentation of the major views on 'information' and the few attempts made to provide a coherent framework for its related conceptual nexus follows. Concerning the nature of 'information' one may distinguish[6] seven major viewpoints. First, traditionally, information

[5] These two broad scientific communities are known to stand quite apart from each other despite both sharing some key foundational problems in addition to the notion of 'information'.

[6] We exclude from our presentation all accounts which do not explicitly tackle the issue of the nature of information.

in terms of the probability of a signal (Shannon and Weaver 1949).[7] Second, the conception of information as order (e.g., De Vree 1996). Third, information in terms of knowledge and meaning at a mentalistic level (Langefors and Samuelson 1976); and, more strongly, information as a mental not a material entity (e.g., Gitt 1989). Fourth, information in terms of the notion of sign as a primitive (e.g., Stamper 1985). Fifth, information conceived in terms, essentially, of the Popperian conception of the three worlds (e.g., Tully 1985).

Sixth, information in terms of truth conditions (see, e.g., Israel and Perry 1990). Finally, information as a basic property of the Universe (e.g., Wiener 1948 & 1950*1954*1988; Rzevski 1985; Stonier 1996); or, at least, as an objective commodity, or intrinsic to external objects (e.g., Dretske 1981; Collier 1990).

Somehow complementary to the above work we have two rather recent works. In the first, Floridi (2011) provides a thorough philosophical treatment of information. It is valuable as philosophy but it does not provide any theory of information. In the second work, Vigo (2013) aims to create a general theory of information. It starts on a sound basis, rightly assuming information depending on context, meaning, and complexity, but it avoids addressing the nature of its defining notions and ends up in forcing extremely rich notions like meaning into existing mathematics. They are simply inadequate.

An adequate theory of 'information' needs to be applicable across the many disciplines based upon, or at least using, it (Gelepithis 1997). This requirement implies that any definition of 'information' should be both wide enough to accommodate animal and machine information and able to be appropriately restricted to address species specific requirements. A second requirement for even an approximately adequate theory of 'information' is to cover also the closely related notions of 'symbol', 'data', 'sign', and 'signal'.

For brevity I will refer to all these notions collectively as the information family notions. Below, I define the above notions within the context of the TNS as the first step for a physical theory of information that can be used across the various disciplines employing 'information'. The notion of 'information is complex and its definition reflects this by being actually a system of four definitions-20/21/22/23. Of course, each of the

[7] See also Kolmogorov (1968) for a common basis between probability and information theories.

constituent defining-notions of information (21–23) stands on its own and is fully defined in terms of the TNS.

Definition-20 Information for a historic human H at time t -symbol Inf(H,t) is an expressed concept, or thought, or system of {concepts, thoughts, symbols, signals, data}.

NB: Before proceeding with the definitions of 'symbol', 'signal' and 'data' to complete definition-20, the following clarification will help. First, the expression 'information for' is different from the expression 'information of'. The latter refers to something internal to H and is discussed and defined (definition-26) in Sect. 3.3.1. This distinction in not usually done in the literature that conflates the two notions (e.g., Barbosa et al. 2020). My second, closely related remark, is that definition-20 synthesises the two major ways that cognitive psychologists use 'information' (Neisser 1988). These two ways, the Gibsonian objective perspective and the cognitive science, internalist, perspective cannot be separated. Neisser (ibid.) draws on both traditions but fails to synthesise the five different senses of 'self' he distinguishes, each of which is established by a different kind of "self-specifying information" (ibid. p. 35). Let me move now to the definitions of the building blocks of information.

Definition-21 Symbol for a human H at time t -abbreviation Sbl(H,t) is a certain configuration of matter meaningful to its producer or interpreter.

NB: Definitions 14b, 15, and 16 apply for the above.

A couple of further clarifications are in order. First, 'symbol' as defined above appears close to Charles W Morris' conception of sign (1938) but it is fundamentally different in being defined in dynamic terms. Put it differently the Morrisian notion of sign appears to be a static conception despite involving an interpretant. For a recent critical view of Morris' theory of signs (Jia 2019).

Second, the most unified alternative theory of symbol is Newell's (1990) -based on the Physical Symbol System Hypothesis (Newell and Simon 1976). For a discussion of Newell's theory of symbols see Sect. 1. 3.

The following definition of signal is slightly but significantly different from that of symbol above. Let us see.

Definition-22 Signal for a human H at time t, is a certain propagated configuration of matter meaningful to a sender or a receiver.

Obviously, this is sharply contrasted to Shannon's theory of syntactic information (Shannon and Weaver 1949). They had explicitly stated the restricted character of their theory and in particular its non-application to semantics. Unfortunately, the non-engineers that followed them tried uncritically and erroneously to generalise it.

In contrast to symbol, signal does not need to be meaningful to both the sender and the receiver. The material of the signal can vary tremendously including light, chemical odours, and patterns of movements. In the following definition neither a sender nor a receiver is required.

Definition-23 Data $=_{\mathrm{df}}$ Potentially meaningful configurations of matter.

The above definition both subsumes the standard scientific conception of data and is related to, but it is distinct from, its epistemological definition. The standard scientific conception of data is captured in OECD's definition (identical to current OECD internet definition) shared worldwide:

> "Characteristics or information, usually numerical, that are collected through observation." (OECD 2007, p. 170).

OECD's definition is useful for a number of applications but it is circular. It is given in terms of information that in its turn is defined in terms of knowledge (ibid. p. 390) that by the examples cited are mostly data or information!

Its epistemological definition is probably best exemplified by the following conception of data as:

> "those propositions of which the truth is known without demonstration" (Russell, 1921, p. 208).

I prefer definition-23 because of its open-ended stance in the theory-ladeness issue as well as of the fact that it is independent of any ***particular*** noémon system. This is a particularly positive feature as an anchor point for the existence of an objective reality that ***may*** have to be interpreted. Please note the possibility, ***not*** necessity, of interpretation—let alone dependance upon the current *Homo sapiens*. This is in sharp contrast to OECD's definition that both implicitly and explicitly, in their explanatory notes accompanying their definitions, refer to humans.

Let me now reminds us of the TNS development up to this point. In the previous chapter, I proposed a theory of representation addressing the first of the conditions of a noémon species and noémon entity. So far in this chapter, I have developed a physicalist theory of meaning for noémon systems. This is a necessary prerequisite for a neurophysiological theory of thinking for noémon species (definition-2) and a materialist theory of thinking for noémon entities (definition-3). We need now to consider the next key definien of noémon systems, namely, 'thinking'. I proceed by considering three types of thinking: Homo sapiens, noémon species in general, and robot. I finish the section by briefly considering an important, special type of thinking of noémon systems, namely, reasoning. The focus will be on human reasoning with a couple of clarificatory remarks on the closely related robot thinking.

3.2.3 Historic Homo Sapiens Thinking and Reasoning

Historic *H. sapiens* thinking appears to be a very restricted viewpoint on *Homo* thinking. So, let me briefly justify my apparently limited approach. Our knowledge on H-thinking is the best we have. All our knowledge on *Homo* thinking is based on less secure grounds. In addition, *Homo* thinking before the advent of WHuLa can be comfortably studied under animal thinking excluding just the historic period of humans. Hence:

Definition-24 H-thinking, T_H, is the *class* of interactions of human meanings, or concepts, or thoughts, or beliefs, or of any combinations of them after the advent of WHuLa. (Earlier version in Gelepithis 2009, p. 12).

The justification for our definition is straightforward. The complexity of the *Homo* (and especially of historic *H. sapiens*) nervous system lead us to take the minimum steps in proposing theoretical constructs. In other words, we should start with the simplest theoretical constructs and build on them more complex ones when data allows us to do so.

The necessity and justification for definition-24 will become clear by considering the following clarificatory remarks concerning the complexity of H- thinking. First, thinking as defined includes imagination, free association, daydreaming, recollection, and in general any process or system of processes involving the semantic structures of an individual human. Instances of such processes can be seen through the numerous senses that the verb 'think' and its derivatives are used in everyday language. For instance in English:

- He thought that John was not in a very good condition.
- She thought that he was a socialist.
- Nicole is lost in thought.
- I cannot think why he did it.
- I thought as much.
- Margarita thought of a simple solution.
- His headache was so strong he could hardly think straight.
- What does B think of climate change?
- He is thinking of applying for the job.
- Brick thinks breathing is necessary for life.

Such an all inclusive definition is a desirable feature of any theory of thinking because it provides the necessary super-ordinate theoretical construct for specifying specialised conditions that identify special types of thinking like the ones mentioned above. Ideally, such specialised types of thinking have to be described in 'bridging' conceptual-neuroscientific terms for a deeper understanding of the phenomenon of thinking. This problem is analogous to the problem of 'hierarchy' in understanding the "different dimensions of the organisation of brain networks" (Hilgetag & Goulas 2020).

Second, our definition includes unconscious and spontaneous thought processes; they are extremely interesting although not yet widely studied (e.g., Christoff et al. 2004; Andrews-Hanna et al. 2018; Fox & Christoff 2018; Mills et al. 2021). This is particularly interesting because such thought processes are quite often intertwined with automatic action processes—a good example is driving automatically. Probably needless to say that specification of the additional elements and associated mechanisms required to sufficiently identify the automatic thinking processes involved in driving is quite complicated and entirely off the limits of this book. Nevertheless, for those interested, a useful starting point should be the mechanisms employed in autonomous vehicles (equivalently: driverless cars, robo- cars, self-driving cars). To be noted that the type of thinking involved in automatic driving by humans is fundamentally different from the type of thinking involved in autonomous vehicles (see below definitions of robot and noémon entity thinking).

Third, definition-24 allows space for the development of a physicalist theory of the creative processes. Presently, the neuroscience of creativity is fraught with data, hypotheses, and viewpoints lacking any coherent thread that may contribute to a theory of creativity. Flaherty (2011) provides an excellent snapshot of some of the relevant problems. Ivancovsky et al. (2024) propose a "novelty-seeking model" that is claimed to underlie both creativity and curiosity. In chapter four we introduce some of the basic open issues concerning creativity and their relations to fundamental mental processes like thinking and understanding.

My fourth remark may be obvious to most readers but it should be stated because of its significance. H-thinking is quite often influenced, in some cases strongly, and in ways that are presently unknown to us, by emotions (chapter-4 of Volume Two, Gelepithis 2024b) and motivation. Keeping in mind this point does not make easier the discovery of the physical mechanisms and neural pathways of thinking, but it can contribute to the development of our critical faculty vis a vis certain techniques assumed to provide solutions to the nature of thinking at the molecular, synaptic, neural circuit, and systems levels (e.g., Roe 2020). Figure 3.3 illustrates some basic relations of thinking and meanings to *Homo* knowledge, consciousness, and emotions, and stresses the importance of the unconscious and conscious parts of the subjective nervous systems. To be recalled and noted, the subjectivity of nervous systems is dual: individual and species-specific.

Finally, it should be noted that H-thinking, as defined, does not imply the reaching of any conclusions (either consciously or unconsciously). However, humans and certain Animalia taxons very often act on the basis of conclusions they have reached consciously. We therefore need definitions of human and animal thinking to capture the fact that there is a type of thinking that starts from somewhere, ends somewhere, and that it is done consciously. I shall call such kind of thinking: reasoning. A very special case of such type of thinking is discussed in Sect. 4.2 (on understanding). The definition of human reasoning is a straightforward restriction of the definition of human thinking. Specifically:

Definition-25 H-reasoning is a form of thinking in which conclusions consciously follow from a system of human beliefs, thoughts and concepts.

NB: To ease expression, I use 'system of premises' for a reference system of human beliefs, thoughts and concepts.

I am well aware that definition-25 runs counter to all definitions of human reasoning as inference process. All such viewpoints, despite their more or less considerable differences, share one common fundamental element characterising the standard conception of inference. Namely, they

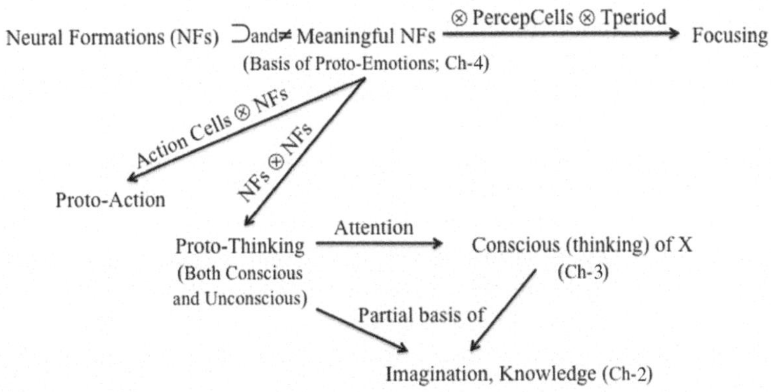

Legend:
⊗ Stands for systemic interactions between;
NFs, Meaningful NFs, and Attention are defined in this chapter.
Chapters 3, 4, & 5 are in Volume Two Consequences (Gelepithis 2024b)

Fig. 3.3 Relations of thinking and meanings to *Homo* knowledge, consciousness, and emotions (The topics of knowledge, consciousness, and emotions are treated in Gelepithis 2024b)

are defined exclusively in terms of statements and their properties (e.g., Sanford 1999).

In sharp contrast to this view, my definition is given in terms of neural formations and their complex physiological mechanisms of inference that may only be conjectured by the system of definitions 14b to 25 inclusive. The difference is of fundamental importance especially in view of the type of meaning specified in the next section and the fact that the linguistic structures of the brain are a subsystem of its overall semantic structure. In particular, this difference affects the range of the inference process. Specifically, it allows non-linguistic conscious processes to influence the drawing of conclusions whereas the standard view, by its definition, does not. In other words, my definition of human reasoning determines a space of inferences vastly greater than the one determined by the language-based inference view. Of course, the complexities introduced by the neural, non-linguistic nature of this definition is clearly a major setback for experimentation. We nevertheless need to encompass them if we are serious about the actual mechanisms involved in human reasoning and not only interested in the linguistic aspects of it however significant and indispensable the latter ones are. The above remarks necessitate further distinctions that in turn both presuppose and demand a lot of empirical research for their establishment.

Let me now briefly consider the nature (i.e., mechanisms) of the WHuLa-based inference process. Usually, it is categorised in two broad classes: deductive and inductive (e.g., Copi 1978; Johnson-Laird 1988; Anderson 1990). This classification depends on the type of argument involved. The key difference between the deductive and inductive types of arguments is that the premises of the latter can *only support* the conclusions whereas premises in a deductive system *entail* the conclusions[8]. In other words, the conclusions of an inductively valid argument are only *probable* whereas those of a deductively valid one are certain. Induction-based systems enable us to make predictions in the presence of conflicting evidence in the premises whereas deduction-based systems cannot. On the other hand the power of deductive modelling lies in the fact that new assertions, obtained through a series of syntactic transformations from the (assumed true) premises, are guaranteed to be true.

This widely used categorisation is nevertheless not satisfactory because, as we know and remarked above, restricts *consideration* of the actual reasoning process. It is well documented that people make mistakes when asked to carry out deductive reasoning tasks (see, for example, Rips & Marcus 1977) or hypothesis formation and evaluation (see, e.g., Anderson 1990). All of the theories proposed to explain the findings concerning language-based reasoning with deductive tasks (e.g., Henle 1962; Ceraso and Provitera 1971; Staudenmayer 1975) assume that subjects do not treat the given tasks according to the prescription of logic. It should be noted that such behaviour is not due to lack of knowing the relevant deductive rules (e.g., Cheng et al. 1986). Similarly, the probabilistic modelling of hypothesis evaluation (essentially Baye's theorem) is at variance with the way people actually carry out hypothesis evaluation (e.g., Anderson 1990 and references cited there).

Despite this widely accepted evidence, the related scientific community continues to favour one or the other of the two types of reasoning: logicist (e.g., Boole 1854*2005; Newell & Simon 1972), and probabilistic

[8] Sometimes inductive reasoning is characterised in terms of its relative generality of its premises and/ or its conclusions. The usual way of such a characterisation is to say that in inductive reasoning one infers generalisations from known instances. For example, on the basis of our past experience we assume that the sun will rise tomorrow.

(e.g., Oaksford and Chater 2009). For my part, human reasoning is based on a complex system of inferential mechanisms influenced by non-linguistic processes and emotions. What is usually called 'the inference process' seems to be a unified system of inductive and deductive reasoning processes that, for humans, is primarily based on the variety of conditionals summarised in Table 3.2, and is affected, probably significantly, from non-linguistic semantic structures.

It is worth noting that at least the first, and possibly the second, of the conditionals listed in Table 3.2 are employed by certain animal taxons. To avoid potential misunderstandings I mean of course the essential character of the first, and possibly the second, of the listed conditionals, not their linguistic statement. In addition, hypothetico-deductive conditionals are at least as powerful as Universal Turing machines (this is easily seen as soon as one realises that a production rule is a special case of a hypothetico-deductive conditional).

Relatively, recently, an unusual type of language-based human reasoning has invoked both interest and criticism. It is called the argumentative theory (Mercier & Sperber 2011) and its objective is "to devise and evaluate arguments intended to persuade". As it is further remarked those involved with it "are not after the truth but after arguments to support their views" (ibid.). The strongest criticism (Narvaez 2011) is its very restricted scope. As a matter of fact argumentative reasoning is much narrower than all previous conceptions of language-based types of reasoning. Expectedly, I am in full agreement with Narvaez when he notes that we need a broader and developmental view of reasoning. Equally, I would support special cases of human reasoning as long as they stick to their restricted scope and do not claim to represent the full scope and complexity of it.

Finally, more recently, work on what has been termed "knowledge-rich reasoning" (essentially a special case of reasoning on the basis of belief systems (definition-19) is promoted "as a new paradigm" (Oaksford & Chater 2020). This approach is modeled in terms of Bayesian probability theory and is founded, liked the argument-based approach, on the assumption that verbal reasoning is a social activity. They furthermore, claim "that [such a process] is prior to understanding individual reasoning" (ibid., p. 308).

In conclusion, logical, argument-based, and Bayesian types of reasoning do not capture the essence of reasoning (or inferential process).

3.2.4 Animal Thinking and Reasoning

Let me now come to the wider notion of animal thinking and reasoning. Specifically:

Definition-24$^{\prime}$**A** An *individual's* thinking of a *particular* animal species ($^{\prime}T_A$), is the interaction of meanings, or concepts, or thoughts, or of any combinations of them of that individual.

I derive it from T_H by two different types of generalisation.

The first generalisation comes from the expansion of the range of species admitted to the space of noémon systems. Although opinions differ, I follow the prevalent, if not dominant, view putting the boundary at the Animalia kingdom. It should be noted that in case adequately new data require new taxa outside the Animalia kingdom to be admitted, one will have to distinguish two cases:

(i). taxa not classifiable as species should be able to be incorporated in definition-3;
(ii). taxa classified as species and lacking nervous system would necessitate an extension of definition-14a.

The coupled definition 14b would not need to be modified except in case that a major biological change in our biological understanding occurs concerning the notions of survival and reproduction.

The second generalisation comes from dropping the belief condition involved in the case of T_H. Although some animal species do perform one or more types of planning, no animal species barring ourselves argue in terms of beliefs.

I want to end my comments on animal thinking by stressing the rather obvious point of the wide diversity of animal thinking caused by the corresponding wide diversity of the sensory-motor part of the nervous system in Animalia. It is an open question whether the principles of interaction of animal meanings and their compounds is different from that of human interactions. It may well turn out that the logic of meaning-related interactions is the same across the animal kingdom without any exception whatsoever, that is, it may well include our species too. I think that it is an interesting project of research to which I will return after the subsection on robot thinking. Before that the notion of animal reasoning may well raise eyebrows. Still:

Definition-25'A An *individual's* reasoning of a *particular* animal species, is a form of animal thinking in which conclusions consciously follow from the system of thoughts and concepts of that individual.

Objections are expected from opponents of animal consciousness. And, of course, such objections will become stronger the wider the range of animals claimed to be able to possess consciousness.

However, animal reasoning is subject to two insuperable hurdles that very considerably restrict it. The first concerns the WHuLa-based type of consciousness that nonhuman animals lack. The second is revealed through analysis of the central and indispensable goal of AI, namely, formalisability of human knowledge. This may sound an unusual restriction but it will become clear after consideration of the robot types of thinking that follows.

3.2.5 Robot Types of Thinking

The above brief discussion of key aspects of the historic *H. sapiens* inferential apparatus brings us naturally to the central objective of AI: formalisability of human knowledge (FHK). The study of our inferential apparatus is related to the Nineteenth century view according to which 'logic' and the psychology of thought were hardly differentiated (cf., George Boole 1854*1958). The FHK issue goes back to the idea of the 'alphabet of human thought' by Leibniz (1646–1716) and, by his acknowledgement, to Ramon Llull (1232–1315). Although the two topics are related and, Leibniz's idea of mapping concepts to numbers and the use of formal rules for number manipulation to also manipulate concepts still has adherents, AI and cognitive science slowly come to accept the inherent limitations of the logicist programme.

On the other hand, the FHK objective has created alternative approaches to the logicist programme. Partly, (some may say primarily) because of these approaches, AISs and robots have come to constitute a breakthrough in the development of tools assisting human thinking and action respectively. Their eventual combination will constitute a further breakthrough. At the very least, (as is the case for AISs), they bring to our attention *consequences* of, and, *gaps* in our knowledge that we ourselves would never have been able to produce or identify respectively. In the case of robots, especially when they incorporate the full AIS representational and reasoning capabilities, we can hardly glimpse their limits (barring limits of human constructability) especially in relation to the possibility of ARE emergence (see discussion in Sect. 2.2). Nevertheless, AI scientists avoid the following fundamental question. What does AIS or robot thinking mean?[9] In the rest of this section, this question is addressed and some closely related issues are discussed.

Since robot (definition-9) is a special and more powerful type of AIS (definition-8), I mainly focus my attention to robot thinking. Since robot action is extremely important in several respects including its feedback relation to its thinking, I will also comment on it to the extent that it affects a robot's thinking. Additionally, I will occasionally refer to AISs since in some cases developments of the latter systems have not been implemented in robots. The following definition sets the scene for our discussion.

Definition-24R Robot thinking, T_R, is the processing of human-based meanings, concepts, thoughts, beliefs, or of any combinations of them by the robot's ***designed*** representational systems capturing their formalisable aspects.

Definition-24_R brings to the fore the FHK issue. It is usually well hidden under the current AI hype that endemically characterises the field since its inception. Although the hype is partially justifiable even for AI scientists, it would serve us all much better if the full extent of the problem was clearly publicised. Let me explicate.

Most, if not all, of the AI hype stems from a partial presentation of a task or/and its solution. Let me illustrate with an example and then consider the problem in its generality. Most human tasks have formal and informal elements. Take for example student education. Some aspects of it, like learning how to program, are mostly formal; others, like learning or teaching how to think, mostly informal. AI systems playing the role of a tutor in a formal domain have already been developed successfully. One of the oldest and most successful implementations is the LISP tutor for teaching the just stated programming language. Therefore, for any task involving formalisable aspects an AIS or robot can be designed and built. On the other hand, all AI R&D programmes are subject to the *limits* of human constructability (Gelepithis 1984; 1991). Because of its

[9] As it was pointed out in sect. 1.1, AI has avoided the critical study of its foundations (see Gelepithis 1984, 2004, 2021).

importance, it should be noted again that AI neither has refuted the argument demonstrating these limits nor has it even seriously considered them despite the fact that several important research programmes repeatedly come across these limits.

The key among these programmes are:

P-1: Representation of common sense knowledge; and
P-2: Ability of representing knowledge changes.

Work on the former includes work on Naive Physics and Naive Psychology. Both of them are investigated for quite some time now (e.g., McCarthy 1959; Hayes 1978*1979; Hobbs & Moore 1985; Davis 1998; Gordon & Hobbs 2004) but progress is slow and no convincing explanation has been proposed. See Davis & Marcus (2015) for a recent view on some of the multiple problems characterising common sense knowledge. A future research programme Naive Societal Relations (aiming to automate some of the huge amounts of socially- and culturally-based common sense knowledge) may be possible and useful. Work on the automation of knowledge changes is more recent (e.g., Bundy 2013) although many common elements with the frame problem (McCarthy & Hayes 1969) can be identified.

AI has chosen to proceed with its engineering objective building on the ideas of the first 25 years of the field. The result is that apart from numerous technical improvements, no conceptual breakthroughs have occurred since the mid 1980s. Although this state of the art is well known to all AI scientists, it will be useful to flesh it out a bit for the benefit of the multi-disciplinary readership of this book.

The design of representational systems *and* associated processing mechanisms able to respectively capture formalisable aspects of human knowledge *and* thinking is the engine of AI. In the AI literature, this 'the engine of AI' is known as the system of KRR formalisms or schemes. Classes of instances of such schemes include semantic networks; production systems; grammars; ANNs; logics (see also below), and a host of recent names usually referring to earlier KRR techniques or recent improvements of such formalisms. Schemes like these in turn employ a variety of reasoning steps like transitivity; implication (→); parsing trees in grammars; propagation functions and weight or threshold adjustment respectively. Some (including distinguished and even pre-eminent

AI scientists) consider the system of KRR formalisms to be analogous to the bioevolutionary process that produced all the variety of types and specialised processes of H-thinking. I think they are grossly mistaken. An argument to support this statement is beyond the remit of this book—albeit it may be implied by the joint results of this two-volume monograph.

Recently, machine learning (probably the earliest AI objective and system of associated techniques (cf, Turing (1950; Feigenbaum 1959) has come to the full attention of the public through the reality of an increasing variety of industrial and home applications and the hype of its advertising proponents. To slightly redress this imbalance, let me briefly comment on its current development.

From the AI perspective an early, good definition of machine learning is the one in the *Encyclopaedia of Artificial Intelligence*:

> "The field of machine learning studies computational methods for acquiring new knowledge, new skills, and new ways to organize existing knowledge." (Carbonell & Langley, 1987, p. 464).

Presently, such computational methods have expanded tremendously and in particular within the subarea of ANNs. I will very briefly focus on a currently hot topic: deep learning employing deep neural networks (a special case of ANNs). Let me start by stressing that the utility of such networks is unquestionable (e.g., Stokes et al. 2020). My whole point is that they do not offer any new insights and even more breakthroughs. This has hesitantly started being realised as Ching et al. (2018, p. 2) note in their review:

> "from an extensive literature review, we find that deep learning has yet to revolutionize biomedicine or definitely resolve any of the most pressing challenges in the field, but promising advances have been made on the prior state of the art."

The team of 36 scientists produced an excellent and comprehensive review that will be of great value to medicine and allied fields. Nevertheless, utility does not imply breakthroughs, and Ching et al. are careful to make the distinction. They even go to the extent of comparing aspects of deep learning algorithms like interpretability with alternative models like Bayesian to found the former wanting. More to our point all the deep learning networks reviewed are improvements of old ideas and earlier systems. Such developments will keep coming (cf, Saxe et al. 2019; Nguyen et al. 2020), but the lack of foundational progress hampers our understanding of ANNs (deep or otherwise) as long as the theoretical principles governing such formalisms remain obscure (Saxe et al. 2019, p. 11538).

Moreover, as indicated above, one should keep in mind that ANNs are far from exhausting the range of KRR formalisms. Actually, the full gamut of formalisms has been used in AI including: mathematical logics like modal, temporal and deontic ones; linear algebra; and of course statistical models. One of the latest efforts is in the application area of Natural Language Processing or Computational Linguistics. It concerns the topic of semantic compositionality. This is an old, well known problem in AI reaching the core of the FHK issue. New methods like category theory (Philips 2019) are proposed and a theme issue (Towards mechanistic models of meaning composition) of *The Royal Society* has been devoted to it (cf, Martin & Baggio 2019). Again, the implementability of semantic composionality is not discussed and the *limits* of human constructability (Gelepithis 1984; 1991) ignored.

My final instance of ignoring the past is a target article in the *Behavioral and Brain Sciences*. Lake et al. (2017) aim to "to examine what it means for a machine to learn or think like a person". This is a very welcome intention and they proposed to tackle the issue by specifying "the essential ingredients for building" such a machine (ibid. p. 2). Unfortunately, although they choose to "focus on two pieces [intuitive physics and intuitive psychology] of developmental start-up software" and provide a good number of recent references, the original and still relevant work of Hayes (1978*1979) on Naïve Physics is not even cited. In addition, the work they refer to hardly advances substantially earlier work on essential ingredients for machine intelligence including work by Anderson & Lebiere (2003) and Gelepithis (2003). Finally, they uncritically adopt terms like 'understanding' (e.g., Eslami et al. 2016) for what is really work on formal inference.

Reinventing the wheel and inappropriate naming are major problems in AI and cognitive science. Fragmentation supports both of them. The excellent foundational work of Newell (1990) remains a glowing exception.

I want to finish this section with an answer and proposed solution to an issue I raised earlier, namely, is there a single neurophysiologically-based logic used across the animal kingdom? My answer is straightforward: I think there is. My proposed solution is very short but rather radical in its nature.

As we saw above, the various classes of KRR formalisms implement a variety of human reasoning mechanisms. I propose that there is a *single* neurophysiological mechanism at the basis of all these mechanisms. In essence this basic neurophysiological mechanism is identified with logic in its sense of valid inference—not in the sense of its multifold instantiations.

Now to the crucial element of my proposal. The proposed mechanism stands for the synthesis of the primitive processes of identification and differentiation of either external or internal stimuli. If that is shown to be true, then the suggested mechanism would hold true both for any noémon system within the animalia taxon and robots. I will call the proposed identification the postulate of physiological logic.

3.3 Discussion

This section: (i) draws two main consequences and suggests a qualitative scheme for partially addressing the related issue of human concept construction (Sect. 3.3.1); and (ii) justifies the TNS theory of meaning and compares my theory of thinking with Hebb's (Sect. 3.3.2).

3.3.1 Consequences and Proposal

Below I outline two major consequences of the theory developed in the previous section. The first concerns the most discussed topic in the philosophy of language, namely the nature of meaning along with its relation between language and thought; I introduce a third type of meaning predicted by the theory. The second concerns the interface between memory and meaning and in particular introduces the memory- meaning postulate. The section finishes off with a proposal concerning the representation (or construction) of concepts—a central problem in memory research.

In Sect. 3.2.1 we introduced the notion of meaningful neural formation (N_m) and the meaning of external stimuli (either perceptual or linguistic). Such meanings constitute a subclass of the N_m class. When the external stimulus is linguistic, its associated meaning usually comes under the heading of linguistic meaning. When the external stimulus is perceptual, its associated meaning has usually been considered under

Grice's notion of natural (or non-linguistic) meaning (see Table 3.2). To complete the range of senses that 'meaning' does cover we need to move into the partly uncharted waters of M and in particular, the relation between our thoughts (definition-18) and other elements of M on the one hand, and our linguistic expressions on the other.

Structured utterances or written expressions, *l*, are taken to convey a person's ideas, beliefs, desires, emotions, motivations, etc. In general and strictly speaking this is not the case. There are many such neural formations, especially whenever they are combined, that cannot be uttered or written precisely; sometimes not at all. To refer to any—or any combination of—such mental states, I will use the words 'skepsis' or 'skepseis' for the singular or plural cases respectively. Furthermore, an expression or utterance of a skepsis is not necessarily meaningful to all hearers. The following definition captures these characteristics:

Definition-26 Skepseis are structures of ***restructured*** neural formations that may or may not involve ***restructured*** N_m, although normally they do.

Now the traditional scientific view holds that:

(1) M (skepsis) = M (*l*); M for meaning.

I hold that (1) can be mistaken and that it usually is, especially when a skepsis is unusual, unconventional, half-baked, vague, novel etc. In all such cases:

(2) M (skepsis) $\approx$ M (*l*).

The symbol $\approx$ stands for 'not necessarily equal'.

It should be noted that the phenomenon indicated by relation (2) is significantly more complex than the phenomenon of semantic underdetermination (e.g., Bach 1994; and Saul 2002; Speaks 2008 for more recent discussions). Actually, the latter (explicitly introduced by Grice 1968) is a special case of the phenomenon referred to by relation (2). Naturally, some skepseis (and more precisely those involving a new type of N_m) constitute a third class of meaning structures in addition to the natural/nonnatural (Grice 1957), or the natural/conventional (e.g., Stevenson 1944) distinctions. In view of the third type of meaning introduced and the slightly misleading traditional classification names, I propose the following three-partite classification: consequential (previously natural); linguistic (previously nonnatural or conventional); and creative. A word of clarification may be needed here with respect to the creative type of meaning that is usually involved in skepseis. It is characterised by the following two conditions:

> (C1): Creative meaning does not involve an S_C like the two types of meanings described by definitions 15 and 16 respectively; and
> (C2): Creative meaning is formed by the *restructuring* of at least one neural formation and possibly of *restructured* novel (definition-15), or prevailed (definition-16) meanings.

It should be noted that all three different types of meaning are characterised by subjectivity. The move towards objectivity requires communication (see next chapter). I should also note that the third, *restructured*, type of meaning is most clearly related to memory (e.g., Bartlett 1932; Wagoner 2019). See below for the meaning-memory relations. The conversational science approach to meaning proposed by Harri-Augstein & Thomas (2001) considers the notion of creative meaning as its fifth level but they provide neither a physicalist basis for it nor the necessary link to communication and understanding (chapter-4). The TNS theory of meaning must be understood in relation to its three partite basis of meaning and the inseparable links of the latter to communication and understanding.

Barring abnormal circumstances, the extreme variety of skepseis is due to the vastness of M, random thinking, creative aspect of thinking, WHuLa, and evolution.

With respect to the latter, NFs have *a history of at least half a billion years*. Genetically, a good number of *Homo sapiens* neural formations may well be at least partly identifiable with neural formations that existed hundreds of millions years ago. Evolution is a near infinite well that modern humans seem to be capable of drawing upon. And this is a key contributor to the creation of new skepseis (i.e., novelty or creativity).

I think it is time for relation (2) to replace assumption (1) as working hypothesis for realistic models of skepseis. Any serious neuroscientific account of meanings and thinking should not push under the carpet the huge complexity involved in the creation of utterances or expressions out of skepseis. At the same time, it has to be realised that:

> An *individual's* language, via scientific knowledge (whenever applicable), augments part of the semantic structure of that *individual's* M.

How the augmented semantic structure affects and is possibly affected by, an *individual's* M is an important open question.

So, when relation (1) is not the case, what is the M(skepsis)? It can be an *l* whose meaning, even for the speaker or scriber, only approximates her skepsis. It may also remain unspoken or unwritten. Although my thesis is based on private evidence, empirical verification is, in principle, possible by linking an AIS to a human's brain.

Furthermore, in accordance with Boden's (1992) distinction between historical and psychological creativity, a historically novel *l* is more likely to be caused by (N, N_m, H, t,), and a psychologically novel *l* by (N_m, H, t,).

A further remark is of interest here. Although we are bound by language we can also extend it thanks to our evolutionary past and our ability to create external representational systems (chapter-2). Could the M(skepsis) be totally and utterly expressed or written at some point in the future? Research on brain imaging aims to eventually read an individual's thoughts. The feasibility of this task remains to be seen. My prediction is that it will for ever remain illusive. My reason for it is the unimaginable complexity of the historic humans' brain, let alone of her constitution as an individual of *H. sapiens*. I want to note here that even an established infeasibility of reading an individual's mind does not imply impossibility of an individual tele- sending her thoughts. Enough of speculation. Let me describe some of the many problems in the specified interface.

The problems are immense because the variety and complexity of human M is staggeringly complex. Their source is threefold: (i) individual; (ii) environmental (including cultural and societal); and (iii) evolutionary. In the next few paragraphs I point out some of these problems and some related work.

To start with, the system of mechanisms, M_e, responsible for the creation of expressions out of an individual's skepseis should be the most complex of all due to the fact that it is, normally, closely knit to both M and the neural aspects of language. This is definitely not helped by the fact that we are largely ignorant of the derivation mechanisms of *l* that vary from the routine to the creative.[10] It is worth noticing that neuroscientific research on cognitive processing (e.g., Abbott 2006) is both at its very beginning and possibly barking on the wrong tree with respect to the level that questions are usually posed (e.g., switching of neural circuits).

Furthermore concerning human language, is there a system of *core* linguistic mechanisms that is at work for all humans (barring pathological cases)? Such a system would be an important human universal. The majority of linguistic approaches postulate syntax or, more recently, the FLN (e.g., Hauser et al 2002) as playing a significant role in human linguistic meaning construction. Syntactic considerations do play a role in creating l, and therefore, $\mathsf{M}(l)$. Nevertheless, that is a far cry from explaining linguistic meaning construction out of skepseis. I think that this is a much more complicated and wide-open issue that the FLN approach may be willing to accept.

As an illustration consider two of the systems of creation mechanisms required during the ontological development of M. First, a system, $\mathbf{M_p}$, that is responsible for creating the system of $\mathbf{N_p}$. The literature on LTM should be able to provide some useful models. Second, a system, $\mathbf{M_{ap}}$, that is responsible for the appearance of the *prevailed* $\mathsf{N_p}$ of $\mathbf{N_p}$. The literature on recall should be useful in this case.

Memories are related to representations and some of them may well be representations. Quite often they are distorted, consciously or unconsciously.

On the basis of the notion of representation introduced in Sect. 2. 2, what are the mechanisms for the genesis and storage of such representations? Would such mechanisms be related to the ones postulated by Rolls (1987) for 'information' representation and processing at the single neuron level? In addition, how could alternative explanations of mental representations (Changeux 1983*1985; Edelman 1987; Edelman and Mountcastle 1978) be applicable to such mechanisms?

Finally, whatever mechanisms for the genesis and storage of representations may be found, how do we, (or any entity capable of representations), come about selecting the most appropriate *essence-preserving simplifications*? What are the mechanisms and scope of such a representational capacity? To what extent can a situation be simplified so that its essential

[10] Wittgenstein's (1953*1976) investigations may be illuminating in this respect if they are read as such rather than as an argument for the nature of meaning.

characteristics are not lost? What are the mechanisms for such simplifications? It appears clear that they need to be related to our capacity for abstraction.

In summary, the naturalistic basis of my theory of meaning redefines the traditional senses of meaning and meaning-related notions in terms of empirically verifiable conditions, and extends the sense of meaning to include the fundamental class of $\mathsf{N_m}$ and its derivative theoretical construct of 'skepsis'. Furthermore, the consequence outlined here implies that language is an expressed and mostly approximate subsystem of thinking. This has consequences for the language-thought issue that fall beyond the scope of this book. For an early but still very valuable introduction to the intricacies of the language-thought interaction the reader is referred to Vygotski (1934*1986). For introduction to the ramifications (Holyoak & Morrison 2005; Johnson-Laird & Wason 1977; Thagard 2002*2006).

The second consequence concerns the interface between memory and meaning. Memory research deals with problems of the full spectrum of organisation levels (i.e., molecular to psychological) and uses several model organisms across the animal kingdom. Human memory, despite sharing common mechanisms with non-human animals, is vastly different too. To a large extent such differences are due to the vast and qualitatively different types of human semantic memory. Its relative neglect within the dominant molecular and systems biology paradigm of memory research should be reversed and my neurophysiological theory of meaning may contribute to this endeavour.

To avoid any potential misunderstanding the following definition will be used as our starting point:

Definition-27 Human memory is the system of interacting processes of acquisition, consolidation, maintenance, modification, retrieval, and integration that involves the semantic structures and associated mechanisms of M.

The above definition is both compatible with standard biological definitions of memory (e.g., Kandel et al. 2014) and complete. It is complete because it defines, in principle, all of its implicit semantic definiens. Any of the processes identified in the above definition may include different subprocesses in explicit and implicit memory. Such an exploration falls beyond the remit of this book. Here, the basic point I want to stress is the relation of human semantic memory and human meanings.

Specifically, the TNS developed so far establishes a *common* naturalistic system-subsystem relation between meaning and memory. In particular, it predicts the following relations: The memory systems of a human constitute a proper subsystem of that individual's semantic system. The latter of course constitutes a proper subsystem of that individual's NFs which is a straightforward consequence of our theory of meaning. I call the former relation the memory-meaning postulate (MMP). Let me briefly justify the specified relations.

Although the distinction between semantic and episodic memory (Tulving 1972, 1983, 2002) has been useful, it obscures the inseparability between memory and meaning. Let me start with the observation that the semantic memory tradition (Collins & Quillian 1969; Collins & Loftus 1975) and its later incarnations as the study of categories and concepts (e.g., Medin and Rips 2005) along with suggestions of meaning theories criteria involving memory (Edelman & Mountcastle 1978), indicate a respectable link between memory and meaning. That link becomes stronger when one further observes that both memory and meaning depend on context, time and the individual concerned. Psychiatry provides numerous cases (e.g., Krystal et al. 1995). Nevertheless, understanding the meaning of an S_C does not imply memorisation of S_C (suggestion that the memory system is a subsystem of the meaning system). In addition, there are instances of meaningless utterances or inscriptions producible by an individual (suggestion that the meaning system is a subsystem of the nervous system). In addition, memory traces (materialised at sub- cellular level: Kandel 2006; Koch 1999) can be identified with meaningful NFs. Finally, The memory-meaning relation can easily be seen at work by considering the restructuring of meaning during or following the process of adaptation to loss.

Instances of such adaptation are ubiquitous (e.g., Neimeyer 2016 and references cited there; Doka & Tucci 2016).

Taking seriously the MMP implies that the key issues of memory research become key problems for any theory of meaning (cf. and contrast with Sutton 2004). Acceptance of the MMP is not in conflict with Roediger's (2008) conclusion of lack of memory laws. It is actually compatible with the huge complexity and interactivity of memory phenomena that is fully recognised by the science of memory community (e.g., Marshall & Bredy 2016; Queenan 2017; Yee et al. 2018; Wagoner 2019). In return, most of the questions on meaning become obsolete and the rest can be translated in the more rigorous framework of memory research to provide a much- needed breath of fresh air.

In the millennium issue of the *Philosophical Transactions of the Royal Society B*, Kandel and Pittenger (1999, p. 2027) reviewed a century of accomplishments in the study of memory along

> "the two major questions that have dominated thinking in this area: the systems question of memory, which concerns where in the brain storage occurs; and the molecular question of memory, which concerns the mechanisms whereby memories are stored and maintained."

With respect to the systems question of memory, a clarification should be made concerning an objection to its very nature. Some have questioned the utility of this endeavour on the basis of a number of apparently negative results concerning the issue of localisation. But, those results and associated argument are really beside the point. For, as Feynman remarks:

> "If we perform sufficiently delicate experiments, we can tell that the earth *is rotating*, but not that it *had rotated*. In other words, we cannot locate its angular position but we tell that it is changing." (Feynman et al. 1963 vol I, pp. 11–3).

In other words, failing to localise memory or neural formations is not against their dynamic existence and therefore their study. How to do it is an open question.

Although work at the molecular level has monopolised the research on memory mechanisms, the possibility of non-synaptic plasticity is explicitly stated as one possible direction of future memory research (cf, definition-14a and related comments).

Kandel and Pittenger (1999, pp. 2042–3) made a second important remark:

> "[w]hile human memory, both explicit and implicit, is likely to employ similar basic mechanism as that of simpler animal systems, it is also doubtlessly unique in other respects."

Unfortunately, no specific suggestions identifying conditions of such uniqueness were made. Meaning results properly incorporated in the memory field (that may well necessitate the development of new memory terms and ideas) can help with both endeavours.

An interesting problem within the MMP area is the construction of human concepts (CHC). Part of its interest comes from its relation to the token-type issue in the philosophy of mind and another part from the anatomic-physiological level of their organisation.

Can we describe the CHC problem in terms of existing quantitative mathematics? I should start by saying that, for the general problem of describing the mechanisms of M, current quantitative mathematics are inadequate because the combinatorial complexity of the elements of M far exceeds the capabilities of even any future quantum computer.

Demonstration of this claim is straightforward by the following simple calculations on the basis of our current knowledge of nervous systems. The current estimate of neurons in humans is 86×10^9. Furthermore, each neuron is estimated to have 1000–10,000 connections. Taking the lower limit of 1000 connections and assuming that each synapse is able of two distinct states:

* The total number of available synaptic patterns is: $2^{86,000,000,000,000}$

Assuming further that only one millionth of these patterns can be mental phenomena,

** The total number of potential mental phenomena is: $2^{85,999,999,999,994}$

I make now the third assumption that only a billion of a billion of a million of these can be conscious. Then:

*** The total number of potentially conscious phenomena is: $2^{85,999,999,999,970}$.

Finally, if a person experiences 1 mental phenomenon per second and we assume that she lives for 120 years, then:

**** A person's total experience over the 120 years is $\sim 4 \times 10^9$ conscious mental phenomena.

Comparisons, and their consequences, are left to the reader.

Nevertheless, proposing conceptual solutions in terms of informal logic (i.e., natural language arguments) *compatible* with current neuroscience, is a feasible and useful exercise. Qualitative mathematics are *compatible* with informal logic and therefore my basic thesis that new mathematics are required (Sect. 1.4 and Gelepithis 2009) is not violated. The rest of this section scratches the surface of the CHC problem and presents my preliminary conceptual solution to it.

A relatively early attempt for a conceptual solution of the CHC problem proposed by Gelepithis (1989). Given the recent interest in graph theory and "network science" (e.g., Bullmore & Sporns 2009;

Faskowitz et al. 2022), I decided to provide an updated summary of that idea in accordance with the theory of meaning of the TNS. The relation between such work and my idea is both tenuous and rather antithetical. In a nutshell, I consider the network science approach as useful for certain goals but as plainly inadequate for addressing the CHC problem. As I will comment below, all current mathematics including my suggestion for a particular topological approach—neighbourhood systems—are inadequate for addressing the complexity of the M space. Nevertheless, they can be fruitfully seen as pathways revealing pitfalls. On this understanding, let me start with that early speculative proposal. Specifically, I presented how the structural (anatomical) part of concepts may be captured by a topological model. In particular, I suggested that:

T-1: Neighbourhoods and families of neighbourhoods capture the anatomical necessity of token and type differentiation; and
T-2: The notion of neighbourhood systems explain the gross anatomical features of M.

Within the theory of thinking presented in this chapter those suggestions are reformulated as follows:

> A topological *neighbourhood* models a synaptic system, that is, an instance of a concept.
> A *family of neighbourhoods* models a family of synaptic systems, i.e., a concept.

A *neighbourhood system* models aspects of the anatomical structure of M.[11] The fundamental weakness of the above suggestions stems from lacking representation of the dynamics of concept construction. Still, if the proposed topological model indeed captures the anatomy of concepts, then parts of the brain might be approximately described in terms of a topological dynamical system characterised by some—yet to be specified—mathematical transformations. That is transformations incorporating an element of unpredictability.

Motivation and initial support for my initial proposal was provided by the following two facts:

[11] For the interested reader, compatibility of neighbourhood topologies to Nm and systems of Nm is argued in Gelepithis (1989).

F-1: The complex interconnections of NS cells (see discussion following definition-14a); and
F-2: The basic cortical organisation principles (e.g., Lamb et al. 1984).

Nevertheless, recently two further sources of support have come to my attention. The first is a late Nineteenth century factual remark by William James:

> "Different feelings may coexist in us without assuming any particular spatial order." (James, 1890, Vol. 2, p. 146)

This fact is the epitome of suggestion for a topological model and against the possibility of geometry being appropriate for describing brain processes and structures. In other words, order is not a prerequisite for phenomena like emotion. The second source is recent research carried out in several quarters. For instance, Cowan (2000) and Mandler (2011) support the proposed hierarchical organisation of M.

A further relation of that model to recent work concerns the notion of N and its instantiated relations to thoughts (definition-18), skepseis (definition-26), objects in one's environment, and language. For instance, a neural formation for an object and a neural formation for a linguistic expression are not necessarily disjoint. They may have certain contexts or N_m in common. As I remarked:

> "neural formations for linguistic expressions and objects are not necessarily separate. Their relations depend on the relations between language and the real-world". (Gelepithis 1989, p. 249).[12]

In particular, concrete and abstract concepts may well overlap.[13] Some current neuroscientific findings support this prediction (e.g., Desai et al. 2018; Dove 2018). In addition, Zdrazilova et al.'s (2018) notion of "multiple representational systems" supports the proposed model's assumption of various modalities contributing to the sense of an object or abstract concept.

[12] An FNS is essentially a neural formation (in 1989 terms) that has been updated to be compatible with current neuroscience.

[13] Abstract concepts constitute a major important class of linguistic concepts.

It should also be noted that my conception of neighbourhoods, families of neighbourhoods, and neighbourhood systems merge nicely with the idea that functional connectivity may be the more massive the larger and more complex the anatomical structures are, and vice versa. This conception is compatible with Adachi et al.'s (2012) proposal of functional connectivity and incorporates Friston et al.'s (1997) definition of effective connectivity as "temporal correlation between spatially remote neurophysiological events".

The weaknesses of my conception stem from the fact that it is an anatomical model of functioning elements lacking representation of the specific or even the gross processes that have caused such an anatomical organisation. For instance, it ignores the fact that concept and all other memory formations necessarily involve molecular dynamics to complement the dynamics of neural formations. This is a task beyond the scope of this book. A related issue is the fact that, to my knowledge, topological dynamics is currently restricted to the use of continuous transformations a feature that I think it is mostly, if not totally, incompatible with both the development and evolution of living systems.

My final comment concerns complexity, not just the combinatorial complexity of the elements of M. A theory of the latter has to take into account basic tenets of the theory of complexity. In general, *complexity*, is a systemic characteristic determined by:

(i) the number of a system's *organisation levels*.[14]
(ii) the number and nature of component interactions at each level.
(iii) the number and nature of interactions among levels.

Overall an organisational level is determined by certain characteristics that cannot be found at any of the lower levels. The systemic transition from one organisational level to a higher one is called emergence. We assume that all level components and their interactions along with any inter-level

[14] Our current knowledge of biology distinguishes a dozen main levels of organisation of living systems, namely: atom, molecule, macromolecule, cell, tissue, organ, system of organs, organism, population, community, ecosystem, and biosphere. Since there is no reason to assume that life exists only on earth, it would be better to talk of 'earthian biosphere' and retain the unqualified term 'biosphere' for the possibility of encompassing non Earthian ones.

interactions are exclusively physical. There is only one *type* of entities involved, namely, material entities.

Organisation levels should be clearly distinguished from explanatory levels. The former concern the ontology of the system and need to be discovered. They are one of the characteristics of natural evolution. Their discovery by humans is not always possible. Quite often we assume certain levels of organisation and our theories depend on such assumptions as well as others. Any human theory of a complex system has to incorporate assumptions on the organisation of the system under investigation. In addition, any human theory has to be described in terms of human language and, for certain topics and purposes, be augmented by a variety of formalisms. This necessity may lead to the introduction of theoretical constructs and explanatory levels (alternatively known as levels of analysis or description levels) that may of may not exist in reality. In other words, theoretical constructs and explanatory levels concern human methodology and may turn out to be superfluous. For instance, the existence of "psychon" (Eccles 1994), and the corresponding 'soul level' are not accepted by the scientific community. More generally and recently, the lack of support for extending the current ontology of fundamental physics with mental constructs has nicely put forward by scientists like Carroll (2021). Of course levels of analysis and their constituent elements may prove to be both real and useful as, for instance, the individual, state, and international levels in world politics (Baylis, et al. 2011). In some cases organisational and description levels can be identified. Quite often description levels become quite a point of contention as in the mid to late 1980s debate in cognitive science.[15]

Until now the factual priority of organisation levels was ignored and debate was centred around descriptive levels. Subsequently, two different questions were asked: Is there a single appropriate level of explanation to describe our theories? If not, can we describe a theory at a certain level in terms of a theory of a lower level? As a result, for many scientists and philosophers, a fundamental issue was the specification of the appropriate analytical level of mental phenomena (e.g., McCauley 1998*1999). However, this viewpoint puts the horses ahead of the cart. We need first

[15] See, for example, Anderson's target article and Open Peer Commentary 1987; Broadbent 1985; Changeux & Dehaene 1989; Marr 1982; Rumelhart and McClelland 1985. For a comprehensive consideration of levels in the framework of the foundations of cognitive science Newell's (1990) is still highly recommended.

to answer the question: What is/(are) the organisational level(s) of mental phenomena? Having answered the latter question, one may wonder what description level would be fully understood by humans.

Empirical identification of the organisation levels of 'mental' phenomena is a very difficult task. A theory that identifies even a single such level and even partially integrates all of our knowledge about it would be a major step forward. One of the conceptual problems of such a sought identification is the possible distinction between a *concrete* mental phenomenon and a class of such phenomena. Another concerns the identification of the organisational levels of certain phenomena like emotions. They seem to span several distinct biological levels.

A full naturalist theory of thinking does not imply a reductionist conception of the human mind. For, as in evolutionary biology the gene is not the object of selection (e.g., Mayr 2004), so meaningful neural formations, and therefore meanings, do not constitute in themselves the criterion of the mental in all of its broadness and noémon species specificity. They provide part of the necessary substratum. They are not adequate. As we saw several levels of additional organisational complexity and novel processes are required. Reductionism at least for psychological, cultural, and societal phenomena characterising historic *H. sapiens* is not possible.

3.3.2 Evaluation

I start with a comparison of my theory of meaning with those reviewed in Sect. 3.1, and continue with an evaluation of the TNS theory of thinking vis a vis that of Hebb (1949, 1980). With respect to the former:

First, the meaning part of TNS satisfies all of the undisputed points made by the earlier theories of meaning as codified in Table 3.2. A recent result (Monroe et al. 2022) provides additional support for definition-14b. Their research has shown that essential genes (like the ones involved in survival and reproduction) have a lower chance of being mutated.

Second, in contrast to Putnam's (1988) argument against the view that 'meanings' (or 'contents') can be seen as 'theoretical entities', our theory has identified the class of N_m as the class of "'psychologically real' entities which have enough of the properties we pre-analytically assign to 'meanings' to warrant an identification." (ibid, p. 4).

Third, definitions 15 & 16 explain meaning as a feedback loop of contextual learning or/and understanding in terms of neural formation mechanisms. Furthermore, the postulated mechanisms get empirical support from Markson and Bloom's (1997) evidence that the system underlying word learning is not specific to language. These two points reinforce each other and taken together weigh considerably against the possibility of word learning being an FLN (faculty of language in the narrow sense) mechanism (Fitch et al. 2005).

Fourth, our analysis provides a naturalistic account of the distinction between token and type meanings that is essentially identical with that of Hebb (1980b for a brief argument). It is therefore unlikely to be convincing to those considering the type-token question a philosophical minefield (Aylwin 1985, p. 44) and even an important topic for serious scholarship (Wetzel 2008). We are though obliged to say that within the TNS, tokens of a type are identified with ${}^{j}N_m$, and the type itself with $\varepsilon(H, t)$. It should be noticed that in the case of Homo sapiens, *prevailed* N_p of higher order N_ms may well capture multiple characteristics of a complex stimulus like that of a beautiful woman.[16] Here we would enter the overlapping phenomena of generalization, categorisation and abstraction but consideration of these issues is beyond the scope of this book.

Fifth, the proposed theory addresses Loar's (1999, p. 546) requirement:

> "A fundamental element of a theory of meaning is where it locates the basis of meaning, in thought, in individual speech, or in social practices."

In the precise sense presented in the previous section the TNS explains why meaning is "located" in all three. It follows that since human meanings are constitutively determined by both a human and her or his environment (physical as well as social and cultural), pure internalism and externalism are bankrupt in either their semantic or epistemological variety. The sort of sophisticated gerrymandering arguments developed in recent literature (e.g., Goldberg 2007; Williamson 2006) evaporate in the light of TNS. Similarly, the coupling between H and her environment (postulated by the dynamicists) can be identified by the links pointed out in the previous section. Almost needless to say that precise specification of

[16] Thanks to Yiannis Kontos for providing me with this example (personal communication).

these links require a lot of interdisciplinary work. The three partite location of the basis of meanings characterising our theory finds support from the conversational science approach too (e.g., Harri-Augstein & Thomas 2001).

Sixth, a most important characteristic of our theory of meaning is its nearly- inseparable connection to emotion. On the basis of our earlier definitions, primitive emotions via the phenomena of survival and reproduction are part of most if not all N_ms. In addition, motivation (i.e., the approach or avoidance tendency of an individual towards a stimulus or a goal) is directly related to the valenced states of an individual and therefore to that individual's N_m systems. Furthermore, since semantic structures are systems of neural formation structures, the question on the relation between emotion and all other mental phenomena breaks down into two new types of questions: (i) what mental phenomena are free of emotions; and (ii) whether there is a level of neurophysiological analysis at which the entanglement of mental phenomena breaks down into simpler physical structures and processes. Gelepithis (2024b, Chapter-4) discusses the major research pathways on emotion in animals and robots and provides the TNS perspective.

Seventh, definitions 14a, 14b, 15, and 16 partly and implicitly characterise consciousness. In particular, the systemic and substantially dynamic nature of attention is closely related to motor activity and therefore to an individual's N_m systems. Usually, that relation is represented by feedback loops. Re-entrant interactions have not been, so far, adequately developed (Sect. 3.3.1 for comments on the staggering complexities involved).

Eighth, I want to make two comments concerning the key point raised against neurophysiological reductionism by Bennett and Hacker (2003), namely, the mereological fallacy. One, I want to point out that this fallacy may remind one, much less strongly or much more ambiguously, already expressed viewpoints (e.g., Wittgenstein 1953 and Dennett 1969 respectively). In any case, it is worth pointing out that this part-whole relation and the serious mistakes its misapplication may produce was made more than 2000 years ago by Aristotle (350*1984c BCE).

Two, for my part I say that *certain* neural formations possess semantic content as a result of the interaction of an appropriate organism with his/her/it environment. As a result, the part-whole principle still holding true, *such* psychological attributes can be attributed to parts of an appropriate nervous system. Of course, *not all* psychological attributes can be attributed to neural systems—not even to the whole nervous system of any member of any species. Such attributes, for example, are those involving behaviour. For instance: Mary plays tennis. The previous comment is mostly in agreement with Bennett & Hacker's claim that neuroscientists misuse the part-whole relation and specifically attribute psychological states to neural systems, and also addresses Searle's (2007, pp. 113–4) avoidance response on this issue, namely: attributing psychological states "to subpersonal entities such as neurons can be harmless as long as it is clear that is a metaphorical use." Finally, the dependence of the behaviour of a noémon species on its environment—in particular its culture, where applicable—can only partly be studied by (cultural) neuroscience. Specifically, the latter can only study those acquired characteristics that have been permanently internalised by an organism. Even so, this is a very difficult task that only a future neuroscience may accomplish.

Finally, I would like to mention that it is encouraging that my neurophysiological grounding, and associated theory, of meaning (originated in Gelepithis 1984) has been recognised—without acknowledgement—in the celebrated symbol grounding problem. Along the same lines, Garagnani et al. (2021) have recently documented direct experimental evidence, in the form of neuroimaging results, confirming my neurophysiological grounding of meaning. Specifically, their evidence concerns novel, previously unencountered items (cf, definition-16).

Comparison of Hebb's and TNS Theory of Thinking

I move now to the comparative evaluation of my theory of thinking. The conceptual structure of Hebb's (1949;1980) theory of thought is based on four concepts: the cell-assembly; the phase-sequence; the notion of attention; and the concept of "intrinsic" cortical organisation. The cell assembly[17] is postulated to be the inevitable result of "any frequently repeated, particular stimulation" and its characteristic properties are believed to be: its slow development; its capability of acting briefly as a closed system; its capability of delivering facilitation to other such systems; and usually, being able to have a specific motor facilitation. On that basis thought is defined as a "phase sequence" (i.e., a series of cell-assemblies).

Hebb's theory has a similar structure up to third-level cell assemblies and also allows subassemblies of 2–3 neurons. The TNS does not add

[17] "A diffuse structure comprising cells in the cortex and diencephalon (and also, perhaps, in the basal ganglia of the cerebrum)".

much to that conception. Nevertheless, the two theories differ in at least *three* crucial points. First, neural formations is a more inclusive construct allowing, for instance, the possibility of non- synaptic plasticity (Kandel & Pittinger 1999; Bollmann & Engert 2009) and of non-neuronal correlates of mental abilities (e.g., Bennett 2007). For instance having delineated a class of N_ms, the mind-body problem collapses.

Second, the immensity of the neurophysiological space of thinking creates a problem for *directed* thinking. To account for that, Hebb (1976) proposed that the exceptionally high frequency of inhibitory neurons may have the essential function of streamlining thought. That may indeed be the case. Given the complexity of the neural formation processes involved we are somehow agnostic on that line of thought. As a theoretical alternative, we suggest the processes of reasoning (Sect. 3.2.2) and of understanding (Sect. 4.2). I also suggest the as yet entirely unknown, in neurophysiological terms, process of perseverance. Remaining in the space of speculation for a bit more, I would say that random thinking, occurring at any, and across any, of the complexity levels of an individual's semantic structures (M), may be triggered easier the richer one's environment is.

Third, and most importantly, Hebb's theory does not include a physicalist, neuroscientifically-based theory of meaning. The same is true for major relatively recent work both in the Hebbian tradition (e.g., Edelman 1987) and in biologically inspired non-linear dynamics (e.g., Freeman 1999). This is a difference of fundamental significance with far reaching consequences (Sect. 3.3.1). Ramachandran (2012, pp. 176 and 178), among several other distinguished neuroscientists, stated the issue clearly:

> "the manner in which neural circuitry embodies meaning is one of the great unsolved mysteries of neuroscience."

My theory of meaning has cracked it. Meanings (both biological and artificial) are materially-based and environmentally (including societally) constrained.

CHAPTER 4

The Nature of Communication: Understanding and Systems of Primitives

> "The most important thing, therefore, that we can know about a man is what he takes for granted, and the most elemental and important facts about a society are those that are seldom debated and generally regarded as settled."
>
> (Wirth, 1929*1954, p. xxiv).
>
> "The book *[On Human Communication]* was first written as an attempt to make a case for the study of human communication as an academic subject. That case still stands, though the nature of such a study is still far from crystal clear."
>
> (Colin Cherry, 1978*1980).
>
> "Science is an endless search for truth. Any representation of reality we develop can be only partial. There is no finality, sometimes no single best representation. There is only deeper understanding, more revealing and enveloping representations."
>
> (Woese 2004, p. 173).

Processes take time. Their orders of magnitude vary tremendously. Currently, they range from hundreds of attoseconds (10^{-18} sec) that is the measured time for an electron motion, to the estimated age of the Universe (13.8 Ga). The process of 'human understanding' has a much shorter duration than the latter. It can vary from around a second to the life time of a person. In the former case the process is usually uninterrupted; in the latter, it is definitely interrupted again and again.

P. A. M. Gelepithis, *Unification of Artificial Intelligence and Psychology*,
https://doi.org/10.1007/978-3-031-68319-0_4

'Human communication' defined, as we shall see below, in terms of mutual human understanding has similar durational and potential discontinuity characteristics. In the general case of noémon systems the processes of 'communication' and 'understanding' are still present and fundamental albeit different in a number of important respects.

In preview of this chapter I want to make two remarks. First, the most important characteristic of the relation between communication and understanding is the fact that the former is a societal process depending on the individual processes of understanding, whereas the latter is an individual process that is societally dependent. Second, despite the very large and increasing literature on human, robot, animal, and even the wider notion of biological communication, the differences and similarities among these kinds of 'communication are not widely studied and studies on the *nature* of communication incorporating its various kinds are practically non existent.

The final chapter of this volume unifies the disciplinary studies of the last two definiens of 'noémon system', namely, communication and understanding. In particular, Sect. 4.1 succinctly reviews the theoretical literature on the nature of communication and proposes a definition of *human* communication that can be used as a theoretical construct across the multitude of disciplines studying it. The proposed definition is in terms of the process of human understanding and its end result, namely, *a* system of human primitives. Section 4.2 starts with an equal succinct review of the literature on *human* understanding, defines the *process* of understanding and briefly introduces the basic phenomena affecting it, discusses in depth its end result (i.e., systems of primitives), justifies the proposed theory of human communication and understanding, and concludes that these processes constitute qualitative invariances of historic *H. sapiens* (H) psychology. Section 4.3 defines communication for *any* NoS (noémon system), discusses its limits among NoSs, argues that the process of NoS-understanding is also an invariance of the space of noémon systems, and compares well known regularities and qualitative invariances of psychology and AI with PriNS and the invariances of the understanding and communication processes.

Naturally, my definitions of human communication and understanding along with those of animal, robot and NoS-wide ones do not automatically make obsolete alternative conceptions of these processes. What they do, nevertheless, do, is bringing to the fore the fundamental building blocks of communication as well as the essential objectives of both communication and understanding. As an interesting and rather significant side offer, the proposed theory of human understanding reveals the transformative capability of the *process* of human understanding. The latter enables an individual to transform her M and the extent of the transformation depends on the depth of the process. Such transformations can reveal the roots of at least four different types of belief systems: pre-scientific; dogmatic; scientific; and hear-say. Many different combinations of these types exist and more basic types could be specified (Sect. 3.2.1 for definition of belief).

4.1 On Human Communication

Communication is basic to all members of any human society (including hermits for at least some considerable time of their lives). But, what is it really? Despite its vast literature, the problem of the *nature* of communication is either ignored or treated in an ad-hoc way within a single discipline. Mattelart and Mattelart (1995*1998) state eleven disciplines involved with its study: Philosophy, history, cybernetics, geography, psychology, biology, sociology, ethnology, economics, political science, and the cognitive sciences! By now this list has become longer. The latest discipline to address 'communication' is cognitive neuroscience through brain imaging techniques (e.g., Noordzij et al. 2009; Anders et al. 2011; Stolk et al. 2014; Leong et al. 2017; Pulvermüller 2018b; Wheatley et al. 2019). Unfortunately, so far, this work has not produced any new insights or theories. It has, of course, provided ample evidence in favour of a physicalist theory of communication and more generally mind, but otherwise has only confirmed the obvious. In the worst case, such work uncritically propagates unfounded or outdated conceptions of key notions involving 'meaning' (see chapter-3).

Ignoring the *nature* of human communication is pervasive. Although it may be expected with textbooks on Human Communication (e.g., Pearson et al. 2011; Littlejohn et al. 2021; Griffin, et al. 2023), it is both surprising and revealing to note that two comprehensive reference works, the *MIT Encyclopaedia of the Cognitive Sciences* (Wilson & Keil 1999) and *A Companion to Cognitive Science* (Bechtel & Graham, 1998) do not include an entry on communication itself. Instead, the former refers the reader to three related entries: on animal communication (Hauser & Marler, 1999); on Grice (Bach, 1999); and on language and communication (Duncan, 1999).[1] The latter refers one to cognitive linguistics (Tomasello, 1998). None of these entries considers the ***nature*** of human communication. If anything a rather non-deep consideration to fundamental phenomena like language and thought is revealed. The same lack of consideration for the nature of communication is essentially the case for any of the contributions in five readers, spanning more than eight decades of research in communication (Cobley 1996; D'Ettorre & Hughes 2008; Pool et al. 1973; Smith 1966; Vaina and Hintikka 1984*1985). It is also true for at least indirectly related work on the social nature of human and animal mind (e.g., Connor 2007; Mead †1934*1962; Moll and Tomasello 2007; Vygotsky †1934*1986). Another use of 'communication' is by works aiming to develop critical consumers of information (e.g., Guerrero et al. 2020). Finally, the view has also been expressed that 'communication' cannot constitute a discipline because it is intrinsically characterised by fragmentation and that should not be of concern (Waisbord 2019). To my knowledge, the best effort to a reference source-book for theories of communication—including concepts, individual theories, and traditions of theories is the *Encyclopedia of Communication Theory* (Littlejohn & Foss 2009). It is an exceptionally well thought and structured reference book in a two-volume set.

With respect to the ad hoc, discipline-based treatment of communication one may distinguish several approaches on its presumed nature. In what follows I stress the prevailing, differentiating perspective of an approach not its full associated theory of conception. In some cases an approach is a combination of several ideas. None of these cases has produced a theory of communication that is part of a unified theory of human 'mind', let alone of noémon systems. Table 4.1 lists the major approaches on the nature of 'communication'.

Table 4.2 tabulates the major advantages and disadvantages of the sufficiently distinct approaches among those listed in Table 4.1.

Among the different conceptions of communication stated above, A-1 and A-6 are the most widely accepted. The conception of 'communication' as an act of sharing signs is one of the oldest and most ramified. It should be noted that perceived in this way, 'communication' gives rise to numerous further splits of interest. As Schramm (1973) remarked: such

[1] Essentially, Grice's important work is primarily on meaning (Table 3.2).

Table 4.1 Approaches to the nature of communication

Number	*Approaches and major references*
A-1	Act of sharing signs (e.g., Cherry 1978*1980, Dimbleby & Burton 1998, Schramm, 1973; Gallese 2003; Witzany 2017a for reviews concerning Archaea)
A-2	The mathematical theory of signal transmission (Shannon and Weaver 1949). Includes code model of communication (e.g., Blackburn 2007)
A-3	Communication as signalling beneficial to sender (e.g., Slater 1983)
A-4	"[T]he social mediation of information" (e.g., Hauser 1996; Matessi et al 2008; Roberts 1973)
A-5	Communication as a means to manage audiences ranging from instructional 'communication' (e.g., Mottet et al. 2006) to political 'communication' (e.g., Stanyer 2007)
A-6	Identification with interaction (e.g., Katz and Danet 1973)
A-7	Communication based on the notion of communicative action (Habermas 1981*1984, 1987)
A-8	"[A]ny exchange of messages between human beings" (e.g., Runcan 1985). Similar to (i)
A-9	Identification with context (e.g., Sperber & Wilson 1995)
A-10	Intention-based (e.g., Messer 1994; Harris 2019)
A-11	Intention to produce understanding (e.g., Searle 1999*2000)
A-12	The practice of producing meanings and their negotiations by participants in a culture (e.g., Schirato and Yell 2000)
A-13	Among humans, the process of responding to each other's symbolic behaviour (e.g., Adler and Rodman 2000)
A-14	Communication as jointly beneficial signalling (e.g., Maynard Smith & Harper 2003).
A-15	"process by which one animal provides information that other animals can incorporate into their decision making." (Bradbury & Vehrencamp 2020).

a relationship is very complex and due to the lack of "general theoretical insights, researchers have typically worked on parts of the relationship". All of them fail to specify their definiens.

Witzany, one of the most recent followers of this view, is the least impressive.

He states that:

> "communication is defined as the sign-mediated interaction between at least two living agents which share a repertoire of signs that are combined (according to syntactic rules) in varying contexts (according to pragmatic rules) to transport content (according to semantic rules)." (Witzany 2017b, p. 3).

Table 4.2 Sufficiently distinct approaches among those listed in Table 4.1

Number	*Comments*
A-1	Captures the necessary element of meaning without defining it
A-2	Very useful syntactic theory of transmission. Not applicable to communication. Still, the code model of communication is extensively used in linguistics
A-6	Too wide a conception to be of any use while
A-7	Major advantage: Part of a theory concerning the foundations of social science. Lacks elaboration of the basic constitutive notions of communication. See *end of this section* for details of the similarities and differences with our system
A-9	Correctly identifies a key element. Fails to take into account mutuality
A-11	View perilously close to propaganda because it rejects mutuality in favour of personal meanings. In his words: "But understanding will consist in the grasp of my meaning." (Searle ibid., p. 145)
A-12	Incorporates the important elements of meaning and negotiation Does not specify best mechanism
A-14	Normative, win–win conception. This is not always the case. Fails to specify mechanisms
A-15	Too general. No mechanisms specified

This definition purported to be applicable across the living world (including RNA consortia see Witzany 2017a for reviews), is simply mistaken by being too rich and demanding in its constitutive conditions while at the same time aiming to be applicable to all living forms. It simply fails to recognise both the vast differences in anatomical, physiological, mental, cultural, and societal organisation of living forms and their consequences.

The interaction theory of communication primarily takes two views. Both of them assume that what is interacted are opinions, feelings, information, etc. They are differentiated by the first viewpoint assuming that the communicandum is known or understood by others; the second type merely shares communicanda (e.g., Arlington & Baird 2005; Benowitz et al. 1984*1985; Murray (1998); Sass (1984*1985). The definiens in both cases are assumed to be well known; a mistaken assumption (Scott 1996; Tomasello et al. 2005).

Additional instances in science viewing communication as mere interaction are more revealing:

(a) Concerning Archaea (e.g., Soucy & Cogarten 2017 for work on lateral gene transfer).
(b) Bacteria (e.g., Williams 2007; Lentini et al. 2017; both for work on chorum sensing; Majumdar & Pal 2017 for work on bacterial 'intelligence'; Majumdar & Pal 2018 for work on chorum sensing and 'information' transfer).

Most 'communication' studies concerning taxonomic groups of the Eykarya domain, barring the animalia kingdom, use 'communication' in various extremely restricted senses of sharing. For instance:

(a) gaze following (Bräuer et al. 2005; Range & Virányi 2011);
(b) pointing (Tauzin et al. 2015);
(c) work on plants (e.g., McGarvey & Croteau 1995; Bonfante & Genre 2015)

Specifically for plants (Farmer & Ryan 1990), 'communication' is even used to refer to activation of defensive plant responses to airborne chemicals (specifically, methyl jasmonate).

One of the most celebrated phenomena of non verbal 'communication' is the waggle dance; originally named the 'language' of bees'. It concerns patterns of honey bees (e.g., Apis mellifera) behaviour that have been interpreted as providing information about promising source food and its characteristic scent along with additional information concerning its distance from the beehive and direction in relation to the sun. Nearly one hundred years ago von Frisch had summarised his observation in a classic treatment in German. The latest results of the work of von Frisch and his team are succinctly summarised in von Frisch & Lindauer (1956). Although they clearly state that the waggle dance "transmits the knowledge of significant facts" (ibid., p. 46), most of the relevant scientific literature until recently insists on talking of 'communication' and 'language'. For contrasting results see Grüter et al. (2008); for a recent review (Ai et al. 2019). Lifting the transmission element of non-human animal behaviour up to the defining characteristic of a presumed non-human animal communication is repetition of the same mistake committed in attempting to characterise human communication (Sect. 4.1). A mistake propagated also by established encyclopaedias. Consider the following definition of animal communication in Britannica:

> "process by which one animal provides information that other animals can incorporate into their decision making." (Bradbury & Vehrencamp 2020).

The rest of this section focuses and defines human communication. In all disciplinary work 'communication' is treated as an orienting term rather than as an explanatory theoretical construct. The strongest objection against the latter use is that 'communication', as opposed to gravity, is assumed to be a socially constructed notion rather than an objective reality and, therefore, any attempt to provide an objective account of it is doomed to failure. Interestingly, this is the view of both those postulating the existence of characteristically social 'facts' (à la Durkheim) and those postulating 'meanings' as the key methodological approach of sociology (à la Weber). This debate in sociology is reflected in the *systems* and *interpretive* perspectives in communication studies (Monge 1977; Putnam 1983). The objection sounds powerful but misses an important point. Both 'gravity' and 'communication' are humanly constructed concepts and both refer to some external phenomena. Their only difference is that 'gravity' has a generally accepted meaning within the Earth-based physicists, whereas 'communication' does not have one within the community of scientists using this notion. It is high time for a conception of communication that could be used as an explanatory tool across the disciplines studying it.

So far, each disciplinary theory of communication has been built on the basis of a single significant feature of it. As we have seen in the previous paragraphs, some have chosen the notion of sharing; some the notion of understanding; and some the notion of meaning in some of its many guises (without addressing it comprehensively). All these three elements are necessary but insufficient on their own. In particular, the 'sharing' element of communication should boil down to the element of mutuality (cf, Habermas 1987) for otherwise it could become biased towards one or the other of the participants. In other words, it has to capture.

> "the inescapable necessity of understanding both oneself and one's adversary in the matrix of the social process" (Mannheim 1929/31*1954, p. 153).

The problem therefore is to provide a *system* of definitions that will capture this fundamental requirement. The following system of three definitions does exactly that. The original version of these definitions can be found in Gelepithis (1984), albeit in a form not reducible to a minimum vocabulary (as the following system does).

Definition-28$_H$ A human H_1 has communicated with H_2 on a topic θ if, and only if:

(i) H1 has understood θ -symbol: U (H1, θ);
(ii) H2 has understood θ -symbol: U (H2, θ);
(iii) U (H1, θ) is output by H1 and understood by H2; and
(iv) U (H2, θ) is output by H2 and understood by H1.

Definition-29$_H$ A human H, at time t, has understood something, θ, if and only if, H can think of θ in terms of *a* system of human primitives that depend on H, θ, and t (symbol $\prod$(H, θ, t), or *a* system of premises.[2]

Definition-30$_H$ π is a primitive of/for H if and only if the meaning of π is immediate for H.

To stress the systemic nature of the above definitions, I will use the abbreviation CUP (Communication—Understanding—Primitives) system whenever I want to refer to all three of them or to stress the systemic nature of their constituent parts.

As it is obvious from an even cursory reading of the above definitions, the first two refer and determine the *end-result* of their corresponding processes (not the processes themselves). My second remark concerns the use of the verb 'to output' instead of alternatives like 'to signal'. My justification is that it is more general than all of the alternatives I could think of. This will be more appreciated in Sect. 4.3 below when I generalise the above definitional system to include an arbitrary NoS able to understand and communicate. A final point should be made. The use of the disjunctive structure 'of/for' in definition-30H is both necessary and significant. Using exclusively 'of' would have meant that a primitive would either exclusively belong to that particular human or that it would be a genuine *Homo* universal. Using 'for' means that a primitive belongs to the class of primitives specified by artificial means like those derived from or based on WHuLa. The best example comes from H- science. Scientific theories

[2] System of premises stands for a reference system of human beliefs, thoughts and concepts.

contain primitives outside the realm of traditional biological evolution. All such primitives do not belong to any human. They are part of the artificial component of H. They are primitives 'for' an individual human (see also remark following definition-30NoS in Sect. 4.3).

According to the TNS developed so far, a large number of species belonging to several classes of the animal kingdom, (at least, mammals, aves, Cephalopoda and insects), exhibit aspects of thinking. In addition, the simplest types of thinking may quite possibly exist in other Eukarea kingdoms as well as in the domains of Archaea and Bacteria. Communication, as systemically defined above and is fully explicated in the following section, is a much more complex process than any type of reasoning, let alone of thinking. That should imply a far lesser number of living entities being able to communicate. We discuss the range of noémon systems capable of understanding and communication in Sect. 4.3.

In what follows I provide a preliminary comparison of my view of the nature of human communication against the major alternative viewpoints. It may be better to be noted here that a full understanding of the following advantages will be possible after one having read at least the next section discussing the building blocks of (human) communication. The same comment applies for the comparison between Jürgen Habermas' Magnum Opus *The Theory of Communicative Action* and our theory of communication that is taken up in the second of the following paragraphs. First, the key advantages of my proposal, so far, include:

(a) It incorporates the three necessary of elements of communication that have been identified by alternative theories into a single system of definitions and defines them in naturalistic terms. No theory had done this before.
(b) It embodies an open, co-operative conception of communication. For, the end result of communication can have one of the following three possibilities: (i) Communicator A accepts communicator's B understanding, or vice versa; (ii) Neither A nor B accept each other's understanding but co-operate until they reach a third, jointly accepted, understanding; and (iii) A and B agree to disagree.
(c) The above definitional system of human communication is part of the minimum vocabulary of the TNS. This again is a unique feature of the proposed theory of communication.

(d) As part of the minimum vocabulary of the TNS, the proposed definitional system is complete (the understanding and primitive system building blocks are fully defined in the next section).
(e) It combines the subjectivity of an individual's understanding with, potentially, the agreed-upon understanding of our species (that is the maximum of possible objectivity of the current historic *H. sapiens*).
(f) Finally, it guards against constructivism's view, namely, each and every one of us is constrained by the individual knowledge space that s/he has constructed.

In relation to the graded nature of human objectivity implied in (e), the issue of human and robotic knowledge is closely related. These topics belong to the Consequences Volume of this monograph (Gelepithis 2024b, Sect. 2.3).

Let me now briefly compare our theory with that of Habermas. First, his theory should be seen from the perspective of his wider objective of setting "The Foundations of Social Science in the Theory of Communication" (Habermas 1987, V.1). Expressed in this general way I am in full agreement. Nevertheless, it all depends on what such a theory boils down to. Concerning the details of the corresponding theories, there are important points of both agreement and differentiation. With respect to the former, the most important points of agreement are the definition of communication in terms of mutual understanding and the indispensable role of meaning in any theory of communication. These are fundamental points of agreement on the basis of which a broader agreement could be reached to bridge our differing theories. Our differentiation stems from a single fundamental difference: I define human understanding in terms of a system of human primitives that are themselves completely defined; Habermas stays at the level of mutual understanding. To appreciate better this analytical difference let us consider an important excerpt from Habermas (ibid., p. 137):

> "Under the functional aspect of *mutual understanding*, communicative action serves to transmit and renew cultural knowledge; under the aspect of *coordinating action*, it serves social integration and the establishment of solidarity; finally, under the aspect of *socialization*, communicative action serves the formation of personal identities."

In terms of these three aspects of Habermas' theory of communication, the following two important differences and one differentiating similarity are pinpointed below. For the TNS theory of communication, *all* knowledge is actually *generated* through the processes reflected in definitions 28–30. His notion of 'renewal' comes close to our notion of 'generation' except for the important fact that it is not specified. Second, for Habermas communication always involves agreement. For us, although agreement is always preferable, there is also the possibility for disagreement (point (b)/(iii) above). Indeed, the latter may vary from disagreeable to potentially painful (Diplomacy is a well known example). The differentiating similarity between the two theories concerns the "formation of personal identities" under the aspect of *socialization*. For Habermas the notion of 'personal identity' is identical to that of Ego identity (influence Freud) and therefore is considerably narrower than our notion of M. Similarly, the notion of *socialization* is essentially identified with "learning how to follow norms and to take on more and more roles" (Habermas 1987, p. 40), whereas in our theory θ is an unrestricted variable ranging over any topic of interest or investigation.

Let us move now to consider the building blocks of human communication, namely, human understanding and system of human primitives.

4.2 Human Understanding and Systems of Primitives

The philosophical roots of the study of human 'understanding' can be traced back at least as far as the times of Plato and Aristotle and their attempts to provide an account for the human mind.[3] More recently, Locke (1690*1975) and Hume (1758*1977) have written treatises on 'human understanding'. For both of them, 'human understanding' was essentially taken to be coextensive with the functioning of the human mind. A conception that is more in tune with that of Plato and Aristotle rather than any of today's workers in the field of human cognition. An exception in tackling understanding as a specific cognitive

[3] This section is an updated version of very small parts of Sects. 3.1 and 4.1 in Gelepithis (1984).

phenomenon can be seen in Sanford's (2003) reader. Rejecting the coextensive assumption helped in focusing on the nature of the phenomenon of understanding.

Nearly universally, understanding is seen as a process. The single exception I am aware of is that of Moravcsik (1979). He has argued that understanding should be seen as the state of mind that yields the insight that unites one's knowledge required to arrive at the solution to a problem. This time I am with the side of the vast majority.

Seen as a process, the study of understanding may conveniently characterised by two orthogonal dimensions: analyticity and temporal duration. Along the analyticity dimension schools of thought are distinguished according to whether they consider human understanding as a process to be further analysed into some simpler notions (the analytic school) or consider it as a primitive process (the hermeneutic school).

The temporal duration of human understanding has not so far taken seriously into consideration despite the fact it can be, and is, applied to the full time scale of human action. It is observed from approximately 10 ms to days, minute, hours, years and more. Examples of the latter case abound in science (I use 'science' to include both physical and social sciences and the humanities). Most of cognitive science is primarily concerned with phenomena whose duration varies from approximately 100 ms to about 10 min. For instance, a simple request like 'please pass me the pepper' takes approximately 1 second. Such phenomena cover all of the cognitive band and most of the rational one as defined by Newell (1990). The large majority of work on understanding falls within the cognitive and rational bands. It usually comes under the name of comprehension. My objective here is to examine the kind of understanding that takes at least a few hours thus falling primarily within the social band of the time scale of human action.

The two orthogonal dimensions of analyticity and temporal scale create four quadrants. Most work falls in the analytic-cognitive quadrant (e.g., Greeno 1977; Johnson-Laird 2003; Just & Carpenter 1987; Schank 1972; St. John & McClelland 1990; Winograd 1972).[4] In the analytic-social quadrant the most important work is that of Pask (1976) and Ziff (1972). Finally, in the hermeneutic-social quadrant the work of Dilthey (1900), Moravcsik (1979), Ricouer (1981) and Habermas (1981*1984;

[4] Johnson Laird's (2003) thesis is that human understanding depends on the construction of mental models from perception, imagination and the comprehension of language.

1987) stand out. Some recent work in the area of mirror neuron systems has attempted to link results in this area to action and in particular the understanding of action (e.g., Jeannerod 2006; Rizzolatti & Sinigaglia 2006). They did not address the issue of understanding per se; they are concerned with our knowledge of the phenomenon under investigation. As such it is an instance of scientific knowledge.

The key conclusion in reviewing the literature on the nature of understanding is that although agreement on its nature has not been reached two attributes of it are virtually universally accepted. First, human understanding always involves the grasp of meaning. Second, human understanding is a process that takes place within individual human. Its localisation is a separate, important, and still unresolved problem. It follows that understanding, at the very least, is a thinking process. As such the former inherits all the characteristics of the latter in addition to its *own* ones. To identify the *own* characteristics of understanding I now turn.

Certainly, thinking processes may, and do, terminate somewhere; but not all of thinking is, or leads to, understanding. One may, for instance, be interrupted while trying to understand something and subsequently fail to catch again the thread of that particular thinking process. Of course, there may be future recall of the interrupted process but the point is that at the time of interruption no understanding may be said to have occurred. So, we conclude that not all terminated thinking processes are processes of understanding.

The important question is: What are the conditions under which understanding has achieved? Work in the cognitive-analytic quadrant takes successful behavior in question-answering tasks, for instance, to constitute an adequate terminating condition. That may be true but it is inapplicable when human understanding is concerned with tasks requiring time scales that fall outside the cognitive and rational bands. Such tasks constitute the bread and butter of the larger part of science. Without loss of generality the subsequent development of my analysis will assume tasks of the latter type being the object of human understanding.

Let us assume then that we witness a case of an undisturbed thinking process. What additional conditions should be fulfilled in order to say that one has understood something? There is a thinking process that will help us to specify these conditions. It may be called alleged understanding, (or misunderstanding), and it occurs whenever people think they have understood something only later to discover that what they had concluded was not the case. The key point in a case of misunderstanding is the fact that one's own predictions or explanations, according to her model or belief system, turn out not to be the case. Assuming there was not any fault in the inference process one concludes that there must have been mistaken premises involved.

A premiss does not have to be fundamental not even well documented for an individual. Premises are, of course, equally effective whether they are true or false as the thinking and behaviour of any person of dogmatic persuasion from football to religion and from politics to ethics can easily demonstrate to observers. A system of premises is far from a secure ground for understanding.

Nevertheless, human reasoning has two interesting and potentially useful characteristics: directionality; and a kind of validity. Directionality in the sense that a human somehow is driven from a system of premises to conclusions. We do not know how but the direction is always present. It is therefore not unreasonable to think that it may be related to to Russell's (1921) and Hebb's (1976) mnemic causation. The 'validity' of human reasoning is reminiscent of mathematical validity despite the fact that the system of an individual's premises is hardly ever checked for errors or inconsistencies (most clearly seen in the cases of dogmatic behaviour mentioned above).

On the basis of the above remarks, I am strongly inclined to think of human understanding as a special type of human reasoning with a more secure grounding that would reduce the number of misunderstandings. What such a grounding be? For my part, a system of primitives is more secure than a system of premises and it appears to be the least insecure system on which to base our understanding. Of course, no system of primitives is ever likely to hold true for all events and phenomena we may come across and want to understand. I think that this is an instance of our limited capabilities. So, I distinguish between an individual's system of primitives $\prod(H, \theta, t)$ and an individual's system of premises. Reasoning processes that eventually end up to a system of primitives I call them processes of *maximum* understanding, those that end up in a system of premises are process of human reasoning (cf, definition 25). Naturally, there are also processes that involve both a system of premises and a half-based system of primitives; I call such processes, processes of *rudimentary* understanding. My thesis on understanding is summarised by the following:

Thesis-1 The end-result of the process of human understanding is determined either by a system of primitives (***maximum*** understanding) or a mixed system of primitives and premises (***rudimentary*** understanding).

The process of understanding itself depends upon a cluster of many other complex processes. Explicitly, the complexity of the process of understanding is characterised by:

- The multiplicity of factors influencing it; and
- The complexity of $\prod(H, \theta, t)$.

I consider each of them in turn.

Figure 4.1 illustrates some of the major phenomena influencing the process of understanding. Any, even cursory, consideration of the factors affecting human understanding would take us far beyond the scope of this book. Nevertheless, a summary statement of some of the most characteristic of these phenomena should be given in order to provide a glimpse of its complexity. Learning may occur without understanding but the latter may require some of the end results of any of the various processes that lead to the acquisition of information or skill.

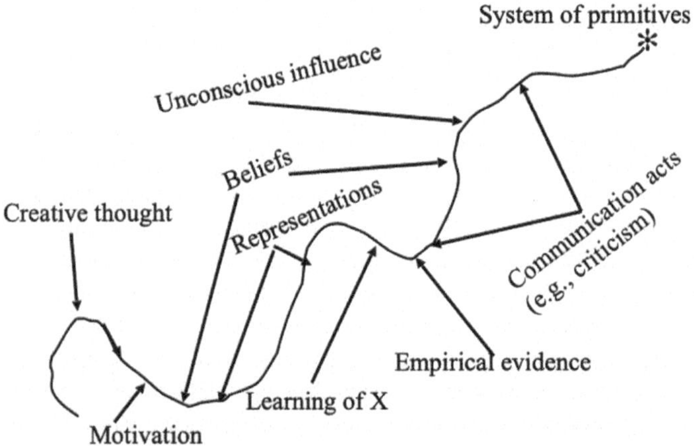

Fig. 4.1 The process of understanding: End result and the major processes and factors influencing it. (Revised from Gelepithis 2005). The order of illustrative types of events is not indicative

Some scientists may consider that learning is treated inadequately in this monograph. Although it is true that the topic of learning is central to AI, Psychology, education and allied fields, it is at best peripheral to the unification of AI and Psychology.

Learning can be significant for the development of mind. But, all learning (barring some self-taught processes) requires an element of communication and all such learning theories involve implicitly or explicitly communication theories. The latter are inextricable linked to theories of understanding. In this clear sense at least, learning is subservient to understanding (e.g., Gelepithis & Goodfellow 1992). Nevertheless, one particular remark has to be made as it is related to Gordon Pask's conversation theory referred to earlier. It is the work of Thomas & Harri-Augstein (1985). Their work argues for learners to take control of their learning process and assists them in building up a repertoire of techniques to that end. Their work is related in opposition to that of Pask, as they rightly consider Pask's approach too formal for their own conception of self-organised learning. In addition, the authors elaborate significantly Kelly's repertory-grid technique developed by Kelly as part of his theory of personal constructs (Kelly 1955).

Nevertheless, all this work is at best peripheral to the theory of communication and understanding developed in this book. And, it is peripheral because it stops short of providing a combined theory of communication and understanding that is necessary for tackling in depth the alternative construction held and developed by people in their lives. From the perspective of the TNS, personal constructs are seen as belief systems (Sect. 3.2.2).

Finally, it should be noted that self-organised learning (Harri-Augstein & Thomas 2001 and 2008) is related but clearly distinct from the notion of understanding as defined within the TNS. Specifically, self-organised learning lacks the directionality and specific type of end result (primitives or/and premisses) characterising both maximum and rudimentary understanding. Self-organised learning is characterised by "the conversational construction, reconstruction and exchange of personally significant relevant and viable meanings with awareness and controlled purposiveness." (Anonymous reviewer). According to this clear definition, self- organised learning restricts restructuring to "personally significant relevant and viable meanings", in sharp contrast to the objective elements (at least at the species level) introduced by the CUP system. For instance, as I have already noted earlier, scientific theories contain primitives outside the realm of traditional biological evolution. Potentially, more significant is the case of theories developed with the help of robot or AI systems.

I want to finish off this subsection on learning with a remark on its relation to conversational science (Harri-Augstein & Thomas 2001 and 2008). The latter offers a humanistic approach to science based on the theory of self-organised learning. This is a very welcome approach but it needs to be augmented in several ways. Their specification falls outside the remits of this book. Nevertheless, I should note the relation between conversational science and the TNS approach and theory developed in this two-volume monograph. In a nutshell, the development of TNS takes into account a component missing from conversational science, namely, H-artificiality. This is a crucial omission with far-reaching ramifications and consequences as it is evidenced in this two-volume monograph. Conversational science is characterised by a traditional evolutionary approach in contrast to TNS's version of the EES hypothesis (Sect. 2.1) that incorporates the component of H-artificiality.

Emotions and interest are two phenomena that are usually neglected or tacitly assumed without further ado. Both strongly influence understanding; their duration and corresponding effects usually vary. Emotions are treated in the Consequences- volume of this monograph. Although communication is not a necessary part of understanding quite often plays a significant role. This is especially the case when an individual wants to broaden or deepen its conception of a particular topic. Such an endeavour nearly inexorably brings in other viewpoints that need to be understood and the process of synthesising such different understandings can require acts of communication. Beliefs (chapter-3) and representations (chapter-2) are themselves complex socio-biological phenomena. Representations in particular can be quite complex artificial constructs like KRR formalisms. Beliefs, usually unconsciously, affect one's understanding through culturally ingrained assumptions. Artificial representation techniques and schemes, existing in abundance in science, affect one's understanding in subtle ways. The influence of language on an individual's understanding is mostly indirect through its well documented influence on human thought and thinking. Motivation, creative thought, empirical evidence and unconscious influences are well known for their affect on individual understanding. Knowledge of their mechanisms does not seem to be in near sight.

I move now to the complexity of the end result of understanding. As we saw above understanding may be *advanced* (i.e., ending into a systems of primitives) or it may be ***rudimentary*** (i.e., ending into an individual's system of preference beliefs). There is an interesting distinction to be made between advanced and rudimentary understanding. On the one hand, the former takes longer to reached than the latter. On the other hand, advanced understanding is less complex than its rudimentary cousin. Because of its relative simplicity my focus in this book is ***advanced*** understanding. In addition, because of considerable similarities between the two cases, the reader may find it interesting to consider the case of ***rudimentary*** understanding and draw differences and further similarities between the two systems.

Let me now proceed with the analysis of advanced understanding. In this case, Definition-29H is cast in terms of "a system of human primitives". It follows that an H may have understood a particular topic in terms of several different systems of primitives. Such systems may be of their own, of someone else's or of a school of thought (established or not). In relation to reasoning, it is widely recognised how easy it is for someone to reason to different conclusions from those of her fellow if their two reference belief systems are different. Please note that above I dropped the use of the qualificatory adjective 'advanced'. In what follows, I will keep the same simplifying practice whenever there is no risk of misunderstanding.

But what meanings count as immediate (definition-30)? Could the set of human primitives be specified? The answer that follows is partly based on Gelepithis (1984). Suppose we are asked to classify the words set, electron, water, pain, and electricity in either one of the following two mutually exclusive sets: (i) the set of primitives P; (ii) its complementary P′.

It seems natural to *me* to place set in P, and electron in P′. What about water and pain? Upon reflection, a lot of people would place water in P′; since water (H2O) is analysable to its constituents parts and these in their turn to electrons (among other similar types of entities). Still, I can think of no one who would not place water in P! Moreover, set and water are two quite different types of primitives. Set is a primitive for a mathematician whereas water is a primitive to anyone and a non-primitive to those with some basic knowledge of chemistry. Therefore, water can be treated as both a primitive and non-primitive by some people depending on their age and education. It will also remain a primitive to others throughout their lives (e.g., my grandmother). Actually, what may be a primitive for someone may be part of a very complicated theory for another (e.g., the quantum theory of water). Coming to pain now, it might seem obvious to everybody that pain should be put in P. Nevertheless, research on pain has produced increasingly sophisticated models of pain (e.g., Dennett 1978; Eisenberger 2015). It follows that one should put pain in the set of P′. Still, having reached the conclusion that:

> "Pain is a multidimensional experience, involving systematic changes in both cognition and emotion: painful stimuli elicit anxiety, capture attention, and motivate action." (Shackman et al. 2015).

hardly makes the case for abandoning the common sense placement of 'pain' in P.[5] My final example is 'electricity'. It can be a primitive for a toddler but it is not a primitive for an electrician or quantum physicist. This is a clear example of age- and knowledge-dependent word that changes its status from primitive to non-primitive.

So, my first conclusion is that primitives are individual- and age-specific. As a result, there is no single definite set of ***individual*** human primitives.

Second, they are also knowledge-, culture-, and species-specific. As an example of cultural primitives consider the host–guest relationship. In India and Hellas for instance, when a potential host invites a potential guest with an expression like 'come at any time', she expects such an invitation to be taken literally. Interestingly, if the recipient is an outsider from, say, the Anglo-Saxon culture such an invitation will definitely not be taken literally but simply interpreted as a kind of friendly invitation. Finally, with respect to species specificity, smile seems to be a primitive of humans and of some other primate species only.

Third, primitives (being a special kind of concepts), inherit all the properties that the latter are characterised by. For instance, they are distinguished into pre- linguistic, speech and WHuLa classes of primitives (cf, the distinct classes of concepts depicted in Fig. 2.4 (Sect. 2.3.3). This distinction opens up a large area of study including the topics of theoretical entities and expressions with sole referent their N_m. The former topic is related to minimum vocabularies and the analytic- synthetic distinction. The latter is part of psychiatric disorders and their studies. More widely, communication as we defined it is distinctly related to the notion of 'good' communication used in psychiatry (e.g., Priebe et al. 2011;

[5] Recent definitions of pain (e.g., Raja et al. 2020) not withstanding.

Ditton-Phare et al. 2015). Although, this topic is clearly beyond the scope of this two-volume monograph, I believe that our model can be quite useful in clinical psychiatric practice.

Let me move into a fourth important point. The fact that the meanings of the elements of a system of primitives are immediate does not imply that they are necessarily atomic (i.e., not able to be split into simpler ones). Of course, sense primitives (i.e., qualia), basic emotions, and words that stand for sense primitives or basic emotions are atomic. All other words are composite to start with. They may be primitives for some people and reducible to simpler ones for others. It depends on the knowledge of each person. A consequence of this point is that the membership of a system of primitives can change with time. A human may split some of the elements of her own $\prod(H, \theta, t)$ into simpler ones or she may actually abandon some. An important special case of a $\prod(H, \theta, t)$ modification is observed in some cases of conceptual change (e.g., Vosniadou & Verschaffel 2004).

A fifth point is that the TNS allows acquired primitives in contrast to Fodor's (1994) strongly innatist account according to which primitives are inherited as part of the structure of the brain. Of course, only linguistic primitives can be acquired.

Sixth, systems of $\prod(H, \theta, t)$ are not in accordance with either Fodor's (1983) modularity thesis or Tooby and Cosmides (1992) massive modularity one. Contra Fodor, systems of $\prod(H, \theta, t)$ are interrelated via thinking or understanding and therefore not encapsulated. Contra massive modularity, a large number of $\prod(H, \theta, t)$ systems are ontogenetically specific and therefore not adaptations.

Seventh, a $\prod(H, \theta, t)$ system is fundamentally different from formal systems of primitives like those identified with pixels or curves (see Schyns et al. 1998 for a discussion).

Eighth, primitives vary both ontogenetically and phylogenetically. Variation during an individual's lifetime presupposes substantial broadening or/and deepening of that individual's belief-horizons, emotions, and overall knowledge. As such a system of primitives for a particular human, a particular group, social group, or humanity at a particular point in time may well be seen as a stepping stone, for that particular entity in his/her/its evolutionary development.

Finally, since primitives are meanings, a $\prod(H, \theta, t)$ is a subsystem of M.

Moreover their characteristics imply that they are quite diverse and diffuse systems of M. This claim is in accordance with fMRI results of brain's semantic organisation (Bookheimer 2002).

In summary, the above analysis of the notion of primitives shows that two of the three variables, H and θ, of $\prod(H, \theta, t)$ are extremely complex. Specifically, H biologically depends on her ontogenetic development and its phylogenetic evolution; societally, depends on his knowledge and culture; and finally depends on her environment. The complexity of the second of the compound variables, θ, is of a different sort. The history of H. sapiens may better characterised by the qualitative and quantitative increase of the range of topics, θ, that humans undertake to investigate or are interested in investigating, rather than its current instantiations in terms of wars and political intrigue. θ is of course directly related to the development of *Homo* science and technology as well as our species enrichment of artistic life and broadening of our weltanschauung from geo- and anthropo-centric viewpoint to an eventually universal one.

Jointly, the H and θ variables determine an evolving, multi-dimensional space of primitives for H. sapiens. Such a space is very closely related to the quest for a unified *Homo* science. Their direct link is the notion of minimum vocabularies introduced in Sect. 1.3. Their difference lies with the fact that "a 'minimum vocabulary' is one in which no word can be defined in terms of the others." (Russell, 1961, p. 45), whereas a system of primitives may well include words that can be defined in terms of others. In other words any minimum vocabulary is a system of primitives but not the other way around. And as Bertrand Russell notes:

> "the whole of any science can be expressed by means of a minimum vocabulary for that science." (ibid.).

I have to add that Russell's conviction is not held by all scientists. I stand within the camp of those scientists that work to demonstrate that Russell's conviction is true.

In connection to science, it is noteworthy that systems of primitives or even minimum vocabularies for a particular domain of investigation may give rise to a 'preferred' minimum vocabulary in that particular domain or at least to a 'preferred' system of primitives. By 'preferred' I mean one that provides deeper explanations and/or wider range of predictions than the original. A well-known example of an early minimum vocabulary is that of the Ionian philosophers for describing the world in terms of a few elements (fire, water, earth, air) and the subsequent development of the 'preferred' atomic and particle physics vocabulary.

To conclude my discussion on primitives, there are three points to be kept in mind. First, the relation from systems of primitives through minimum vocabularies to disciplinary, interdisciplinary and eventually H-science unification. Second, the evolving nature of the system of *H. sapiens* primitives and to a lesser extent of those of individual humans. Both are due to the ever expanding body of knowledge of both individual humans and our species. The rather obvious relation of human knowledge to the processes of understanding and communication is addressed in the next chapter. Third, a fundamental similarity among primitive systems across the biological world. I develop this point in the next section where I also discuss the relation among human, robotic, and ARE primitive systems.

Let me now present my justification for the proposed theory of understanding. First, it provides necessary and sufficient conditions for human understanding which:

(a) capture the fact that understanding always involve the grasp of meaning; (b) capture the process nature of understanding; (c) capture the two most significant aspects of the analytic tradition, namely, (c_1) systematicity (since understanding involves a sequence of steps; although neither necessarily formal nor necessarily conscious); and (c_2) the requirements of context and motivation as contributing factors in human understanding; (d) are not in conflict with the hermeneutic approach in cases of completely unconscious understanding.

Second, it does not violate our common sense of understanding as described by most dictionaries and encyclopaedias (e.g., Oxford, Longman, Britannica) and used in both scientific and vernacular language.

Third, understanding and therefore communication can operate across both the conscious/unconscious divide and the pre-linguistic, speech and WHuLa stages of human evolution providing the deep and complexly integrated characteristic of human behaviour. It should be noted, in case it is not immediately obvious that conscious understanding can be quite effortful (because of the complexity of the $\prod(H, \theta, t)$ that is required to be specified) and may take considerable amount of time depending on the topic.

Fourth, it naturalises a key part of the process of human understanding by making the end result of it empirically investigable. This may well happen through primitives-based descriptions. I consider brain imaging an impossible means for the empirical investigation of scientific understanding. On the other hand, for completely unconscious understanding processes brain imaging may be useful.

Fifth, the integrative character of understanding seems to be in accordance with the integrative character of the brain. This remark is most clearly seen to be applicable to memory research. As we saw in Sect. 3.3.1, the primary brain structures responsible for lasting meanings and concepts are the LTM structures (follows from the MMP). This is in full accordance with the increasing tendency in memory research to talk of the restructuring 'characteristic' of memory (e.g., Kandel et al. 2014; Ofengenden 2014). I expect that relating such results with a human's system of primitives should provide exciting results. In contrast to the above remark, the following one is rather speculative. Specifically, one may claim that the context dependence of the end result of understanding in the form of $\prod(H, \theta, t)$ is in accordance with the context-related functions of the right hemisphere while the process nature of it seems to be in accordance with the left one (Bookheimer 2002). Although I am responsible for making this second remark, I am quite skeptical of the implied differentiation between left and right brain hemispheres.

Sixth, jointly, the processes of communication and understanding structure *Homo sapiens* knowledge.[6] Specifically, each and every terminated process of advanced understanding, through its $\prod(H, \theta, t)$ structures and modifies to some extent the semantic structures and space of mental phenomena of an individual human. Here the reader should keep in mind that similar results more often happen in the case of rudimentary understanding. An instance of this restructuring has been shown as a result of the very close relation between understanding and explanation characterising the communication between learners and tutors (Gelepithis and Goodfellow 1992). And, also, the pivotal characteristic of understanding in the knowledge nexus provides support for its role in explaining the integrative nature of phenomena like surprise (Foster & Keane 2015). Finally, the iterative use of the communication and understanding processes explains the inseparability of the individual and collective aspects of human knowledge. This enables one to demonstrate the mistake of the presumed objective-subjective divide.

[6] For a novel conception of *Homo* knowledge and its far-ranging consequences see Gelepithis (2024b, Chapter-2).

Seventh, the proposed theory can be straightforwardly generalised to any animal taxon (see next section). Appropriate taxon primitives can contribute to the design of methodologies that are less biased in favour of humans, thus addressing Emery & Clayton's (2008) important design requirement of cognitive tests.

Eighth, since understanding depends on *one's* own primitives, its end result may well vary very significantly from person to person depending on the $\prod(H, \theta, t)$ used by each person on a particular topic. As a result a human's ***advanced*** understanding of a particular topic is in terms of a minimum vocabulary for that topic and human.

Ninth, the combination of definitions 28H and 29H and the associated analysis of human primitives cover all types of understanding determined by the four quadrants. In particular it covers the cognitive-hermeneutic quadrant whenever immediate understanding is involved.

Tenth, genuine understanding of a topic (θ) by two humans H1 and H2 does not imply that H1 and H2 can communicate. This result holds true in general between any noémon entities able to understand something. It follows from the nature of $\prod(H, \theta, t)$.

Eleventh, human understanding can be formal (when it is expressed in purely linguistic terms), and it is informal in all other cases. The latter consequence follows from the existence of sense primitives and the relation between sense, speech and WHuLa primitives. I will make use of this result in the next section when addressing the issue of robotic understanding and communication.

Twelfth, the rudimentary and advanced types of understanding specified earlier are not the only types of understanding possible. Actually, there can be a number of different types each corresponding to the particular 'depth' an individual's understanding ends up. The 'depth' of such an understanding can be specified as the number of primitives involved in a system of premises. It can vary from zero primitives corresponding to the most rudimentary type of understanding, to the most advanced type of understanding characterised by the minimum possible number of primitives coupled with zero premises. In accordance with this point, one can see that the process of understanding may well help in identifying further steps required in order to deepen one's understanding. In this sense, the process of human understanding is like a compass.

Thirteenth, by now the reader may well be tempted to agree with the presented TNS theory of communication, but she may be worried by the apparent lack of verifiability. To start with, one can easily verify, the *process* of human understanding is independent of both the individual understander and of time. This does not contradict the fact that the *end result* of complete-understanding of any noémon system does depend on the individual understander, the phenomenon under consideration and the period that it happens. In other words, the process of human understanding, regardless of the extreme variability of $\prod$(NoS, θ, t), invariably ends up into *a* system of primitives. I therefore propose that the process of human understanding is an invariance of qualitative structure of historic *H. sapiens* psychology. And this could be verified (see also the verifiability remarks I made in Sect. 3.2).

It is worth noting that the proposed invariance of the human understanding process does not imply that it is a characteristic of human nature in the sense employed by evolutionary psychologists (e.g., Tooby and Cosmides 1992). For human understanding is not a developmental program. It is a complex brain process affected by both ontogenetic, cultural and environmental factors.

Could the proposed invariance look firmly at the face of well known human regularities? If yes, could it the generalised process of understanding, introduced in the next section, be accepted as a qualitative invariance of the space of noémon systems? In other words, the question is: could this kind of complex neural process be generalised so that it becomes a NoS-law of qualitative structure? An answer to this question requires first to inquire on the generalisability of the process of human communication to a NoS-wide notion of communication. These three related questions constitute the topic of the following section.

I grasp the opportunity here to add a brief comment in relation to the recent trend for replication studies across both the natural (e.g., Lash & Vandenbroucke 2012) and social sciences (e.g., Crandall & Sherman 2016; Fiala et al. 2022) and references cited there). If such efforts are taken as trying to standardise science in its widest sense, they run the risk of either failing or stifling the blossoming of some research seeds.

4.3 Scope and Limits

Sections 4.1 and 4.2 reviewed the literature on the fundamental sociobiological processes of human understanding and communication and extended the TNS by developing theoretical constructs for both of them for the human case. In this section we:

(a) discuss the possibility of extending the theory of human understanding and communication to other classes of S (e.g., nonhuman noémon species, AISs, and robots).;
(b) conclude that the process of understanding is an invariance of qualitative structure for the full space of noémon systems (Sect. 1.2); and
(c) introduce three levels of law generality for noémon systems phenomena and tabulate a number of regularities and qualitative invariances in terms of these three levels.

It should be noted that to delineate (let alone discuss) the major known classes of noémon systems that are capable of the processes of understanding and communication is a major problem requiring a lot of empirical work to be carried out. Such work will also considerably contribute to clarification of the multiple relations among the *pivotal* system of notions of S (Sect. 1.3/C-1).

To proceed with such an investigation we need appropriate definitions for the classes of noémon systems considered as well as for the members of S in general. As it will be seen our initial system of definitions 28–30 will only need to be modified slightly with respect to their format. That simplifies presentation and does not necessitate definitions for all the classes considered. The general definition for noémon systems and the definition for the animalia taxon should be adequate. The reader can easily obtain similar definitions for any class of noémon systems. Some care in the wording of definitions for an arbitrary class can be met by a couple of clarificatory remarks following the said definitions. We start with the system of definitions for an arbitrary NoS followed by the sequential introduction of the definitions for animal understanding and communication as the need arises. I chose animals because it includes humans and we shall be able to draw a further crucial difference between historic *H. sapiens* and other animal species.

Definition-28NoS A specific noémon system, NoS1, has communicated with NoS2 on a topic θ if, and only if:

(a) NoS1 has understood θ -symbol: U (NoS1, θ);
(b) NoS2 has understood θ -symbol: U (NoS2, θ);
(c) U (NoS1, θ) is output by NoS1 and understood by NoS2; and
(d) U (NoS2, θ) is output by NoS2 and understood by NoS1.

Definition-29NoS A noémon system, NoS, has understood something, θ, iff NoS can think of θ in terms of a system of primitives (symbol: ∏(NoS, θ, t), or *a* system of premises.

Definition-30NoS π is a primitive *of/for* a NoS if and only if the meaning of π is immediate *of/for* that NoS.

For simplicity of presentation and ease of comparison I retained the same serial number as that for the human definitional system of communication and understanding while replacing the subscript for an individual human H (e.g., $^{\mathsf{I}}\mathsf{A}$ for individual I of a particular animal species A, B for bacteria, *R* for robots, etc.). The key difference between the H and the general NoS systems of definitions concerns the definition of 'understanding'. In the former case the definition is given in terms of *a* system of *human* primitives or *human* premises. In the latter, the definition is given in terms of *a* system of *own* primitives or premises. The difference is crucial. The notions human primitives or premises incorporate the notion of 'own'. Neither of the generalised notions of primitives or premises incorporate the notion of 'own'. In other words, a NoS may understand a θ in terms of its own 'primitives or premises' or in terms of 'primitives or premises' that are not its own. The classical example is an AIS. The aforepointed difference is reflected in the use of the disjunctive construction of/ for in definition-30NoS (see also remark following definition-29H). The differences between human 'primitives' and 'premises' and the corresponding types of ***advanced*** and ***rudimentary*** human understanding are discussed in Sect. 4.2. The generalisation from 'human primitives or premises' to NoS-level 'primitives or premises' is straightforward and is omitted here. Whether animal primitives and animal premises can be distinguished as clearly as in the case of humans will be partly addressed below and, in general, is an open issue.

Let me now come to the notion of animal understanding that is the constitutive process of animal communication. The former's definition will both clarify further the above distinction and illustrate the diversity of the evolutionary process. The process of animal communication will be introduced later in discussing communication between noémon systems. For reasons stated in the previous section and they are also applicable here, I will focus on primitives.

Definition-29$^{\mathsf{I}}\mathbf{A}$ An $^{\mathsf{I}}\mathsf{A}$, at time t, has understood something, θ, if and only if, $^{\mathsf{I}}\mathsf{A}$ can think of θ in terms of *a* system of animal primitives that depend on $^{\mathsf{I}}\mathsf{A}$, θ, and t (symbol ∏($^{\mathsf{I}}\mathsf{A}$, θ, t).

Definition-30$^{\prime}$A π is a primitive of ^{I}A if and only if the meaning *of* π is immediate for ^{I}A.

The point that should be stressed here concerns definition-30^{I}A. In contrast to both definition-30H and definition-30NoS, the definition of animal primitives uses exclusively 'of'. In other words, animal primitives characterise the particular NoS that instantiates definition-30^{I}A and that identifies the corresponding particular representation system of the instantiated NoS. Animal representational systems differ markedly between taxa and possibly between species of the same genus. Bats, spiders and octopuses are obvious examples of representational diversity among taxa and *Homo* is an extremely interesting case of genus diversification. The above remarks bring us naturally to the next question.

Definition-29^{I}A is characterised by the theoretical construct $\prod(^{I}A, \theta, t)$. In what ways do animal primitive systems differ from, or they are similar to, the $\prod(H, \theta, t)$? At the very least, classes like aves, Cephalopoda, mammalia, and insects do possess systems of sense primitives that can be used for a variety of mental phenomena including thinking. Therefore, at this class-level of biological organisation, there should be at least this type of nonhuman animal understanding. For clarity and brevity reasons I call it sensorial animal understanding. It is actually quite similar to human sensorial understanding. Their differences stem from the differing range of senses characterising each taxon as well as the varied extent of a particular sense for a certain species. Sensorial animal understanding should be quite extensive within the animal kingdom.

Although animal thinking can be either conscious or unconscious animal reasoning and hence understanding can only be conscious. This imposes a restriction on the class of understanding noémon systems. Animal understanding is further restricted whenever communication is also practiced among conspecifics. Here we have a first difference between human and animal understanding. The latter involves the two types we just distinguished, the former also involves at least WHuLa-based understanding in addition to the other two types. There is also possibility for a fourth category of human understanding. It will be the case if and when it is beyond doubt demonstrated that even the stronger animal communication systems fall short of human speech. In summary, there are two types of animal understanding and at least three types of human understanding. This implies considerably more interesting research work for comparative psychology.

Animalia-wide primitives or primitive animal appetites (e.g., Rolls 1999) seem to include hunger, thirst, and lust (at least in the sense of reproduction motivation). Such primitives may well be related to basic emotional primitives required for the faculty based approach to human emotions. Finally, it should be noted that non- human animals (e.g., bats, dolphins, aves) are born with their own system of sense primitives and therefore it should not be impossible that some animals may have developed a different system of basic emotions from that claimed to exist for humans.

Could sensorial understanding be a trait outside the Eukarea domain, or of the non-animal kingdoms, or at least of the animal kingdom in general? I do not know. Evolution ensures at least a few common primitives across all living forms (e.g., survival and reproduction; cf, definition-14b). Along these lines, biological thinking should be quite wide spread and may be argued to include proto-thinking like simple reflex arcs. Animal reasoning though is a very different story (cf, Sect. 3. 2). Therefore, sensorial animal understanding seems to be constrained to relative complex organisms possessing nervous systems.

Even if sensorial animal understanding is established to characterise only the above four aforementioned classes of animals, it can be quite revealing. This follows from the key differentiating factor of sensorial animal understanding, namely, the range of objects and phenomena that it is applicable to. This range (symbol, θ), varies depending on the number of senses and their associated sensitivities comprising the sensory system of a species and therefore of its corresponding system of primitives. Sensorial animal (including humans) understanding should be found to be both similar and different among species. Now to the key, unique, difference between human and animal understanding.

The $\prod(H, \theta, t)$ may contain linguistic primitives that did not exist before the appearance of WHuLa (Sect. 2.3.3). Whenever this is the case the corresponding human linguistic understanding is fundamentally different even from human sensorial understanding and, a fortiori, any other form of sensorial understanding. A good example illustrating WHuLa-based understanding is a scientific theory (e.g., gravitational theory, DNA sequencing theory, plate tectonics).

In conclusion, nonhuman animals possess one type of understanding, namely, sensorial understanding, while humans possess the additional ability of WHuLa-based theoretic understanding that may involve even unobserved theoretical constructs. The potential complexity of sensorial animal understanding is an open issue. For instance, even for the classes of mammals, aves, Cephalopoda and insects sensorial understanding can be very limited. This limitation is indeed the case when a $\prod(A, \theta, t)$ is identified with a system of discrete θs each of which is further identified with a discrete primitive. For instance, three discrete calls corresponding to the predators 'eagle', 'leopard', and 'snake' for a primate species (Egnor et al. 2004) can easily be identified with three discrete primitives. So, primates have at least a 'flat' system of primitives. By 'flat' I mean having a 'depth' of one (1) step. Where, the depth of a system of primitives I take it to be measurable in terms of the steps required for the process of advanced understanding to reach it. It is very likely that at least Primates and Aves have deeper systems of primitives caused by relatively complex systems of communication. Humans, for instance, have systems of primitives at three levels of complexity (sensorial, oral, and written language). In general, a $\prod(NoS, \theta, t)$ may be instantiated at several levels of complexity depending on the complexity of their communication system.

The next point of our discussion on noémon systems understanding concerns the cases of robots and possible AREs.

Robots (and the wider class of AISs), by design, are only capable of formal interaction. In other words they are only capable of processing uninterpreted systems of information and appropriately represented human knowledge (e.g., in terms of any of the various KRR systems developed in AI). I had pointed out the nature of this limitation over thirty years ago as well as the possible emergence of AREs:

> "But of course, this limitation is only a human limitation. Machines may themselves develop their own premises through their own use of sensors and processing capabilities that we initially provided them with. This possibility may sound remote but we have no reasons to believe that it is impossible. Indeed, it is logically sound and in accordance with at least one of our theories for the emergence of human intelligence.
>
> It follows that one should distinguish between 'machine understanding' in terms of un-interpreted human premises, what one should really call 'machine-executed human understanding'; and machine understanding in terms of machine premises that humans may not necessarily know about. Similarly, one should distinguish between machine-exhibited human intelligence and machine intelligence proper. The former is already with us; the latter may well be too." (Gelepithis 1991, p. 266).

In the much broader context of this monograph we have distinguished between robots and possible AREs and we have suggested certain prerequisites for the development of the latter in compatibility with the limits of human constructability (Sect. 2.2). In this and all chapters in Gelepithis (2024b), we consider both robots and possible AREs within the context of each individual chapter. Figure 4.2 summarises our discussion of the different key types of NoS-understanding.

With respect to Robot understanding the key element, that is usually ignored, is that any robot's sensory system and therefore sensorial understanding is eventually based on KRR formalisms that provide the robot's underlying reasoning. The non- sensorial robot understanding is fundamentally identical in kind with formalised human understanding. Nevertheless, there is a quantitative difference in favour of robot understanding. It is in this sense that we talk of enhanced, human-based, formal understanding of robots (Fig. 4.2). Concerning AREs the important point to be kept in mind is that they will indeed develop their *own*-understanding in case an R_0 emerges. The latter possibility is discussed in Sect. 2.2.

On the basis of the above analysis, one is justified to claim invariance for the NoS-wide understanding (definition-29NoS). All of the points

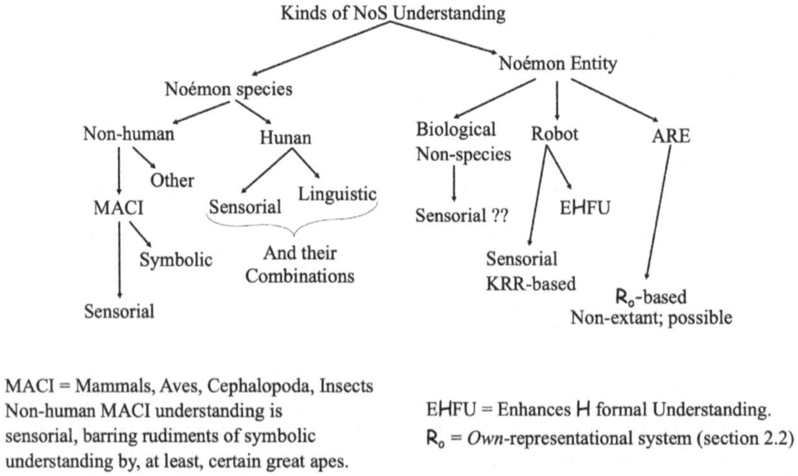

Fig. 4.2 Kinds of noémon systems understanding (see text for details)

supporting the human invariance claim and not depended on nervous systems are directly generalisable for the NoS-wide understanding.

Since an invariance is a kind of law, it would be interesting to compare the various kinds of understanding invariances to some well-known human regularities and laws of qualitative structure in terms of a law's range of applicability. Table 4.3 associates descriptions of some well known laws to the three types of laws distinguished on the basis of their range of applicability in Sect. 1.3/C-4.

I move now to the issue of communication and focus on some of the major similarities and differences between human and nonhuman processes of communication.

Table 4.4 summarises the key points concerning the scope and limits of communication among certain selected classes of noémon systems. In what follows I provide some further details and make some additional remarks.

Table 4.3 Selected examples of Laws of noémon systems

Description	*Type*
Power law of practice (Snoddy 1926)	Confirmed S_H- wide law (human invariance). Possibly applicable to other biological species
Hebb's law (Hebb 1949)	Confirmed S_C-wide law for several animalia classes
Fitts' Law (Fitts 1954)	Confirmed S_H- wide law (human invariance)
STM constraint (Miller 1956; Cowan 2000)	Confirmed S_H- wide law (human invariance)
(PSSH): The Physical Symbol Systems Hypothesis (Newell & Simon 1976)	Proposed S-wide law (qualitative)
Computer systems hierarchy (Newell 1990)	Confirmed S_{AIS}—wide law (Von Neumann architecture)
Constraints of human neural architecture	Confirmed S_H- wide law (human invariance). Extension to an Animalia-wide law possible
Principle of Noémon Systems (PriNS)	Proposed S-wide law (qualitative). See discussion of the relation between PSSH and PriNS in Sect. 2.1
The understanding process	Proposed S-wide law (qualitative). Empirically testable consequences for, at least, biological species

Table 4.4 Communication: Remarks on its scope and limits

Communication among	*Remarks*
Humans	Communication is in general possible. Limitations are due to substantial knowledge differences, belief systems and some pathologies
Humans–Mammals	Partial sensorial communication with some mammals (e.g., dogs). Partial linguistic communication with great apes species
Humans–AISs or robots	Communication impossible (Gelepithis 1984, 1991); *formal interaction* possible
Humans–ARE (should they may emerge)	Above comment applies and additionally the communication gap on the basis of ARE's and humans *own*-understandings will increase
Robots and AISs	Human-based formal interaction. Results can be better than the corresponding formal interaction between humans
Robots or AISs–ARE	Human-based formal interaction; Communication might be developed
ARE–ARE	Unknown-to-humans type of communication possible
Archaea	Mutualist and commensalist interactions
Bacteria	Quorum sensing type of interaction Mutualist, commensalist, and parasitic interactions

See text for details and further remarks. AREs are not extant noémon systems; Yet, their existence is possible (see Sect. 2.2).

I start with the issue of communication between animals. For ease of reference let me state the definition of that type of communication and note that our earlier discussion concerning the diversity of animal representational systems is of outmost importance for the possibility of communication between animal taxa. In other words, communication between different animal species is both constrained by the diversity of animal representational systems and facilitated by the continuity of the evolutionary process. In addition, the differences between human and animal understandings should be kept in mind. It follows that the earlier general definition of NoS-communication, eventually, differs significantly from the following definition of animal communication.

Definition-28$_A$ An individual member I1 of a particular animal species A (^{I1}A) has communicated with ^{I2}A on a topic θ if, and only if:

(a) ^{I1}A has understood θ -symbol: U (^{I1}A, θ);
(b) ^{I2}A has understood θ -symbol: U (^{I2}A, θ);
(c) U (^{I1}A, θ) is output by ^{I1}A and understood ^{I2}A; and
(d) U (^{I2}A, θ is output by ^{I2}A and understood by ^{I1}A.

It can easily be seen that the differentiating factor between the two definitions are the animal taxon constraint and through that the range θ and the corresponding system of primitives that, in general, differs from species to species. It is indeed obvious that the same type of differentiating factor applies for communication among any other type of noémon system.

Before proceeding I should make clear the relation between our definition of animal communication and those of Maynard Smith & Harper (2003) and Bradbury & Vehrencamp (2020). Their similarity is that all three definitions are grounded on meaning. Nevertheless, both Maynard Smith & Harper and Bradbury & Vehrencamp do not provide an overall theory of meaning as we do. The key difference between their definitions and mine is that the process of understanding is implicit in their conceptions in sharp contrast with its explicit and complete specification of it in my definition. It should also be noted that animal communication is usually centred around signalling theory (e.g., Maynard Smith & Harper 2003; Weaver et al. 2017) and in particular on whether a signal is honest or not (e.g., Johnstone 1999; Blount et al. 2009; Számadó et al. 2019).

The case of interspecies communication and, in general, communication between different types of noémon systems is quite complicated.

Overall, as we saw in Sect. 4.1, animal species communicate by means of diverse behavioural patterns including odours, electric discharges, vocal sounds, facial expressions, dances, and pointing—among others. This diversity is realised by a correspondingly wide range of primitive systems limited only by the lack of a *WHuLa-kind* of primitives. Of course, this is a severe restriction. Nonhuman animal communication is, consequently, substantially restricted by the comparatively very limited range of θ that can be signalled about through a sense-based primitives system. An interesting difference between human and animal communication is that animal communicators are not able to agree to disagree. In intraspecies communication, the range of θ spans the type of food, other survival situations like warning of predators, and mating concerns including evaluation of potential mates. In complex species the range of θ includes breeding conditions, displays of aggression, submission, and threat.

In interspecies interactions mating concerns, and survival in the form of mutualist, commensalist, and amensalist systems fail to fulfil the conditions of communication. They are mere interactions of mutual benefit. In contrast, the existence of animal sensorial communication between different species, by means of emotions, seems to have been done and dusted; at least for the particular case of human–dog communication. Albuquerque et al. (2016) have answered it to the affirmative without having left much room for disagreement. The important question now is how does interspecies communication of emotions does happen. Can there be any other basis apart from that of expressed emotions? If not, then the case for basic universal types of emotions is strengthened considerably.

So far we have considered in very general terms the conditions of communication concerning non-human biological noémon systems. In the rest of this section, I want to:

(1) Very briefly comment on the work on *interaction* among AISs, robots, and humans;
(2) Very briefly remark on the work on *communication* between humans on the one hand and AISs or robots on the other; and
(3) State a couple of remarks on the *possible* relation between historic *H. sapiens* and AREs with respects to the contents of this chapter.

The first issue is technically challenging and societally extremely complicated. A few words on both follow. With the increasing use of robots and AISs in diverse fields of social life the issue of interaction among them as well as between them and humans is of central importance and technically both challenging well attended (e.g., Ching et al. 2018; Armitage & Kaindl 2020; Stokes et al. 2020). My first comment in relation to HRI (Human–Robot Interaction) is that the necessary and fundamental work on ethical and legal issues is lagging behind despite efforts to that end (e.g., Boden et al. 2011*2017; Deng 2015; Delvaux 2016; Kerbe 2016; Crawford et al. 2019; Tzachor et al. 2020; Verheij 2020). My second point applies to the whole of AI, although probably it is more pronounced within the HRI community. It concerns the way humanity faces, develops and disseminates the AI objectives and enterprise but need to be at least aired. To this end it is encouraging that certain leading learned societies and universities started addressing the AI narratives (e.g., The Royal Society, see Cave et al. 2018). The way AI is perceived and portrayed in the West and particularly the English-speaking part of it is to a large extent mistaken and counterproductive in the long term. A case at point is the work on social and communicative robots. It is amazing that all such work (e.g., Williams et al. 2015; Hoorn 2018; Guzman & Lewis 2020; Hepp 2020) avoids tackling any of the foundational questions in (robot) communication. Even a Frontiers Research Topic with the grand title *Investigating Human Nature and Communication Through Robots* fails to discuss any of the many related foundational issues in any of the ten papers that constitute it (Nishio et al. eds 2017). Finally, it should be realised by the AI community that it is not enough to avoid using communication and essentially renaming it interaction. A lot of useful and very challenging work remains to be done on the latter. The former delineates limits that should be understood and respected. Formal interactions are devoid of any kind of meaning, communication is inextricably linked to meanings.

With respect to the second issue I only want to re-state an earlier argument of mine in recent terminology. So, here it is in a nutshell. Human-robotic communication requires mutual understanding. The latter requires the sharing of primitives between robots and humans. Sense primitives for robots need to be build. That can be done by providing them with sensors. Formalised linguistic primitives for robots can incorporated in robot design by the use of KRR systems. The problem is that built sensors could not provide interpretation because they are formal by design. Similarly, formalised linguistic primitives lack meaning. Since a Turing machine does not and cannot know the meaning of any of the instructions it implements and executes (e.g., Knuth 1977) the meanings of both the sense and linguistic primitives must be described to an AIS. Now, the only means we, humans, have to describe anything to robots is through formalised human language in the form of KRR formalisms. In particular, we need language to describe the meanings of the sensorial primitives to an AIS and language itself is sense-primitives based. This is a vicious circle impossible to break. In other words, AI (including robotics and the AGI initiative) is unable to imbue an AIS with meanings (sensory, motor, or of any other type) because any meanings need to be described to an AIS and this has been shown to be impossible because of the nature of human language and the associated limits of human constructability (Gelepithis 1984, 1991). It is encouraging that some have at last realised that AISs do not understand human language (e.g., Hutson 2021). It would be better for the AI community to eventually accept that AISs cannot in principle understand human language and neither can communicate with humans.

It is worth noting that the argument is entirely compatible with Robotics and AI work that produces AISs exhibiting higher-than-human intelligent performance or recognising and producing emotions. For, such amazing performance and stunning capabilities are caused by a combination of speed and appropriate formal knowledge representations schemes capturing any *formalisable* aspect of human knowledge, consciousness and emotions. Similar reasoning and conclusions apply to robots.

The third issue, although still in the realm of mere possibility, is too important to be ignored (see Sect. 2.2). Here, my remarks are in relation to the contents of this chapter: understanding and communication. The possible emergence of an ARE type of noémon system presupposes the development, by an AIS or robot, of the ability of *fundamentally* changing their initial design features specified by humans. The difficulty of such a developmental ability consists in breaking the human constructability constraint in a way that enables them to develop their *own* primitives and therefore the ability of *own* understanding and, consequently, *own* communication. Incidentally, one can easily verify that the definitional characteristics of ARE concerning understanding, communication, and primitives are fully compatible with the definition of ARE (definition-10; Sect. 2.2).

Whether the initial human-based design features and associated formal human knowledge would be retained by AREs could be kept beyond human knowledge. Such a possibility, most likely, would be counter to human interests. In case of developing *own* primitive systems without any human basis, the development of AREs, and therefore possible actions, would be unknowable to us. Such a possible evolutionary step is, of course, quite distinct from the emergence of a new hybrid *Homo* species based on a combination of AI and biotechnology.

Communication among AREs would, of course, be possible and it would depend on the ARE-type of understanding they could develop. The end result of such an understanding would be in terms of ARE-primitives that could be fundamentally different from those of humans and of any other biological noémon system. ARE *own*-understanding and associated primitives require the development of an *own*- representational system (Sect. 2.2).

The limits of both human constructability and communication between historic *H. sapiens* and robots are traceable back to the FHK issue (Sect. 3.2.2). To investigate the latter one need to consider the nature of *Homo* knowledge (Gelepithis 2024b, chapter-2).

Correction to: Unification of Artificial Intelligence and Psychology

Correction to:
P. A. M. Gelepithis, *Unification of Artificial Intelligence and Psychology*, https://doi.org/10.1007/978-3-031-68319-0

The book was inadvertently published with few errors, which are corrected now. The missing rows in the table, references, as well as the revised author biography have been corrected.

The updated version of the book can be found at
https://doi.org/10.1007/978-3-031-68319-0

P. A. M. Gelepithis, *Unification of Artificial Intelligence and Psychology*,
https://doi.org/10.1007/978-3-031-68319-0_5

Epilogue

Let me start this epilogue with a summary statement of the constitutive theories of the TNS so far, continue with the key link connecting the two volumes of *Unification of Artificial Intelligence and Psychology*, and finish it off with a brief comment.

As I have shown in the first chapter, the necessity for the introduction of a new approach and constitutive notion is based on the fact that 'mind', 'designed intelligence', and 'neuron', the constitutive notions of psychology, AI, and neuroscience, are inadequately specified. Such inadequacies create methodological and unification problems that become worse when (unconsciously) held belief systems influence a constitutive notion. The noémon system theoretical construct is a completely defined constitutive notion for S. That entailed development of *complete* theories for its three definiens—representation, thinking, communication. A theory is descriptively *complete* if it is describable in terms of primitive systems (i.e., systems of primitive terms).

The theory of representation developed in the second chapter ultimately rests on two primitive terms: 'goal' and 'meaningful material formation'. The former is specific to the theory of representation. The latter is characteristic of all theories of noémon systems. In the special case

P. A. M. Gelepithis, *Unification of Artificial Intelligence and Psychology*,
https://doi.org/10.1007/978-3-031-68319-0

of noémon biological species the notion of 'meaningful material formation' becomes the special category of 'meaningful neural formation'. The theory has reached three major conclusions. First, a complete definition of AI, that is, a definition expressed in terms of primitive notions. Second, a novel argument and result on the AGI and superintelligence debates on the relation between humans and robots. Third, a radical solution to the gradualist (continuity vs discontinuity) debate in terms of *written* human language. The latter is argued to be the determining tool-factor and a major transition in the evolution of *Homo* artificiality.

The theory of thinking developed in the third chapter is squarely based on the basic notions of meaningful neural and material formations. The major consequence of the theory is the memory-meaning postulate that bridges the philosophical and neuroscientific studies of meaning. The focus and extended discussion of human thinking reveals interesting relations between traditional fields and enables a clear description of the similarities and differences between human and animal thinking.

The major point in our discussion of robot thinking is the relation of the latter to the issue of formalisability of human knowledge. An important issue that requires special treatment as part of the huge topic of *Homo* knowledge (Gelepithis 2024b).

The theory of communication developed in the final chapter of the first volume brings to the fore the inseparable relation between the communication and understanding processes. It also highlights the most important characteristic of that relation, namely: communication is a societal process depending on the individual processes of understanding, whereas the latter is an individual process that is societally dependent. The key result of the theory is that the processes of understanding and communication restructure and augment *Homo sapiens* knowledge. A result that is fully appreciated when it is seen in relation to the extension of the theory of human understanding to include robot understanding and the limits of human–robot communication.

The key link connecting the two volumes of *Unification of Artificial Intelligence and Psychology* is the natural relation between foundations and consequences implied by them. As we saw in this volume, all entities of S experience and exhibit the following three fundamental phenomena:

representation, thinking, communication. They are describable in terms of the corresponding *minimum* PSN (pivotal system of notions proposed in Sect. 1.3). Certain classes of noémon systems have developed additional mechanisms that enable them to experience and exhibit aspects of knowledge, consciousness, and emotion. These phenomena are describable in terms of the corresponding PSN and presuppose the evolution of the phenomena describable in terms of the *minimum* PSN. The theories of knowledge, consciousness and emotion developed in the second volume are based on the foundational part of the TNS developed in the first one. They also strengthen and in a sense widen the foundations of the TNS. Not surprisingly, they carry their own major consequences.

Table A.1 expands the above key link by codifying the results of the current constitutive theories of the TNS across the 2 volumes and stating some of the future work required.

I come now to my brief comment. It concerns the evolution of human nature and the nature of noémon systems in general. Evolution affects all phenomena and may be affected by the evolution of some of them. In particular, the evolution of *Homo* artificiality is the driving force for the evolution of all pivotal phenomena denoted by the PSN. As such it is the unifying thread of psychology and AI. In cooperation with AISs and Robots, the latest events of the evolution of H-artificiality, humans started transforming their science, their individual nature, and they may well influence the nature of *Homo sapiens*. A physicalist theory of noémon systems is a must. This book makes a small first step to this end, the companion volume-2 adds a further component to the prospective science of noémon systems.

Table A.1 The TNS unification: Currently constitutive theories and future work

The unification of artificial intelligence and psychology	
Volume one foundations	*Volume two consequences*
Demonstrates inadequacies of traditional constitutive notions of Cognitive Science Establishes necessity of single new constitutive notion for Cognitive Science Proposes and fully explicates the notion of noémon system as the single constitutive notion for the study of animals, robots and hybrid systems The definiens of noémon system are completely described in terms of the corresponding theories of representation, thinking, and communication Discusses the defining characteristics of historic *Homo sapiens* and its differences from animals and robots Provides the first complete definition of Artificial Intelligence and explains the mental gap issue	Extends the foundational unification of Artificial Intelligence and Psychology to cover the pivotal phenomena of knowledge, consciousness, and emotions Mathematics constitutes a socio-cultural ramification of the Written Human Language transition Philosophy is an attitude towards belief systems; it is not knowledge. We are experiencing a philosophy-to-science transition, i.e., eventually all the work of philosophers will be carried out by scientists There is no fundamental difference between natural sciences, social sciences, and the arts AI consciousness is impossible while *own*-AI consciousness is possible If *own*-AI were to be materialised, major human characteristics/capabilities like thinking, understanding and emotions could also be materialised. They would *fundamentally* differ from their human counterparts The *probability* of *own*-AI is presently minuscule but it is increasing. Its materialisation requires the element of chance Novel explanation of individual human nature
Phenomena unified: Meaning, memory, information, belief, thinking, concepts, emotion, representation, understanding, communication, knowledge, consciousness, human nature *Additional phenomena that need to be unified by a complete theory of noémon systems*: Autonomy in dynamic unpredictable environments, Human neonate's development capabilities, Values, Creativity, Human language acquisition, Beauty, Truth, Morality, Sociality of our species, H-civilisations, Future evolution of *Homo sapiens*	

Appendix-1: Inadequacies of AI Definitions to Date

In Sect. 2.2 we completely defined AI in a way we justified to be preferable to the definition of Newell on the basis of a more expressive minimum vocabulary (Sect. 1.3). Table A.2 states and refutes all the major definitions of AI.

Definitions are an indispensable characteristic of language and they are, mostly unconsciously, used all the time by everybody. Their significance becomes particularly clear in science and, more generally, whenever substantial and effective communication is required or desired. A definition is complete if and only if all its definiens are described in terms of (systems of) primitives. Errors occur whenever a definition: (i) is too wide; (ii) is too narrow; (iii) is circular; or (iv) involves obscure definiens.

P. A. M. Gelepithis, *Unification of Artificial Intelligence and Psychology*, https://doi.org/10.1007/978-3-031-68319-0

Table A.2 Definitions of AI (1968–2020, chronological order)

Definitions of AI (1968–2020, chronological order)	
AI is …	*Remarks*
"an attempt to build intelligent machines without any prejudice toward making the system simple, biological, or humanoid." (Minsky 1968, p. 7)	Circular definition. Circularity is attempted to be circumvented by making appeal to what humans commonly consider to be or characterise as 'intelligent' or 'intelligence'. (cf, Luger's (2002) related remark below)
"Although there is much practical good that can come of more intelligent machines, the fundamental theoretical goal of the discipline is understanding intelligent processes ***independent*** of their particular physical realisation." (Goldstein & Papert 1977 pp. 84–85)	A functionalist definition of the theoretical objective of AI. Key notion of 'intelligent processes' is left undefined. It also carries the weaknesses of the functionalist hypothesis
"the study of the computational problems posed by the interrelated natural phenomena of reasoning, perception, language and learning." (Pentland & Fischler 1983 p 18)	It is not circular but includes undefined terms (e.g., reasoning, language) that are not explicated and therefore they are no more clear than the definiendum. It is also relatively narrow as it does not include action
"Really what AI is, potentially, is the algorithmic study of processes in every field of inquiry". (Schank 1983 p 7)	Extremely wide (but, not too-wide) definition of AI. It does not take into account thelimits of human constructability
"Artificial intelligence is the study of knowledge representations and their use in language, reasoning, learning, and problem solving." (Sowa 1984, p. 22)	Implicitly circular: 'knowledge' is not defined. Comments on Pentland & Fischler (1983) above also applicable to this definition
"The engineering science of concepts" Michie (1985)	Succinct and accurate. The notion of 'concept' is left undefined
"the science of intelligence", where "intelligence" is a coherent repertoire of generic information—processing strategies, each of which solves a type of problem in a computationally efficient way, using knowledge of certain types, organised in a specific way, and using specific and locally appropriate control strategies." (Chandrasekaran, 1990, p.42)	A computational theory of intelligence, where the latter is inadequately 'defined' in terms of the ***undefined*** notions of information and knowledge. Nothing new offered

(continued)

Table A.2 (continued)

Definitions of AI (1968–2020, chronological order)	
AI is …	*Remarks*
"AI is the study of the mechanisms of intelligence and all supporting technologies, extending to perception and motion, namely robotics." Newell, 1990, p. 40) "A system is intelligent to the degree that it approximates a knowledge-level system." (Ibid, p. 90)	Based on a clearly stated theoretical framework part of which—the PSS approach to AI—is also experimentally supported Its single inadequacy is Newell's conception of knowledge as belief (see Sect. 1.1.2 and Chapter 2 Volume Two—Consequences; Gelepithis 2024b)
1. "The central goals of Artificial Intelligence are to make computers more useful and to understand the principles which make intelligence possible." (Winston 1977, p. 1) 2. "Artificial Intelligence is [t]he study of the computations that make it possible to perceive, reason, and act." (Winston 1992, p. 5)	Similar to previous circular definitions of AI Similar to Pentland & Fischler (1983) Ps. Both definitions part of key textbook
"the branch of computer science that is concerned with the automation of intelligent behavior." (Luger, 2002, p. 1)	Luger himself remarks: "this definition suffers from the fact that intelligence itself is not very well defined or understood. Although most of us are certain that we know intelligent behavior when we see it, it is doubtful that anyone could come close to defining intelligence in a way that would be specific enough to help in the evaluation of a supposedly intelligent computer program, while still capturing the vitality and complexity of the human mind." (cf, my remark at the top of this table)
"the study of agents that receive percepts from the environment and perform actions. Each agent implements a function that maps percept sequences to actions". Russell, S. J., & Norvig 2003, p. vii	Black- box type definition. The fundamental notion of 'agent' is not defined
Intelligence as " adaptation with insufficient knowledge and resources". (Wang 2008)	Incomplete definition; key definiens undefined

(continued)

Table A.2 (continued)

Definitions of AI (1968–2020, chronological order)	
AI is …	*Remarks*
"is the field that studies *the synthesis and analysis of computational agents that act intelligently.*" An agent is something that acts in an environment An agent acts **intelligently** when: (i) what it does is appropriate for its circumstances and its goals, (ii) it is flexible to changing environments and changing goals, (iii) it learns from experience, and (iv) it makes appropriate choices given its perceptual and computational limitations A **computational** agent is an agent whose decisions about its actions can be explained in terms of computation." (Poole & Mackworth, 2017)	Essentially equivalent to Newell's (1990) definition Ps. Poole and Mackworth remark that: "An agent typically cannot observe the state of the world directly; it has only a finite memory and it does not have unlimited time to act."
"Artificial Intelligence (AI) is a branch of computer science that deals with the development of algorithms that seek to simulate human intelligence" (Kapoor et al., 2019)	Similar to previous circular definitions o f A I (i. e., u n d e f i n e d u s e o f 'intelligent')
The goal of AI is: "the scientific understanding of the mechanisms underlying thought and intelligent behavior and their embodiment in machines." (AAAI website, 4 April 2018, 13 November 2023)	Similar to previous circular definitions o f A I (i. e., u n d e f i n e d u s e o f 'intelligent')

NB: The *Journal of Artificial General Intelligence*, Volume **11**, Issue 2, February 2020, pp. 1–100, published a Special Issue "On Defining Artificial Intelligence". Unfortunately, the result was inconclusive and revealed the deep rooted differences of opinion among AI-ists.

Appendix-2: Definitions

Root-Conception (equivalently, **Definition-1**): Noémon system, is a system that consists of at least one individual I of a noémon species, or at least one noémon entity, E, not belonging to a species, or a combination of the above and tools that at least one noémon entity E or individual I can use.

Definition-2 Noémon species is a species whose individuals fulfil at least the first two of the following conditions:

(a) Possess *own*-representational systems (e.g., sensory, motor).
(b) Possess the ability of thinking.
(c) Are able to communicate among themselves, and possibly individuals of other species.
(d) Are able to create *permanent* external representations.

Definition-3 E_n is a system fulfilling at least the first two of the following three conditions:

(a) Possess representational systems (e.g., sensory, motor).
(b) Possess the ability of thinking.
(c) Is able to communicate with other noémon entities.

P. A. M. Gelepithis, *Unification of Artificial Intelligence and Psychology*,
https://doi.org/10.1007/978-3-031-68319-0

Definition-4 For a human H, an external representation of a situation B *is* an artificial construction C_a of her characterised by the properties:

(a) C_a is a simplification of B; and
(b) C_a preserves, at least some of, the essential characteristics of B.

Definition-5 For a human H, a NS representation of a situation B *is* a 'meaningful' structure of 'neural formations', C_n such that:

(a) C_n is a simplification of B; and
(b) C_n tends to preserve the essential characteristics of B.

Definition-6 A representation of a situation, say, B, *is* a construction, C, characterised by the properties:

(a) C simplifies B; and
(b) C preserves the essential characteristics of B.

Definition-7 AI is the study, design, and development of artificially-intelligent systems (AISs) and robots. *Where*:

Definition-8 An AIS is a system that fulfils the following conditions:

(a) Possess representational systems of human knowledge.
(b) Possess the ability of thinking.
(c) (a) and (b) are designed and built by humans.

Definition-9 Robot, *R*, is an AIS possessing, in addition, a motor system that enables it to move in and affect its environment.

Definition-10 An E_n possesses its *own* representational system, R_o, if and only if, R_o is independent of the language of another kind of noémon entity E^*_n.

Definition-11 An autonomous robot entity, (ARE) is a noémon entity that may *only* partly be designed and built by humans that fulfils the following conditions:

(a) Possess R_o (e.g., sensory, motor, knowledge); and
(b) Possess the ability of thinking.

Definition-12 Culture Y of a multi-member noémon system Z is:

(a) the system of socially learned and inheritable behaviours between generations that Y has evolved to become;
(b) Y is being developed by members or groups of Z; and
(c) Y may affect the development of any member or group of Z.

Definition-13a Homo artificiality at time t, is the degree to which *Homo*-at-t has incorporated the tools constructed by it by time t.

Definition-13b Artificiality of a noémon system is the degree to which it constructs and incorporates tools in its development or evolution.

Definition-14a For an human H, I call 'neural formation' (symbol N), a structure of *interacting* sub-cellular components across a region of H's nervous system (NS).

Definition-14b For an human H, a specific neural formation N is meaningful, (symbol N_m), iff N is able to influence the survival or reproduction of H.

Definition-15 The meaning of a novel S_c, for the human H at time t, is whatever N_m is *created* by the interaction of S_c and H at time t.

Definition-16 The meaning of a previously encountered S_c, for the human H, at time t, is the *prevailed* N_p of $\mathbf{N_p}$.

Definition-14b ^{I}A For an individual member I of a particular animal species A (^{I}A), a neural formation N is meaningful (symbol N_m), if and only if N is able to influence the survival or reproduction of ^{I}A.

Definition-17 Let $^{1}N_m$ be the first neural formation *created* by the specific triad (S_{c1}, H, t_1). Then the *system* of all $^{j}N_m$ (j a natural number) of human H that have been created by time t later than t1 I call it a concept of H up to t and symbolise it by ε(H, t).

Definition-18 σ is a thought (equivalent idea) of human H if and only if σ is a flexible, not necessarily permanent structure of concepts and/or N_m (definition-14b), that encompasses the possibility of action by H.

Definition-19 Belief of H = def A structure of NFs and meaningful NFs of H on the basis of which H is prepared to act, argue, or live by.

Definition-20 Information for a historic human H at time t -symbol Inf(H,t) is an expressed concept, or thought, or system of {concepts, thoughts, symbols, signals, data}.

Definition-21 Symbol for a human H at time t -abbreviation Sbl(H,t) is a certain configuration of matter meaningful to its producer or interpreter.

Definition-22 Signal for a human H at time t, is a certain propagated configuration of matter meaningful to a sender or a receiver.

Definition-23 Data $=_{df}$ Potentially meaningful configurations of matter.

Definition-24 H-thinking, T_H, is the *class* of interactions of human meanings, or concepts, or thoughts, or beliefs, or of any combinations of them after the advent of WHuLa.

Definition-25 H-reasoning is a form of thinking in which conclusions consciously follow from a system of human beliefs, thoughts and concepts.

*Definition-24^I**A*** An *individual's* thinking of a *particular* animal species ($^I T_A$), is the interaction of meanings, or concepts, or thoughts, or of any combinations of them of that individual.

*Definition-25^I**A*** An *individual's* reasoning of a *particular* animal species, is a form of animal thinking in which conclusions consciously follow from the system of thoughts and concepts of that individual.

Definition-24$_R$. Robot thinking, T_R, is the processing of human-based meanings, concepts, thoughts, beliefs, or of any combinations of them by the robot's ***designed*** representational systems capturing their formalisable aspects.

Definition-26 Skepseis are structures of ***restructured*** NFs that may or may not involve ***restructured*** N_m, although normally they do.

Definition-27 Human declarative memory is the system of interacting processes of acquisition, consolidation, maintenance, modification, retrieval, and integration that involves the semantic structures and associated mechanisms of M.

Definition-28$_H$. A human H_1 has communicated with H_2 on a topic θ if, and only if:

(i) H_1 has understood θ -symbol: U (H1, θ);
(ii) H_2 has understood θ -symbol: U (H2, θ);
(iii) U (H1, θ) is output by H1 and understood by H2; and
(iv) U (H2, θ) is output by H2 and understood by H1.

Definition-29$_H$ A human H, at time t, has understood something, θ, if and only if, H can think of θ in terms of *a* system of human primitives that depend on H, θ, and t (symbol ∏(H, θ, t), or *a* system of premises.

Definition-30$_H$ π is a primitive of/for H if and only if the meaning of π is immediate for H.

Definition-28$_{NoS}$ A specific noémon system, NoS1, has communicated with NoS2 on a topic θ if, and only if:

(a) NoS1 has understood θ -symbol: U (NoS1, θ);
(b) NoS2 has understood θ -symbol: U (NoS2, θ);
(c) U (NoS1, θ) is output by NoS1 and understood by NoS2; and
(d) U (NoS2, θ) is output by NoS2 and understood by NoS1.

Definition-29$_{NoS}$ A noémon system, NoS, has understood something, θ, iff NoS can think of θ in terms of a system of primitives (symbol: ∏(NoS, θ, t), or *a* system of premises.

Definition-30$_{NoS}$ π is a primitive of/for NoS if and only if the meaning of π is immediate for NoS.

Definition-29^{I}A An ^{I}A, at time t, has understood something, θ, if and only if, ^{I}A can think of θ in terms of *a* system of animal primitives that depend on ^{I}A, θ, and t (symbol ∏(^{I}A, θ, t).

Definition-30^{I}A π is a primitive of ^{I}A if and only if the meaning of π is immediate for ^{I}A.

Definition-28$_A$ An individual member I1 of a particular animal species A (^{I1}A) has communicated with ^{I2}A on a topic θ if, and only if:

(a) ^{I1}A has understood θ -symbol: U (^{I1}A, θ);
(b) ^{I2}A has understood θ -symbol: U (^{I2}A, θ);
(c) U (^{I1}A, θ) is output by ^{I1}A and understood ^{I2}A; and
(d) U (^{I2}A, θ is output by ^{I2}A and understood by ^{I1}A.

Contents of Volume Two

P. A. M. Gelepithis, *Unification of Artificial Intelligence and Psychology*, https://doi.org/10.1007/978-3-031-68319-0

References

Abbott, L. F. (2006). Where are the switches on this thing? In J. L. van Hemmen & T. J. Sejnowski (Eds.), *23 Problems in systems neuroscience* (pp. 423–431). Oxford University Press.

Abbracchio, M. P., Burnstock, G., Verkhratsky, A., & Zimmermann, H. (2009). Purinergic signalling in the nervous system: An overview. *Trends in Neurosciences,* **32**(1), 19–29.

Adachi, Y., Osada, T., Sporns, O., Watanabe, T., Matsui, T., Miyamoto, K., & Miyashita, Y. (2012). Functional connectivity between anatomically unconnected areas is shaped by collective network-level effects in the macaque cortex. *Cerebral Cortex,* **22**(7), 1586–1592. https://doi.org/10.1093/cercor/bhr234

Adler, R. B., & Rodman, G. (2000). *Understanding human communication.* Harcourt College Publishers.

Adolphs, R. (2015). The unsolved problems of neuroscience. *Trends in Cognitive Sciences,* **19**(4), 173–175.

Ai, H., Okada, R., Sakura, M., Wachtler, T., & Ikeno, H. (2019). Neuroethology of the waggle dance: How followers interact with the waggle dancer and detect spatial information. *Insects,* **10**, 336. https://doi.org/10.3390/insects10100336

Alberti, M., Correa, C., Marzluff, J. M., Hendry, A. P., Palkovacs, E. P., Gotanda, K. M., Hunt, V. M., Apgar, T. M., & Zhou, Y. (2017). Global urban signatures of phenotypic change in animal and plant populations. *PNAS,* **114**(34), 8951–8956.

P. A. M. Gelepithis, *Unification of Artificial Intelligence and Psychology*,
https://doi.org/10.1007/978-3-031-68319-0

Albuquerque, N., Guo, K., Wilkinson, A., Savalli, C., Otta, E., & Mills, D. (2016). Dogs recognize dog and human emotions. *Biology Letters,* **12**(1), 20150883. https://doi.org/10.1098/rsbl.2015.0883

Allen, N. J., & Barres, B. A. (2009). Glia—More than just Brain Glue. *Nature,* **457**, 675–677.

American Anthropological Association (2017). http://www.americananthro.org/

Anders, S., Heinzle, J., Weiskiph, N., Ethofer, T., & Haynes, J.-D. (2011). Flow of affective information between communicating brains. *NeuroImage,* **54**, 439–446.

Anderson, J. R. (1983). *The architecture of cognition.* Harvard University Press.

Anderson, J. R. (1987). Methodologies for studying human knowledge. *Behavioral and Brain Sciences,* **10**, 467–505.

Anderson, J. R. (1990). *The adaptive character of thought.* Lawrence Erlbaum Associates.

Anderson, J. R. (1993). *Rules of the mind.* Lawrence Erlbaum Associates, Inc.

Anderson, J. R. (2018). Chimpanzees and death. *Phil. Trans. R. Soc. B* **373**: 20170257. http://dx.doi.org/10.1098/rstb.2017.0257.

Anderson, J. R., & Bower, G. H. (1973). *Human associative memory.* Winston and Sons.

Anderson, J. R., & Lebiere, C. L. (1998). *The atomic components of thought.* Erlbaum.

Anderson, J. R., & Lebiere, C. L. (2003). The Newell test for a theory of cognition. *Behavioral & Brain Sciences,* **26**, 587–637.

Anderson, J. R., Bothell, D., Dyrne, M. D., Douglass, S., Lebiere, C., & Qin, Y. (2004). An integrated theory of the mind. *Psychological Review,* **111**(4), 1036–1060.

Andrews-Hanna, J. R., Irving, Z. C., Fox, K. C. R., Spreng, R. N., & Christoff, K. (2018). The neuroscience of spontaneous thought: An evolving, interdisciplinary field. In K. C. R. Fox & K. Christoff (Eds.), *The Oxford handbook of spontaneous thought: Mind-wandering, creativity, and dreaming.* OUP.

Ardesch, D. J., Scholtens, L. H., Lim, L., Preuss, T. M., Rilling, J. K., & van den Heuvel, M. P. (2019). Evolutionary expansion of connectivity between multimodal association areas in the human brain compared with chimpanzees. *PNAS,* **116**(14), 7101–7106.

Aristotle (4th c. BCE*1984a). Posterior analytics. In J. Barnes (Ed), *The complete works of Aristotle: The revised Oxford translation,* (Vol. One). Princeton University Press.

Aristotle (4th c. BCE*1984b). Poetics. In J. Barnes (Ed), *The complete works of Aristotle: The revised oxford translation*, (Vol. Two). Princeton University Press.

Aristotle (4th c. BCE*1984c). Physics. In J. Barnes (Ed), *The complete works of Aristotle: The revised oxford translation*, (Vol. Two). Princeton University Press.

Arlington, J. W., & Baird, J. A. (Eds). (2005). *Why language matters for theory of mind*. Oxford University Press.

Armitage, C., & Kaindl, M. (2020). Getting with the program. *Nature,* **588**, 138–141.

Armstrong, D. M. (1968). *A materialist theory of the mind*. Routledge & Kegan Paul.

Ashby, F. G. (1999). A neuropsychological theory of positive affect and its influence on cognition. *Psychological Review,* **106**(3), 529–550.

Ashby, R. W. (1960). *Design for a Brain: The origin of adaptive behaviour*. John Wiley & Sons Inc.

Avise, J. C., & Ayala, F. J. (2010). In the light of evolution IV: The human condition. *PNAS,* **107**(suppl. 2), 8897–8901.

Aylwin, S. (1985). *Structure in thought and felling*. Routledge.

Baars, B. J., & Franklin, S. (2007). An architectural model of conscious and unconscious brain functions: Global workspace theory and IDA. *Neural Networks,* **20**, 955–961.

Bach, K. (1994). Conversational implicature. *Mind & Language,* **9**(2), 124–162.

Bach, K. (1999). Meaning. In R. A. Wilson & F. C. Keil (Eds.), *The MIT Encyclopedia of the cognitive sciences* (pp. 513–514). The MIT Press.

Baldwin, J. C. (1986). *George Herbert Mead: A unifying theory for sociology*. Sage.

Barbosa, L. S., Marshall, W., Streipert, S., Albantakis, L., & Tononi, G. (2020). A measure for intrinsic information. *Scientific Reports,* **10**, 18803. https://doi.org/10.1038/s41598-020-75943-4

Barnier, A. J., & Sutton, J. (2008). From individual to collective memory: Theoretical and empirical perspectives. *Memory,* **16**(3), 177–182.

Barres, B. A. (2008). The mystery and magic of glia: A perspective on their roles in health and disease. *Neuron,* **60**, 430–440.

Barsalou, L. W., & Wiemer-Hastings, K. (2005). Situating abstract concepts. In D. Pecher & R. Zwaan (Eds.), *Grounding cognition: The role of perception and action in memory, language, and thought* (pp. 129–163). Cambridge University Press.

Barsalou, L. W., Dutriaux, L., & Scheepers, C. (2018). Moving beyond the distinction between concrete and abstract concepts. *Philosophical Transactions of the Royal Society B,* **373**, 20170144. https://doi.org/10.1098/rstb.2017.0144

Bartlett, F. C. (1932). *Remembering: A study in experimental and social psychology*. Cambridge University Press.

Bassett, D. S., & Sporns, O. (2017). Network neuroscience. *Natural Neuroscience,* **20**(3), 353–364.

Bates, L. A., Sayialel, K. N., Njirani, N. W., Moss, C. J., Poole, J. H., & Byrne, R. W. (2007). Elephants classify human ethnic groups by odor and garment color. *Current Biology*. https://doi.org/10.1016/j.cub.2007.09.060

Bateson, G. (1972). *Steps to an ecology of mind: Collected essays in anthropology, psychiatry, evolution, and epistemology*. University of Chicago Press.

Baylis, J., Smith, S., Owens, P., et al. (2011). *The globalization of world politics: An introduction to international relations* (5th ed.). Oxford University Press.

Bechtel, W. (1998). Representations and cognitive explanations: Assessing the dynamicist's challenge in cognitive science. *Cognitive Science*, **22**, 295–318.

Bechtel, W., & Graham, G. (1998*1999). Preface. In W. Bechtel, & G. Graham, (Eds.), *A companion to cognitive science*. Blackwell Publishers Ltd.

Beck, B. B. (1980). *The use and manufacture of tools by animals*. Garland STPM Press.

Belmonte, J. C. I., Callaway, E. M., Caddick, S. J., Churchland, P., Feng, G., Homanics, G. E., Lee, K.-F., Leopold, D. A., Miller, C. T., Mitchell, J. F., Mitalipov, S., Moutri, A. R., Movshon, J. A., Okano, H., Reynolds, J. H., Ringach, D. L., Sejnowski, T. J., Silva, A. C., Strick, P. L., … Zhang, F. (2015). Brains, genes, and primates. *Neuron*, **86**, 617–6314.

Bennett, M. R. (2007a). Neuroscience and philosophy. In M. Bennett, D. Dennett, P. Hacker, & J. R. Searle (Eds.), *Neuroscience and philosophy: Brain, mind, and language* (pp. 49–69). Columbia University Press.

Bennett, M. R. (2007b). Development of the concept of mind. *Australian and New Zealand Journal of Psychiatry*, **41**, 943–956.

Bennett, M. R., & Hacker, P. M. S. (2003). *Philosophical foundations of neuroscience*. Blackwell Publishing.

Benowitz, L. I., Bear, D. M., Mesulam M-M., Rosenthal, R., Zaidel, E., & Sperry, R. W. (1984*1985). Contributions of the right cerebral hemisphere in perceiving paralinguistic cues of emotion. In J. Hintikka, & L. Vaina (Eds.), *Cognitive constraints on communications: Representation and processes*, D. Reidel Publishing Company.

Bentley, R. A., Hahn, M. W., & Shannon, S. J. (2004). Random drift and culture change. *Proceedings of the Royal Society of London, Series b: Biological Sciences*, **271**, 1443–1450.

Bernardi, G. (2012). The use of tools by wrasses (Labridae). *Coral Reefs*, **31**, 39.

Bertolaso, M., & Dieli, A. M. (2017). Cancer and intercellular cooperation. *Royal Society Open Science*, **4**, 170470. https://doi.org/10.1098/rsos.170470

Bess, M. D. (2008). A historian's perspective on human biological enhancement. *Technology and Culture*, **49**, 114–126.

Bickerton, D. (1990). *Language and species*. University of Chicago Press.

Birch, J. (2017). The inclusive fitness controversy: Finding a way forward. *Royal Society Open Science,* **4**, 170335. https://doi.org/10.1098/rsos.170335

Birch, J., Schnell, A. K., & Clayton, N. S. (2020). Dimensions of animal consciousness. *Trends in Cognitive Sciences,* **24**(10), 789–801.

Birch, J., & Heyes, C. (2021). The cultural evolution of cultural evolution. *Phil. Trans. r. Soc. B,* **376**, 20200051. https://doi.org/10.1098/rstb.2020.0051

Birch, J., Burn, C., Schnell, A., Browning, H., & Crump, A. (2021). *Review of the evidence of sentience in cephalopod molluscs and decapod crustaceans.* November 2021, report commissioned via LSE Consulting.

Biro, D., Haslam, M., & Rutz, C. (2013). Tool use as adaptation. *Philosophical Transactions of the Royal Society B,* **368**, 20120408. https://doi.org/10.1098/rstb.2012.0408

Blackburn, P. L. (2007). *The code model of communication: A powerful metaphor in linguistic metatheory*. SIL International.

Blakemore, S.-J., Wolpert, D. M., & Frith, C. D. (2002). Abnormalities in the awareness of action. *Trends in Cognitive Sciences,* **6**, 237–242.

Bloomfield, L. (1933). *Language*. Holt, Rinehart & Winston

Bobay, L. M., & Ochman, H. (2018). Biological species in the viral world. *PNAS,* **115**(23), 6040–6045.

Boden, M. A. (1992). *The creative mind: Myths and mechanisms*. Sphere Books Ltd.

Boden, M. A. (2001). Life and cognition. In J. Branquinho (Ed.), *The foundations of cognitive science* (pp. 11–22). Oxford University Press.

Boden, M. A., Bryson, J., Caldwell, D., Dautenhahn, K., Edwards, L., Kember, S., Newman, P., Parry, V., Pegman, G., Rodden, T., Sorrell, T., Wallis, M., Whitby, B. & Winfield, A (2011*2017). Principles of robotics: regulating robots in the real world. *Connection Science*, **29**, 124–129.

Boivin, N. L., Zeder, M. A., Fuller, D. Q., Crowther, A., Larson, G., Erlandson, J. M., Denham, T., & Petraglia, M. D. (2016). Ecological consequences of human niche construction: Examining long-term anthropogenic shaping of global species distributions. *PNAS,* **113**(23), 6388–6396.

Bollmann, J. H., & Engert, F. (2009). Subcellular topography of visually driven dendritic activity in the vertebrate visual system. *Neuron,* **61**, 895–905.

Bolton, D., & Hill, J. (2004). *Mind, meaning and mental disorder: The nature of causal explanation in psychology and psychiatry* (2nd ed.). Oxford University Press.

Bonduriansky, R., & Day, T. (2009). Nongenetic inheritance and its evolutionary implications. *The Annual Review of Ecology, Evolution, and Systematics, 2009*(**40**), 103–125.

Bonfante, P., & Genre, A. (2015). Arbuscular mycorrhizal dialogues: Do you speak 'plantish' or 'fungish'? *Trends in Plant Science,* **20**(3), 150–154.

Bookheimer, S. (2002). Functional MRI of language: New approaches to understanding the cortical organization of semantic processing. *Annual Review of Neuroscience,* **25**, 151–188.

Boole, G. (1854*2005). *An investigation of the laws of thought, on which are founded the mathematical theories of logic and probabilities*. Project Gutenberg.

Borghi, A. M., Barca, L., Binkofski, F., & Tummolini, L. (2018a). Varieties of abstract concepts: Development, use and representation in the brain. *Philosophical Transactions of the Royal Society B,* **373**, 20170121. https://doi.org/10.1098/rstb.2017.0121

Borghi, A. M., Barca, L., Binkofski, F., & Tummolini, L. (2018b). Abstract concepts, language and sociality: From acquisition to inner speech. *Philosophical Transactions of the Royal Society B,* **373**, 20170134. https://doi.org/10.1098/rstb.2017.0134

Borst, C. V. ed. (1970). *The mind/brain identity theory.* Macmillan Publishers Ltd.

Boyd, R., & Richerson, P. J. (1996). Why culture is common, but cultural evolution is rare. In W. G. Runciman, J. M. Smith, & R. I. M. Dunbar (Eds.), *Evolution of social behaviour patterns in primates and man* (pp. 77–93). Oxford University Press.

Bradbury, J. W., & Vehrencamp, S. L. (2020). Animal communication. *Encyclopaedia Britannica.* https://www.britannica.com/science/animal-communication.

Branquinho, J. (ed.). 2001. *The foundations of cognitive science.* Oxford University Press.

Bräuer, J., Call, J., & Tomasello, M. (2005). All great ape species follow gaze to distant locations and around barriers. *Journal of Comparative Psychology,* **119**(2), 145–154.

Brette, R. (2019). Is coding a relevant metaphor for the brain? *Behavioral and Brain Sciences*. https://doi.org/10.1017/S0140525X19000049

Brigandt, I., & Love, A. (2017). Reductionism in Biology. In Edward N. Zalta (Ed.) *The Stanford Encyclopedia of Philosophy (Spring 2017 Edition).*

Broadbent, D. E. (1985). A question of levels: Comments on McClelland and Rumelhart. *Journal of Experimental Psychology: General,* **114**, 189–192.

Broadbent, D. E. (1989). Lasting representations and temporary processes. In H. L. Roediger, III, & F. I. M. Craik, LEA (Eds.), *Varieties of memory and consciousness: Essays in honour of endel tulving.*

Brock, D. A., Douglas, T. E., Queller, D. C., & Strassmann, J. E. (2011). Primitive agriculture in a social amoeba. *Nature,* **469**, 393–396. https://doi.org/10.1038/nature09668

Brooks, R. A. (2012). Avoid the cerebral blind alley. *Nature, 482*, 462. Part of: Is the brain a good model for machine intelligence *Nature*, **482**, 462–463.

Brooks, R. A. (1991). Intelligence without representation. *Artificial Intelligence*, **47**, 139–159.

Bullmore, E., & Sporns, O. (2009). Complex brain networks: Graph theoretical analysis of structural and functional systems. *Nature Reviews Neuroscience*, **10**(3), 186–198.

Bundy, A. (2013). The interaction of representation and reasoning. *Proceedings of the Royal Society A*, **469**, 20130194. https://doi.org/10.1098/rspa.2013.0194

Bunge, M. (1980). *The mind-body problem: A psychobiological approach*. Pergamon Press.

Buss, D. M. (2009). *Evolutionary psychology: The new science of the mind* (3rd ed.). Pearson international edition.

Butler, S. (1872). *Erewhon or over the range*. Printed by Ballantyne and Company: Edinburgh and London.

Butz, M. V. (2016). Toward a unified sub-symbolic, computational theory of cognition. *Frontiers in Psychology*, 7, 925.

Buzsáki, G. (2010). Neural syntax: Cell assemblies, synapsembles, and readers. *Neuron*, **68**, 362–385.

Byrne, R. W., Barnard, P. J., Davidson, I., et al. (2004). Understanding culture across species. *TRENDS in Cognitive Sciences*, **8**(8), 341–346.

Carbonell, J. G., & Langley, P. (1987). Learning, machine. *The Encyclopaedia of Artificial Intelligence*, *II*, 464–488.

Carlson, T., Tovar, D. A., Alink, A., & Kriegeskorte, N. (2013). Representational dynamics of object vision: The first 1000 ms. *Journal of Vision*, **13**(10), 1–19.

Carmen, R. A., Geher, G., Glass, D. J., Guitar, A. E., Grandis, T. L., Johnsen, L., Philip, M. M., Newmark, R. L., Trouton, G. T., & Tauber, B. R. (2013). Evolution integrated across all islands of the human behavioral archipelago: All psychology as evolutionary psychology. *EvoS Journal: The Journal of the Evolutionary Studies Consortium*, **5**(1), 108–126.

Carroll, S. M. (2021). Consciousness and the laws of physics. *Journal of Consciousness Studies*, **28**(9–10), 16–31.

Catania, A. C. (2013). A natural science of behavior. *Review of General Psychology*, **17**(2), 133–139.

Cave, S., et al. (2018). *Portrayals and perceptions of AI and why they matter*. The Royal Society.

Ceraso, J., & Provitera, A. (1971). Sources of error in syllogistic reasoning. *Cognitive Psychology*, **2**, 400–410.

Ceruti, M., & Damiano, L. (2018). Plural embodiment(s) of mind genealogy and guidelines for a radically embodied approach to mind and consciousness. *Frontiers in Psychology*, **9**, 2204.

Chalmers, D. J. (Ed.). (2002). *Philosophy of mind: Classical and contemporary readings*. Westview Press.

Chandrasekaran, B. (1990). What kind of information processing is intelligence: A perspective on AI paradigms and a proposal. In D. Partridge & Y. Wilks (Eds.), *The foundations of artificial intelligence: A sourcebook* (pp. 14–46). Cambridge University Press.

Changeux, J-P. (1983*1985). *Neuronal man: The biology of mind*. Trans. by L. Garey. Oxford University Press.

Changeux, J.-P., & Dehaene, S. (1989). Neuronal models of cognitive functions. *Cognition,* **33**, 63–109.

Chapman, C. A., & Huffman, M. A. (2018). Why do we want to think humans are different? *Animal Sentience, 2018*(**163**), 1–8.

Charlesworth, J. C., Beloe, C., Watters, C., & Burns, B. P. (2017). Quorum sensing in archaea: Recent advances and emerging directions. In G. Witzany (Ed.), *Biocommunication of archaea*. Springer International Publishing.

Checkland, P. (1992). Information systems and systems thinking: Time to unite? In W. W. Cotteman & J. A. Senn (Eds.), *Challenges and strategies for research in systems development*. John Wiley and Sons.

Cheng, P. W., Holyoak, K. J., Nisbett, R. E., & Oliver, L. M. (1986). Pragmatic versus syntactic approaches to training deductive reasoning. *Cognitive Psychology,* **18**, 293–328.

Cherry, C. (1978). *On human communication: A review, a survey, and a criticism* (3rd ed.). The MIT Press.

Ching, T., et al. (2018). Opportunities and obstacles for deep learning in biology and medicine. *Journal of the Royal Society, Interface,* **15**, 20170387. https://doi.org/10.1098/rsif.2017.0387

Chomsky, N. (1959). A review of B. F. Skinner's verbal behavior. *Language,* **35**(1), 26–58.

Chomsky, N. (1965). *Aspects of the theory of syntax*. Cambridge, Mass, MIT Press.

Chomsky, N. (1995). Language and nature. *Mind,* **104**, 1–61.

Chomsky, N. (2000). *Linguistics and brain science*. The Noam Chomsky Website.

Christiansen, M. H., & Chater, N. (2008). Language as shaped by the brain. *Behavioral and Brain Sciences,* **31**, 489–558.

Christoff, K., Ream, J. M., & Gabrieli, J. D. E. (2004). Neural basis of spontaneous thought processes. *Cortex,* **40**, 623–630.

Churchland, P. S., & Sejnowski, T. J. (1992). *The computational brain*. The MIT Press.

Claidière, N., Scott-Phillips, T. C., & Sperber, D. (2014). How Darwinian is cultural evolution. *Philosophical Transactions of the Royal Society B,* **369**, 20130368. https://doi.org/10.1098/rstb.2013.0368

Clark, A. (2013). Whatever next? Predictive brains, situated agents, and the future of cognitive science. *Behavioral and Brain Sciences*, **73** pages including Commentary.

Clark, A., & Chalmers, D. (1998*2008). Appendix: The extended mind. (pp. 220–232, 251–253). In A. Clark (2008). *Supersizing the mind: embodiment, action, and cognitive extension.* OUP. The appendix first appeared as "The Extended Mind" in Analysis **58**(1), 7–19.

Clark, A. & Toribio, J. (1994). Doing without representing? *Synthese*, **101**, 401–431.

Cleeremans, A. (2010). The grand challenge for psychology: integrate and fire!. *Frontiers in Psychology*, **1**, 12.

Cobley, P. (Ed.). (1996). *The communication theory reader.* Routledge.

Collard, M., & Wood, B. (2015). Defining the Genus Homo. In W. Henke, & I. Tattersall (Eds.). *Handbook of Paleoanthropology*, (pp. 2107–2144).

Collier, J. D. (1990). Intrinsic information. In P. P. Hanson (Ed.), *Information, language, and cognition.* The University of British Columbia Press.

Collins, A. M., & Quillian, M. R. (1969). Retrieval time from semantic memory. *Journal of Verbal Learning and Verbal Behavior,* **8**, 240–248.

Collins, A. M., & Loftus, E. F. (1975). A spreading activation theory of semantic memory. *Psychological Review,* **82**, 407–428.

Connor, R. C. (2007). Dolphin social intelligence: Complex alliance relationships in bottlenose dolphins and a consideration of selective environments for extreme brain size evolution in mammals. *Philosophical Transactions of the Royal Society B,* **362**, 587–602.

Copi, I. M. (1978). *Introduction to Logic* (5th ed.). Collier Macmillan.

Cowan, N. (2000). The magical number 4 in short-term memory: A reconsideration of mental storage capacity. *Behavioral and Brain Sciences* **24**, 87–185 (including Open Peer Commentary).

Crandall, C. S., & Sherman, J. W. (2016). On the scientific superiority of conceptual replications for scientific progress. *Journal of Experimental Social Psychology,* **66**, 93–99.

Crawford, K., Dobbe, R., Dryer, T., & Whitaker, M. (2019). *AI now 2019 report.* AI Now Institute.

Crick, F., & Koch, C. (1998). Consciousness and neuroscience. *Cerebral Cortex,* **8**, 97–107.

Christoff, K., & Fox, K. C. R. (Eds.). (2018). *The Oxford handbook of spontaneous thought: Mind-wandering, creativity, and dreaming.* Oxford University Press.

Cromwell, H. C., & Panksepp, J. (2011). Rethinking the cognitive revolution from a neural perspective: How overuse/misuse of the term 'cognition' and the neglect of affective controls in behavioral neuroscience could be delaying progress in understanding the BrainMind. *Neuroscience & Biobehavioral Reviews,* **35**(9), 2026–2035.

Cuccio, V., & Gallese, V. (2018). A Peircean account of concepts: grounding abstraction in phylogeny through a comparative neuroscientific perspective. *Philosophical Transactions of the Royal Society B,* **373**, 1752.

d'Errico, F., & Stringer, C. B. (2011). Evolution, revolution or saltation scenario for the emergence of modern cultures? *Philosophical Transactions of the Royal Society B*, **366**, 1060–1069.

Dancy, C. L., Ritter, F. E., Berry, K., & Klein, L. C. (2015). Using a cognitive architecture with a physiological substrate to represent effects of psychological stress on cognition. *Computational and Mathematical Organization Theory*, **21**(1), 90–114.

Darwin, C. (1859*2006). On the origin of species. In: *From so simple a beginning: The four great books of Charles Darwin*. Edited, with introductions by Edward O. Wilson. W. W. Norton & Company.

Darwin, C. (1871*1981). The descent of man, and selection in relation to sex. In *From so simple a beginning: The four great books of Charles Darwin*. Edited, with introductions by Edward O. Wilson. W. W. Norton & Company.

Darwin, C. (1872*2006). Expression of emotions in the man and animals. In *From so simple a beginning: The four great books of Charles Darwin*. Edited, with introductions by Edward O. Wilson. W. W. Norton & Company.

Davidson, D. (1967). Truth and meaning. *Synthese*, **17**, 304–323.

Davidson, D. (2001). What thought requires. In J. Branquinho (Ed.), *The foundations of cognitive science* (pp. 121–132). Oxford University Press.

Davies, E. B. (2010). *Why beliefs matter: Reflections on the nature of science*. Oxford University Press.

Davis, E. (1998). The Naïve physics perplex. *AI Magazine*, **19**(4), 51–79.

Davis, E., & Marcus, G. (2015). Commonsense reasoning and commonsense knowledge in artificial intelligence. *Communications of the ACM*, **58**(9), 92–103.

Dawkins, R. (1989a). *The selfish Gene, New Edition* Oxford University Press.

Dawkins, R. (1989b). The evolution of evolvability. In C. Langton (Ed.). *Artificial Life*, (pp. 201–220). Addison-Wesley.

Dawkins, R. (1982*2017). *The Extended Phenotype*. Oxford University Press.

Dawson, M. R. D. (2013). *Mind, body, world: Foundations of cognitive science*. AU Press.

D'Ettorre, P., & Hughes, D. P. (2008). *Sociobiology of communication: An interdisciplinary perspective*. Oxford University Press.

De Vree, J. K. (1996). A note on information, order, stability and adaptability. *Bio Systems*, **38**(2&3), 221–227.

Deacon, T. W. (2010). A role for relaxed selection in the evolution of the language capacity. *PNAS*, **107**(suppl. 2), 9000–9006.

Dean, L. G., Kendal, R. L., Schapiro, S. J., Thierry, B., & Laland, K. N. (2012). Identification of the social and cognitive processes underlying human cumulative culture. *Science*, **335**(6072), 1114–1118.

Dean, L. G., Vale, G. L., Laland, K. N., Flynn, E., & Kendal, R. L. (2013). Human cumulative culture: a comparative perspective. *Biological Review*, **89**, 284–301. https://doi.org/10.1111/brv.12053

Delvaux, M. (2016). *DRAFT REPORT with recommendations to the Commission on Civil Law and Rules on Robotics* (2015/2103 (INL)). European Parliament 2014–2019.

Deng, B. (2015). The robot's dilemma. *Nature*, **523**, 24–26.

Dennett, D. C. (1969). *Content and consciousness*. Routledge & Kegan Paul.

Dennett, D. C. (1978). Why you can't make a computer that feels pain. *Synthese*, **38**, 415–456.

Dennett, D. C. (1988). *The intentional stance*. The MIT Press, Bradford Books.

Dennett, D. C. & McKay, R. (2006). A continuum of mindfulness. *Behavioral and Brain Sciences*, **29**(4), 353–354.

Desai, R. H., Reilly, M., & van Dam, W. (2018). The multifaceted abstract brain. *Philosophical Transactions of the Royal Society B*, **373**, 20170122.

Dewey, J. (1931). *Individualism old and new*. George Allen & Unwin.

Di Paolo, E., & De Jaegher, H. (2012). The interactive brain hypothesis. *Frontiers in Human Neuroscience*, **6**, 163. https://doi.org/10.3389/fnhum.2012.00163

Dietrich, E. (2007). Representation. In P. Thagard (Ed.), *Philosophy and psychology of cognitive science*. Elsevier.

Dilthey, (1900*1976). The development of hermeneutics. In H. P. Pickman (Ed.). *Dilthey Selected writings*, Cambridge University Press.

Dimbleby, R., & Burton, G. (1998). *More than words: An introduction to communication* (3rd ed.). Routledge.

Diringer, D. (1968). *THE ALPHABET: A Key to the History of Mankind*. Third Edition completely revised with the collaboration of Reinhold Regensburger. Hutchinson of London.

Ditton-Phare, P., Halpin, S., Sandhu, H., Kelly, B., Vamos, M., Outram, S., Bylund, C. L., Levin, T., Kissane, D., Cohen, M., & Loughland, C. (2015). Communication skills in psychiatry training. *Australasian Psychiatry*. https://doi.org/10.1177/1039856215590026

Dityatev, A., & Rusakov, D. A. (2011). Molecular signals of plasticity at the tetrapartite synapse. *Current Opinion in Neurobiology*, **21**(2), 353–359.

Doka, K., & Tucci, A. (eds.). (2016). *Managing conflict, finding meaning*. Hospice Foundation of America.

Dove, G. (2018). Language as a disruptive technology: Abstract concepts, embodiment and the flexible mind. *Philosophical Transactions of the Royal Society B*, **373**, 20170135.

Dretske, F. I. (1981). *Knowledge and the flow of information*. Oxford, Blackwell.

Driscoll, L. N., Pettit, N. L., Minderer, M., Chettih, S. N., & Harvey, C. D. (2017). Dynamic reorganization of neuronal activity patterns in parietal cortex. *Cell* **170**, 986–999.

Duncan, S. (1999). Language and communication. In R. A. Wilson & F. C. Keil (Eds.), *The MIT encyclopedia of the cognitive sciences* (pp. 438–441). The MIT Press.

Dyer, G., et al. (2005). Towards Y3K: A 2004 Perspective on Hominisation with some Emphasis on Educational Systems. *Review of Administration and Informatics.* **17**(2), 1–17.

Eccles, J. C. (1973). Preface. In E. Polten's (Ed.), *Critique of the psycho-physical identity theory.* Mouton.

Eccles, J. C. (1994). *How the self controls its brain.* Springer-Verlag.

Edelman, G. M. (1978). Group selection and phasic reentrant signaling: a theory of higher brain function. In G. M. Edelman & V. B. Mountcastle (Eds.), *The mindful brain: Cortical organization and the group- selective theory of higher brain function* (pp. 51–100). MIT Press.

Edelman, G. M. (1987). *Neural Darwinism: The theory of neuronal.* Basic Books.

Edelman, G. M. (1992). *Bright air, brilliant fire: On the matter of the mind.* Basic Books.

Edelman, G. M., & Mountcastle, V. B. (1978). *The mindful brain: Cortical organization and the group-selective theory of higher brain functions.* The MIT Press.

Edelman, S. (1998). Representation is representation of similarities. *Behavioral and Brain Sciences,* **21**, 449–498.

Egnor, R., Miller, C., & Hauser, M. (2004). Nonhuman primate communication. In *Encyclopedia of language & linguistics—Second Edition.*

Eisenberger, NI. (2015). Social pain and the brain: Controversies, questions, and where to go from here. *Annual Review of Psychology,* **66**, 601–629.

Eliasmith, C. (2013). *How to build the brain: a neural architecture for biological cognition.* OUP.

Elstob, M. (2018). *Explaining Free Will.* Printed and distributed by Amazon.

Emery, N. J. (2006). Cognitive ornithology: The evolution of avian intelligence. *Philosophical Transactions of the Royal Society B,* **361**, 23–43. https://doi.org/10.1098/rstb.2005.1736

Emery, N. J., & Clayton, N. S. (2008). Imaginative scrub-jays, causal rooks, and a liberal application of Occam's aftershave. *Behavioral and Brain Sciences,* **31**, 134–135.

Eslami, S. M. A., Heess, N., Weber, T., Tassa, Y., Kavukcuoglu, K., & Hinton, G. E. (2016). Attend, infer, repeat: Fast scene understanding with generative models. *arXiv preprint* arXiv:1603.08575.

Farber, I., Peterman, W., & Churchland, P. S. (2001). The view from here: The nonsymbolic structure of spatial representation. In J. Branquinho (Ed.), *The foundations of cognitive science* (pp. 55–76). Oxford University Press.

Farmer, E. E., & Ryan, C. A. (1990). Interplant communication: Airborne methyl jasmonate induces synthesis of proteinase inhibitors in plant leaves. *Proceedings of the National Academy of Sciences of the United States of America,* **87**, 7713–7716.

Faskowitz, J., et al. (2022). Edges in brain networks: Contributions to models of structure and function. *Network Neuroscience,* **6**(1), 1–28.

Feigenbaum, E. A. (1959). *An information-processing theory of verbal learning.* Ph.D. Dissertation, Carnegie Institute of Technology. Pittsburgh, Penn., USA

Feigl, H. (1960). Mind-body, not a pseudoproblem. In S. Hook (Ed.), *Dimensions of mind.* New York University Press.

Feldman, M. W., & Ramachandran, S. (2018). Missing compared to what? Revisiting heritability, genes and culture. *Philosophical Transactions of the Royal Society B,* **373**, 20170064. https://doi.org/10.1098/rstb.2017.0064

Feynman, R., & Leighton, R. B. (1963). *The feynman lectures on physics*. Addison Wesley.

Fiala, N., Neubauer, F., & Peters, J. (2022). *Do economists replicate? Ruhr Economic Papers, No. 939*, RWI - Leibniz-Institut für Wirtschaftsforschung, Essen, https://doi.org/10.4419/96973100.

Fiske, A. P. (1992). The four elementary forms of sociality: Framework for a unified theory of social relations. *Psychological Review,* **99**(4), 689–723.

Fitch, W. T. (2011). The evolution of syntax: An exaptationist perspective. *Frontiers in Evolutionary Neuroscience,* **3**, 1.

Fitch, W. T., Hauser, M. D., & Chomsky, N. (2005). The evolution of the language faculty: Clarifications and implications. *Cognition,* **97**, 179–210.

Fitts, P. M. (1954). The information capacity of the human motor system in controlling the amplitude of movement. *Journal of Experimental Psychology,* **47**, 381–391.

FitzPatrick, W. J. (2017). Human altruism, evolution and moral philosophy. *R. Soc. Open Sci.,* **4**, 170441. https://doi.org/10.1098/rsos.170441

Flaherty, A. W. (2011). Brain illness and creativity: mechanisms and treatment risks. *Canadian Journal of Psychiatry,* **56**(3), 132–143.

Floridi, L. (2011). *The philosophy of information.* OUP.

Fodor, J. A. (1980). Methodological solipsism considered as a research strategy in cognitive psychology. *Behavioral and Brain Sciences,* **3**, 63–109.

Fodor, J. A. (1998). *Concepts: Where cognitive science went wrong*. OUP.

Foerder, P., Galloway, M., Barthel, T., Moore, D. E., III., & Reiss, D. (2011). Insightful problem solving in an Asian elephant. *PLoS ONE,* **6**(8), e23251.

Fogarty, L., Strimling, P., & Laland, K. N. (2011). The evolution of teaching. *Evolution,* **65**–*10*, 2760–2770.

Foley, R. A. (2016). Mosaic evolution and the pattern of transitions in the hominin lineage. *Philosophical Transactions of the Royal Society B,* **371**, 20150244. https://doi.org/10.1098/rstb.2015.0244

Foster, M. I., & Keane, M. T. (2015). Surprise as an ideal case for the interplay of cognition and emotion. *Behavioral and Brain Sciences,* **38**, e74. https://doi.org/10.1017/S0140525X14000958

Fox, E. (2018). Perspectives from affective science on understanding the nature of emotion. *Brain and Neuroscience Advances,* **2**, 1–8.

Freeman, W. J. (1999). *How brains make up their minds*. Phoenix.

Freud, S. (1895*2001). Project for a Scientific Psychology. In J. Strachey (Ed.). *The standard edition of the complete psychological works of Sigmund Freud*, Volume I, Vintage, The Hogarth Press.

Friston, K. J., Buechel, C., Fink, G. R., Morris, J., Rolls, E., & Dolan, R. J. (1997). Psychophysiological and modulatory interactions in neuroimaging. *NeuroImage,* **6**(3), 218–229.

Froese, T., & Ziemke, T. (2009). Enactive artificial intelligence: Investigating the systemic organization of life and mind. *Artificial Intelligence,* **173**, 466–500.

Fullford, K. W. M., Thornton, T., & Graham, G. (Eds.). (2006). *Oxford handbook of philosophy and psychiatry*. Oxford University Press.

Gallese, V. (2003). The manifold nature of interpersonal relations: The quest for a common mechanism. *Philosophical Transactions of the Royal Society of London B,* **358**(1431), 517–528.

Gallistel, C. R. (1990). Representations in animal cognition: An introduction. *Cognition,* **37**, 1–22.

Garagnani, M., Kirilina, E., & Pulvermüller, F. (2021). Semantic grounding of novel spoken words in the primary visual cortex. *Frontiers in Human Neuroscience,* **15**, 581847. https://doi.org/10.3389/fnhum.2021.581847

Geertz, C. (1973). *The interpretation of cultures: Selected essays*. Basic Books.

Gelb, I. (1963). *A study of writing, second edition*. University of Chicago Press.

Gelepithis, P. A. M. (1984). *On the foundations of artificial intelligence and human cognition*. PhD Thesis, Dept. of Cybernetics, Brunel University, England.

Gelepithis, P. A. M. (1988). Survey of theories of meaning. *Cognitive Systems,* **2**, 141–162.

Gelepithis, P. A. M. (1989). Knowledge, truth, time, and topological spaces. In *Proceedings of the 12th International Congress on Cybernetics,* (pp. 247–256), Namur.

Gelepithis, P. A. M. (1991). The possibility of machine intelligence and the impossibility of human–machine communication. *Cybernetica,* **XXXIV**, *4*, 255–268.

Gelepithis, P. A. M. (1997). A rudimentary theory of information: Consequences for information science and information systems. *World Futures* **49**, pp 263–274. Reprinted in *The Quest for a Unified Theory of Information*. Hofkirchner, W. (ed.), Gordon and Breach Publishers.

Gelepithis, P. A. M. (1999). Embodiments of theories of mind: A review and comparison. In M. P. Bekakos, M. Sambandham, & D. J. Evans (Eds.), *Computational methods and neural networks* (pp. 235–264). Dynamic Publishers Inc.

Gelepithis, P. A. M. (2001a). *Νοήμονα Συστήματα, Τόμος-1: Αναπαράσταση Γνώσης, Κοινωνικές και Ψυχολογικές Επιπτώσεις της Τεχνητής Νοημοσύνης*. Εκδόσεις Σταμούλη, Αθήνα, Ελλάς. *(Noémon Systems Volume-1: Knowledge Representation, Social and Psychological Impact of Artificial Intelligence*. Stamoulis Editions, Averof St., Athens, Hellas).

Gelepithis, P. A. M. (2001b). Complex intelligent systems: Juxtaposition of foundational notions and a research agenda. *Entropy*, **2001**(3), 247–258.

Gelepithis, P. A. M. (2003). Criteria and evaluation of cognitive theories. *Behavioral and Brain Sciences*, **26**, 607–609.

Gelepithis, P. A. M. (2004). Remarks on the foundations of cybernetics and cognitive science. *Kybernetes*, **33**, 9–10.

Gelepithis, P. A. M. (2005). Knowledge, IT and the Firm. In: *Encyclopedia of information science and technology*, (Vol. I–V, pp 1783–1787), M. KhosrowPour, Editor-in-Chief. Idea Group Reference, Hershey.

Gelepithis, P. A. M. (2009). Outline of a new approach to the nature of mind. *Oxford University Research Archive*. (p. 42) http://ora.ouls.ox.ac.uk/objects/uuid:0c28b7dfd3dc-4786-95fde6c8886f4341.

Gelepithis, P. A. M. (2024b). *Unification of artificial intelligence and psychology: Volume Two—Consequences*. Palgrave Macmillan, Springer Nature.

Giaume, C., Koulakoff, A., Roux, L., Holcman, D., & Rouach, N. (2010). Astroglia networks: A step further in neuroglia and gliovascular interactions. *Nature Reviews Neuroscience*, **11**, 87–99. https://doi.org/10.1038/nrn2757

Ginsborg, H. (2012). Meaning, understanding and normativity. *The Aristotelian Society Supplementary*, **86**(1), 127–146.

Gintis, H. (2007). A framework for the unification of behavioral sciences. *Behavioral and Brain Sciences*, **30**, 1–16.

Gitt, W. (1989). Information: The third fundamental quantity. *Siemens Review*, *56*, 6.

Glüer, K., & Wikforss, Å. (2015). Meaning normativism: Against the simple argument. *Organon*, **F22**, 63–73.

Godfrey-Smith, P. (2017). *Other minds: The octopus and the evolution of intelligent life*. William Collins.

Gold, I., & Stoljar, D. (1999). A neuron doctrine in the philosophy of neuroscience. *Behavioral and Brain Sciences*, **22**, 809–869.

Goldberg, S. D. (Ed.). (2007). *Internalism and externalism in semantics and epistemology*. Oxford University Press.

Goldstein, I., & Papert, S. (1977). Artificial intelligence, language, and the study of knowledge. *Cognitive Science,* **1**(1), 84–123.

Goody, J., & Watt, I. (1963). The consequences of literacy. *Comparative Studies in Society and History,* **5**(3), 304–345.

Gordon, A. S., & Hobbs, J. R. (2004). Formalizations of commonsense psychology. *AI Magazine,* **25**(4), 49–62.

Gosden, C. (2008). Social ontologies. *Philosophical Transactions of the Royal Society B,* **363**, 2003–2010. https://doi.org/10.1098/rstb.2008.0013

Gould, S. J. (1980). Is a new and general theory of evolution emerging? *Paleobiology,* **6**(1), 119–130.

Grace, K., Salvatier, J., Dafoe, A., Zhang, B., & Evans, O. (2018). Viewpoint: When will ai exceed human performance? Evidence from AI experts. *Journal of Artificial Intelligence Research,* **62**, 729–754.

Grafen, A. (2007). The formal Darwinism project: A mid-term report. *Journal of Evolutionary Biology,* **20**(4), 1243–1254. https://doi.org/10.1111/j.1420-9101.2007.01321.x

Greeno, J. G. (1977). Process of understanding in problem solving. In N. J. Castellan Jr., D. B. Pisoni, & G. R. Potts (Eds.), *Cognitive theory* (Vol. **2**, pp. 43–83). Laurence Erlbaum Associates.

Greenspan, S. I., & Shanker, S. G. (2004). *The first idea: How symbols, language, and intelligence evolved from our primate ancestors to modern humans*. Da Capo Press.

Greslehner, G. P. (2018). The "unreasonable effectiveness of mathematics" in biology and the fallacy from complexity. In G. M. Mras, P. Weingartner & B. Ritter (eds.). *Contributions of the Austrian Ludwig Wittgenstein Society Volume XXVI. Philosophy of Logic and Mathematics. Contributions of the 41st International Wittgenstein Symposium*, Austrian Ludwig Wittgenstein Society: pp. 70–72, 2018

Grice, H. P. (1957). Meaning. *Philosophical Review,* **66**, 377–388.

Grice, H. P. (1968). Utterer's meaning, sentence-meaning and word-meaning. *Foundations of Language* **4**, 225–242; reprinted in Searle JR (1971).

Grice, H. P. (1969). Utterer's meaning and intention.*The Philosophical Review,* **78**(2), 147–177.

Griffin, E., Ledbetter, A., & Sparks, G (2023). *A first look at communication theory*. 11th Edition. McGraw Hill

Grilner, S. (2014). Megascience efforts and the brain. *Neuron,* **82**, 1209–1211.

Grünbaum, A. (1989). The pseudo-problem of creation in physical cosmology. *Philosophy of Science,* **56**(3), 373–394.

Grüter, C., Sol Balbuena, M., & Farina, W. M. (2008). Informational conflicts created by the waggle dance. *Proceeding of the Royal Society B,* **275**, 1321–1327. https://doi.org/10.1098/rspb.2008.0186

Gu, L., Poddar, S., Lin, Y., Long, Z., Zhang, D., Zhang, Q., Shu, L., Qiu, X., Kam, M., Javey, A., & Fan, Z. (2020). A biomimetic eye with a hemispherical perovskite nanowire array retina. *Nature,* **581**, 278–282.

Güçlütürk, Y., et al. (2017). Visualising apparent personality analysis with deep residual networks. In *2017 IEEE International Conference on Computer Vision Workshops (ICCVW)*, pp. 3101–3109. Venice, Italy.

Guerrero, L. K., Ersen, P. A., & Affix, W. A. (2020). *Close encounters: Communication in relationships* (6th ed.). Sage Publications.

Guillery, R. W. (2005). Observations of synaptic structures: Origins of the neuron doctrine and its current status. *Philosophical Transactions of the Royal Society B,* **360**, 1281–1307. https://doi.org/10.1098/rstb.2003.1459

Guzman, A. L., & Lewis, S. C. (2020). Artificial intelligence and communication: A human–machine communication research agenda. *New Media & Society,* **22**(1), 70–86.

Habermas, J. (1981*1984). *The theory of communicative action, Volume 1: Reason and the Rationalization of Society.* Polity Press.

Habermas, J. (1987). *The theory of communicative action, Volume 2:Lifeworld and system: A critique of functionalist reason.* Polity Press.

Hagoort, P. (2005). On Broca, brain, and binding: A new framework. *TRENDS in Cognitive Sciences,* **9**(9), 416–423.

Hall, E. T. (1959). *The silent language.* Doubleday.

Harmand, S., et al. (2015). 3.3 -million-year-old stone tools from Lomekwi 3, West Turkana, Kenya. *Nature* **521**, 310–315. 3.3-million-year-old stone tools from Lomekwi 3, West Turkana, Kenya. https://doi.org/10.1038/nature14464.

Harri-Augstein, E. S., & Thomas, L. F. (2001). Conversational science and advanced learning technologies (ALT): Designing tools for a conversational pedagogy based on self-organised learning. *Kybernetes,* **30**(7–8), 921–954.

Harri-Augstein, E. S., & Thomas, L. F. (2008). A Conversational framework for self- organised learning: Modelling personal meaning for effective action in the world. In R. Luppicini (Ed.), *Handbook of conversation design for instructional applications* (pp. 308–342). Information Science Reference.

Harris, D. W. (2019). Intention recognition as the mechanism of human communication. In A. Sullivan (Ed.), *Sensation, thoughts, language: Essays in honor of Brian Loar.* Routledge.

Hattiangadi, A. (2006). Is meaning normative? *Mind & Language,* **21**(2), 220–240.

Hauser, M. D., & Marler, P. (1999). Animal communication. In R. A. Wilson & F. C. Keil (Eds.), *The MIT encyclopedia of the cognitive sciences* (pp. 22–24). The MIT Press.

Hauser, M. D. (1996). *The evolution of communication.* MIT Press.

Hauser, M. D., Chomsky, N., & Fitch, W. T. (2002). The faculty of language: What is it, who has it, and how did it evolve? *Science,* **298**, 1569–1579.

Hayes, P. J. (1978*1979). The Naïve physics manifesto. In D. Michie (Ed.). *Expert systems in the micro-electronic age* (pp. 242–270). Edinburgh University Press.

Hebb, D. O. (1949). *The organisation of behaviour.* John Wiley and Sons.

Hebb, D. O. (1980a). *Essay on mind.* Lawrence Erlbaum Associates.

Hebb, D. O. (1980b). The structure of thought. In P. W. Jusczyk & R. M. Klein (Eds.), *The nature of thought: Essays in honor of D. O. Hebb* (pp. 19–35). Laurence Erlbaum Associates.

Heim, S., et al. (2012). The language-number interface in the brain: a complex paramedic study of quantifiers and quantities. *Frontiers in Evolutionary Neuroscience,* **4**, 4.

Heisenberg, W. (1958*1989). *Physics and Philosophy: The revolution in modern science.* Penguin Books.

Henle, M. (1962). On the relation between logic and thinking. *Psychological Review,* **69**, 366–378.

Henrich, J., Boyd, R., & Richerson, P. J. (2008). Five misunderstandings about cultural evolution. *Human Nature,* **19**, 119–137.

Henriques, G. R. (2003). The tree of knowledge system and the theoretical unification of psychology. *Review of General Psychology, 7*(2), 150–182.

Henriques, G. R. (2008). The problem of psychology and the integration of human knowledge: Contrasting Wilson's consilience with the tree of knowledge system. *Theory & Psychology,* **18**(6), 731–755.

Henriques, G. R. (2011). *A new unified theory of psychology.* Springer.

Hepp, A. (2020). Artificial companions, social bots and work bots: Communicative robots as research objects of media and communication studies. *Media, Culture & Society,* **42**(7–8), 1410–1426.

Herman, L. M., Richards, D. G., & Wolz, J. P. (1984). Comprehension of sentences by bottlenosed dolphins. *Cognition,* **16**, 129–219.

Herman, L. M., Uyeyama, R. K., & Pack, A. A. (2008). Bottlenose dolphins understand relationships between concepts. *Behavioral and Brain Sciences,* **31**(2), 139–140.

Hewlett, B. S. (2016). Evolutionary cultural anthropology: Containing ebola outbreaks and explaining hunter-gatherer childhoods. *Current Anthropology,* **57**(S13), S27–S37.

Heyes, C. (2019a). Précis of cognitive gadgets: The cultural evolution of thinking. *Behavioral and Brain Sciences,* **42**, 1–13.

Heyes, C. (2019b). Author's response: Cognition blindness and cognitive gadgets. *Behavioral and Brain Sciences,* **42**, 42–47.

Higginbotham, J. T. (2001). On referential semantics and cognitive science. In J. Branquinho (Ed.), *The foundations of cognitive science* (pp. 145–156). Oxford University Press.

Hilgetag, C. C., Goulas, A. (2020). 'Hierarchy' in the organization of brain networks. *Philosophical Transactions of the Royal Society B* **375**: 20190319. https://doi.org/10.1098/rstb.2019.0319.

Blount, J. D., et al. (2009). Warning displays may function as honest signals of toxicity.Proc. *R. Soc. B*, (2009) 276, 871–877.

Hippocrates of Cos (400 B.C.E.) *On the sacred disease.* The Internet Classics Archive. Trans by F. Davis)

Hobbs, J. R., & Moore, R. (Eds.). (1985). *Formal theories of the commonsense world.* Ablex Publishing.

Hockett, C. F. (1960) The Origin of Speech, Scientific American 203, 88–111 Reprinted in: Wang, William S-Y. (1982) *Human Communication: Language and Its Psychobiological Bases*, Scientific American pp. 4–12.

Holyoak, K. J., & Morrison, R. G. (Eds.). (2005). *The Cambridge handbook of thinking and reasoning.* Cambridge University Press.

Holyoak, K. J., & Morrison, R. G. (2005). Thinking and reasoning: A reader's guide. In K. J. Holyoak & R. G. Morrison (Eds.), *The Cambridge handbook of thinking and reasoning* (pp. 1–9). Cambridge University Press.

Hoorn, F. J. (2018). Theory of robot communication: I. The medium is the communication partner. *arXiv:cs*, 2502565(v1), pp. 1–21.

Hume, D. (1758*1977). *An inquiry concerning human understanding.* Bobbs-Merill Co., U.S.A.

Hunt, E. B. (1989). Cognitive science: definition, status, and questions. *Annual Review of Psychology,* **40**, 603–629.

Hunt, G. R., Gray, R. D., & Taylor, A. H. (2013). Why is tool use rare in animals? In C. M. Sanz, J. Call, & C. Boesch (Eds.), *Tool use in animals: Cognition and ecology.* Cambridge University Press.

Hunt, H. T. (2005). Why psychology is/is not traditional science: The self referential bases of psychological research and theory. *Review of General Psychology,* **9**(4), 358–374.

Hurford, J. R. (2003). The neural basis of predicate-argument structure. *Behavioral and Brain Sciences,* **26**, 261–316.

Hutson, M. (2021). The language machines. *Nature,* **591**(4), 22–25.

Huxley, J. (1942*1974). *Evolution: The modern synthesis*, 3rd ed. Allen & Unwin

Israel, D., & Perry, J. (1990). What is information? In P. P. Hanson (Ed.), *Information, language, and cognition.* The University of British Columbia Press.

Ivancovsky, T., et al. (2024). A shared novelty-seeking basis for creativity and curiosity. *Behavioral and Brain Sciences,* **47**, e89.

Jacobs, I. F., von Bayern, A., & Osvath, M. (2016). A novel tool-use mode in animals: New Caledonian crows insert tools to transport objects. *Animal Cognition,* **19**, 1249–1252.

James, W. (1890). *The principles of psychology*, (Vol. 1, 2). Authorised edition by Dover Publications.

James, W. (1892). *Psychology—Briefer course.* Henry Holt & Company. New York.

Jeannerod, M. (2006). *Motor cognition: What actions tell the self*. Oxford University Press.

Jia, H. (2019). Foundations of the theory of signs (1938): A critique. *Chinese Semiotic Studies,* **15**(1), 1–14.

Johnson-Laird, P. N. (1977). Procedural semantics. *Cognition,* **5**, 189–214.

Johnson-Laird, P. N. (1983). *Mental models: Towards a cognitive science of language, inference, and consciousness.* Cambridge University Press.

Johnson-Laird, P. N. (1988). A computational analysis of consciousness. In A. J. Marcel & E. Bisiach (Eds.), *Consciousness in contemporary science.* Oxford University Press.

Johnson-Laird, P. N. (2003). Models, causation, and explanation. In A. J. Sanford (Ed.), *The nature and limits of human understanding.* T&T Clark.

Johnson-Laird, P. N. (2005). Mental models and thought. In K. J. Holyoak, & R. G. Morrison, (Eds.). (2005a). *The Cambridge handbook of thinking and reasoning.* Cambridge University Press.

Johnson-Laird, P. N., & Wason, P. C. (Eds.). (1977). *Thinking: Readings in cognitive science.* Cambridge University Press.

Johnstone, R. A. (1999). Signaling of need, sibling competition, and the cost of honesty. *PNAS,* **96**(22), 12644–12649.

Jones, T. B., & Kamil, A. C. (1973). Tool-making and tool-using in the northern blue jay. *Science,* **180**(4090), 1076–1078.

Just, M. A., & Carpenter, P. A. (1987). *The psychology of reading and language comprehension.* Allyn and Bacon.

Kaku, M. (2014). *El futuro de nuestra mente: El reto científico para entender, mejorar y fortalecer nuestra mente.* Penguin Random House.

Kandel, E. R. (2006). *In search of memory: The emergence of a new science of mind.* W. W. Norton & Company.

Kandel, E. R., & Pittinger, C. (1999). The past, the future and the biology of memory storage. *Philosophical Transactions of the Royal Society B,* **354**, 2027–2052.

Kandel, E. R., Dudai, Y., & Mayford, M. R. (2014). The molecular and systems biology of memory. *Cell,* **157**, 163–186.

Kapoor, R., Walters, S. P., & Al-Aswad, L. A. (2019). The current state of artificial intelligence in ophthalmology. *Survey of Ophthalmology,* **64**(2), 233–240.

Katz, E., & Danet, B. (1973). Communication between bureaucracy and the public: A review of the literature. In I. S. Pool, F. W. Frey, W. Schramm, N. Maccoby, & E. B. Parker (Eds.), *Handbook of communication*. Rand McNally College Publishing Company.

Katz, J. J., & Fodor, J. A. (1963). The structure of a semantic theory. *Language,* **39**(2), 170–210.

Kaufman, C. D., Liu, S. C., Cvetkovic, C., Lee, C. A., Naseri Kouzehgarani, G., Gillette, R., Bashir, R., & Gillette, M. U. (2020). Emergence of functional neuromuscular junctions in an engineered, multicellular spinal cord-muscle bioactuator. *APL Bioengineering,* **4**, 026104.

Kay, K. N., et al. (2008). Identifying natural images from human brain activity. *Nature,* **452**, 3353–3355.

Kelso, J. A. S. (1995). *Dynamic patterns: The self-organization of brain and behavior*. The MIT Press.

Kelly, G. (1955). *The psychology of personal constructs*. (Volumes One & Two). W. W. Norton & Company Inc.

Kerbe, W. (2016). What is life--In everyday understanding? A Focus group study on lay perspectives on the term life. *Artificial Life,* **22**, 119–133. https://doi.org/10.1162/ARTL_a_00181

Kimbel, W. H., & Villmoare, B. (2016). From australopithecus to homo: The transition that wasn't. *Philosophical Transactions of the Royal Society B,* **371**, 20150248.

Kimble, G. A. (1994). A frame of reference for psychology. *American Psychologist,* **49**(6), 510–519.

Klump, B. C. (2019). Of crows and tools. *Science,* **366**(6468), 965

Knuth, D. E. (1977*1997). *The art of computer programming, Volume 1: Fundamental algorithms, Third Edition*. Addison Wesley.

Koch, C. (1999). Computing in single neurons. In R. A. Wilson & F. C. Keil (Eds.), *The MIT encyclopedia of the cognitive sciences* (pp. 174–176). The MIT Press.

Koch, S. (1981). The nature and limits of psychological knowledge: Lessons of a Century qua "Science." *American Psychologist,* **36**, 257–269.

Kolmogorov, A. N. (1968). Logical basis for information theory and probability theory. *IEEE Transactions on Information Theory,* **14**, 662–664.

Kolodny, O. (2018). Integrative studies of cultural evolution: crossing disciplinary boundaries to produce new insights. *Phil. Trans. R. Soc. B* **373**: 20170048. http://dx.doi.org/10.1098/rstb.2017.0048.

Kotseruba, I., & Tsotsos, J. K. (2020). 40 years of cognitive architectures: Core cognitive abilities and practical applications. *Artificial Intelligence Review*, **53**, 17–94.

Köhler, W. (1927). *The mentality of Apes*, Translated from the Second Revised Edition by E. Winter. Kegan Paul. First edition 1925. Originally appeared in 1917.

Krichbaum, S., Davila, A., Lazarowski, L., & Katz, J. S. (2020). Animal cognition. Oxford research encyclopedia psychology. *Trends in Cognitive Sciences*, **17**(8), 401–412.

Kriegeskorte, N., & Kievit, R. A. (2013). Representational geometry: integrating cognition, computation, and the brain. *Trends in Cognitive Sciences*, **17**(8), 401-412.

Krutzen, M., Kreicker, S., MacLeod, C. D., Learmonth, J., Kopps, A. M., Walsham, P., & Allen, S. J. (2014). Cultural transmission of tool use by Indo-Pacific bottlenose dolphins (*Tursiops* sp.). provides access to a novel foraging niche. *Proceedings of the Royal Society B: Biological Sciences*, **281**, 20140374. https://doi.org/10.1098/rspb.2014.0374

Krystal, J. H., Bennett, A. L., Bremner, F. D., Southwick, S. M., & Charney, D. S. (1995). Toward a cognitive neuroscience of dissociation and altered memory functions in post-traumatic stress disorder. In M. J. Friedman, D. S. Charney, & A. Y. Deutsch (Eds.), *Neurobiological and clinical consequences of stress: From normal adaptation of post-traumatic stress disorder* (pp. 239–269). Lippincott-Raven.

Kuhn, T. S. (1977). Objectivity, value judgement, and theory choice. In T. S. Kuhn (Ed.), *The essential tension: Selected studies in scientific tradition and change* (pp. 435–450). University of Chicago Press.

Kukla, A. (1992). Unification as a goal for psychology. *American Psychologist*, **47**, 1054–1055.

Külpe, O. (1893). *Grundriss der Psychologie. Auf experimenteller Grundlage dargestellt*. Leipzig: Wilhelm Engelmann; translated into English by E.B. Titchener as Külpe, O. (1895). *Outlines of Psychology. Based upon the Results of Experimental Investigation*. Swan Sonnenschein.

Kurto, K., & Itskov, V. (2008). Cell groups reveal structure of stimulus space. *PLOS Computational Biology*, **4**, 1–13.

Laird, J. E. (2012). *The soar cognitive architecture*. The MIT Press.

Laird, J. E., Lebiere, C., & Rosenbloom, P. S. (2017). *A standard model of the mind: Toward a common computational framework across artificial intelligence, cognitive science, neuroscience, and robotics* (pp. 13–26). AI Magazine.

Lake, B. M., Ullman, T. D., Tenenbaum, J. B., & Gershman, S. J. (2017). Building machines that learn and think like people. *Behavioral and Brain Sciences*. https://doi.org/10.1017/S0140525X16001837

Laland, K. N., Uller, T., Feldman, M., Sterelny, K., Müller, G. B., Moczek, A., Jablonka, E., & Odling-Smee, J. (2014). Does evolutionary theory need a rethink? Yes, urgently. *Nature,* **514**, 161–164.

Laland, K. N., Uller, T., Feldman, M. W., Sterelny, K., Müller, G. B., Moczek, A., Jablonka, E., & Odling-Smee, J. (2015). The extended evolutionary synthesis: Its structure, assumptions and predictions. *Proceedings of the Royal Society B,* **282**, 20151019.

Lallouette, J., De Pitta, M., Ben-Jacob, E., & Berry, H. (2014). Sparse short-distance connections enhance calcium wave propagation in a 3D model of astrocyte networks. *Frontiers in Computational Neuroscience,* **8**(45), 1–18.

Lamb, J. F., et al. (1984). *Essentials of physiology* (2nd ed.). Blackwell Scientific Publications.

Langefors, B., & Samuelson, K. (1976). *Information and data systems.* Petrocelli/Charte.

Langton, C. G. (Ed.). (1995). *Artificial life: An overview.* The MIT Press.

Lash, T. L., & Vandenbroucke, J. P. (2012). Should preregistration of epidemiologic study protocols become compulsory? Reflections and a counterproposal. *Epidemiology,* **23**(2), 184–188.

Leahey, T. H. (2022). *Fundamentals of cognitive science: Minds, brain, magic, and evolution.* Routledge.

Lentini, R., Martín, N. Y., Forlin, M., Belmonte, L., Fontana, J., Cornella, M., Martini, L., Tamburini, S., Bentley, W. E., Jousson, O., & Mansy, S. S. (2017). Two-way chemical communication between artificial and natural cells. *ACS Central Science,* **3**, 117–123.

Leong, V., Byrne, E., Clackson, K., Georgieva, S., Lam, S., & Wass, S. (2017). Speaker gaze increases information coupling between infant and adult brains. *PNAS,* **114**(50), 13290–13295.

Lepore, E., & Smith, B. C. (Eds.). (2006). *The Oxford handbook of philosophy of language.* Oxford University Press.

Leshinskaya, A., & Caramazza, A. (2016). For a cognitive neuroscience of concepts: Moving beyond the grounding issue. *Psychonomic Bulletin & Review,* **23**, 991–1001. https://doi.org/10.3758/s13423-015-0870-z

Lewens, T. (2017). Human nature, human culture: The case of cultural evolution. *Interface Focus,* 7, 20170018. https://doi.org/10.1098/rsfs.2017.0018

Li, M., Liu, J., & Tsien, J. Z. (2016). Theory of connectivity: Nature and nurture of cell assemblies and cognitive computation. *Frontiers in Neural Circuits,* **10**, 34.

Lickliter, R., & Honeycutt, H. (2013). A developmental evolutionary framework for psychology. *Review of General Psychology,* **17**(2), 184–189.

Lieberman, P. (2007). The evolution of human speech: Its anatomical and neural bases. *Current Anthropology,* **48**(1), 39–66.

Lieder, F., & Griffiths, T. L. (2019). Resource-rational analysis: understanding human cognition as the optimal use of limited computational resources. *Behavioral and Brain Sciences*, Vol. **43**, e1.

Lind, J., et al. (2013). Dating human cultural capacity using phylogenetic principles. *Scientific Reports,* **3**, 1785. https://doi.org/10.1038/srep01785

Litman, L., & Reber, A. S. (2005). Implicit cognition and thought. In K. J. Holyoak, & R. G. Morrison, (Eds.). (2005a). *The Cambridge handbook of thinking and reasoning*. Cambridge University Press.

Littlejohn, S. W., & Foss, K. A. (Eds.). (2009). *Encyclopedia of communication theory*. SAGE Publications.

Littlejohn, S. W., Foss, K. A., & Wetzel, J. G. (2021). *Theories of human communication* (12th ed.). Waveband Press.

Loar, B. (1999). Meaning. In R. Audi (Ed.), *The Cambridge dictionary of philosophy* (2nd ed.). Cambridge University Press.

Locke, J. (1690*1975). *An Essay concerning human understanding*. Oxford University Press.

Longino, H. E. (1990). *Science as social knowledge: Values and objectivity in scientific inquiry*. Princeton University Press.

Lucas, A. J., Kings, M., Whittle, D., Davey, E., Happé, F., Caldwell, C. A., & Thornton, A. (2020). The value of teaching increases with tool complexity in cumulative cultural evolution. *Proceedings of the Royal Society B,* **287**, 20201885.

Luger, G. F. (2002). *Artificial intelligence: Structures and strategies for complex problem solving* (4th ed.). Addison Wesley.

Luria, A. R. (1965*68). *A little book about a vast memory: The mind of a mnemonist*. Basic Books, Inc., Publishers. N.Y., London. Trans from the Russian by Lynn Solotaroff. With a Foreword by Jerome S. Bruner.

Lurz, R. W. (2007) In Defense of Wordless Thoughts About Thoughts. *Mind & Language*, **22**: 270–96.

Lyons, J. (1981). *Language and linguistics: An introduction*. Cambridge University Press.

Macdonald, G., & Papineau, D. (2006). Introduction. In G. Macdonald & D. Papineau (Eds.), *Teleosemantics*. Oxford University Press.

Macfarlane, A. (1996). Individualism. In A. Cupers & J. Cupers (Eds.), *The social science encyclopedia* (2nd ed.). Routledge.

Machlup, F., & Mansfield, U. (Eds.). (1983). *The study of information: Interdisciplinary messages*. John Wiley & Sons.

MacLean, E. L. (2016) Unraveling the evolution of uniquely human cognition. *PNAS* June 7, 2016 **113**(23), 6348–6354.

Majumdar, S., & Pal, S. (2017). Bacterial intelligence: Imitation games, time-sharing, and long-range quantum coherence. *Journal of Cell Communication Signal,* **11**, 281–284.

Majumdar, S., & Pal, S. (2018). Information transmission in microbial, and fungal communication: From classical to quantum. *Journal of Cell Communication and Signalling,* **12**, 491–502.

Mallet, J. (2007). *Species, concepts of encyclopedia of biodiversity.*

Mandler, G. (2011). From association to organization. *Current Directions in Psychological Science,* **20**(4), 232–235.

Mannheim, K. (1929/31/54*1954). *Ideology and Utopia: An introduction to the sociology of knowledge.* With a Preface by L. Wirth. Routledge & Kegan Paul, London. First published in German in 1929.

Mannu, M., & Ottoni, E. B. (2009). The enhanced tool-kit of two groups of monkeys in the Caatinga: Tool making, associative use, and secondary tools. *American Journal of Primatology,* **71**(3), 242–251. https://doi.org/10.1002/ajp.20642

Margolis, E., & Lawrence, S. (2007). The ontology of concepts—Abstract objects or mental representations? *Noûs,* **41**(4), 561–593.

Margolis, E., & Lawrence, S. (2019). Concepts. In Edward N. Zalta (Ed). *The stanford encyclopedia of philosophy* (Summer 2019 Edition).

Marijuan, P. C. (1996). First conference on foundations of information science: From computers and quantum physics to cells, nervous systems, and societies. *Bio Systems,* **38**(2&3), 135–140.

Markson, L., & Bloom, P. (1997). Evidence against a dedicated system of word learning in children. *Nature,* **385**, 813–815.

Markus, H. R., & Kitayama, S. (1991). Culture and the self: Implications for cognition, emotion, and motivation. *Psychological Review,* **98**, 224–253.

Marsh, T., & Boag, S. (2014). Unifying psychology: Shared ontology, and the continuum of practical applications. *Review of General Psychology,* **18**(1), 49–59.

Marshall, P., & Bredy, T. W. (2016). Cognitive neuroepigenetics: the next evolution in our understanding of the molecular mechanisms underlying learning and memory? *Npj Science of Learning,* **1**, 16014.

Martin, A. E., & Baggio, G. (2019). Modelling meaning composition from formalism to mechanism. *Philosophical Transactions of the Royal Society B,* **375**, 20190298. https://doi.org/10.1098/rstb.2019.0298

Marupaka, N., Iyer, L. R., & Minai, A. A. (2012). Connectivity and thought: The influence of semantic network structure in a neurodynamical model of thinking. *Neural Networks,* **32**, 147–158.

Marwick, B. (2003). Pleistocene exchange networks as evidence for the evolution of language. *Cambridge Archaeological Journal,* **13**(1), 67–81.

Maslen, H., Douglas, T., Kadosh, R. C., Levy, N., & Savulescu, J. (2014). The regulation of cognitive enhancement devices: Extending the medical model. *Journal of Law and the Biosciences.* https://doi.org/10.1093/jlb/lst003

Matessi, G., Matos, R. J., & Dabelsteen, T. (2008). Communication in social networks of territorial animals: networking at different levels in birds and other systems. In P. d'Ettorre, & D. P. Hughes (Eds.). *Sociobiology of communication: An interdisciplinary perspective*, (pp. 33–53). Oxford University Press.

Mattelart, A., & Mattelart, M. (1995*1998). *Theories of communication: A short introduction*, trans. Taponier, S. G., & Cohen, J. A. SAGE Publications Ltd.

Maynard Smith, J., & Szathmáry, E. (1997). *The major transitions in evolution.* Revised edition. OUP, Oxford. First edition 1995, Freeman.

Maynard Smith, J. & Harper, D. (2003). *Animal signals*. Oxford University Press.

Mayr, E. (2004). *What makes biology unique? Considerations on the autonomy of a scientific discipline*. Cambridge University Press.

McBrearty, S., & Brooks, A. S. (2000). The revolution that wasn't: a new interpretation of the origin of modern human behavior. *Journal of Human Evolution*, **39**, 453–563.

McCarthy, J., & Hayes, P. J. (1969). Some philosophical problems from the standpoint of artificial intelligence. *Machine Intelligence*, **4**, 463–502.

McCarthy, J., Minsky, M. L., Rochester, N., Shannon, C. E. (1955). A proposal for the Dartmouth Summer Research Project on Artificial Intelligence. August 31, 1955. http://www-formal.stanford.edu/jmc/history/dartmouth/dartmouth.html (20/4/2017).

McCauley, R. N. (1988). Epistemology in an age of cognitive science. *Philosophical Psychology,* **1**(2), 143–152.

McCulloch, W. S., & Pitts, W. H. (1943*1988). A logical calculus of the ideas immanent i nervous activity. In W. S. McCulloch (Ed.). *Embodiments of mind.* MIT Press. Originally in *Bulletin of Mathematical Biophysics,* **5**, 115–133.

McDowell, J. (1994). *Mind and world*. The MIT Press.

McGann, M., De Jaegher, H., & Di Paolo, E. (2013). Enaction and psychology. *Review of General Psychology,* **17**(2), 203–209.

McGarvey, D. J., & Croteau, R. (1995). Terpenoid metabolism. *The Plant Cell,* 7, 1015–1026.

McPherron, S. P., et al. (2010). Evidence for stone-tool-assisted consumption of animal tissues before 3.39 million years ago at Kikika, Ethiopia. *Nature,* **466**, 857–860. https://doi.org/10.1038/nature09248

Mead, G. H. (†1934*1962). *Mind, self and society: From the standpoint of a social behaviorist*. University of Chicago Press.

Medin, D. L., & Rips, L. J. (2005). Concepts and categories: Memory, meaning, and metaphysics. In K. J. Holyoak & R. G. Morrison (Eds.), *The Cambridge handbook of thinking and reasoning* (pp. 37–72). Cambridge University Press.

Mensen, A., et al. (2017). EEG differentiation analysis and stimulus set meaningfulness. *Frontiers in Psychology,* **8**, 1748.

Mercier, H., & Sperber, D. (2011). Why do humans reason? Arguments for an argumentative theory. *Behavioral and Brain Sciences,* **34**(2), 57–74.
Messer, D. I. (1994). *The development of communication: From social interaction to language*. John Wiley & Sons.
Mesoudi, A. (2017). Pursuing Darwin's curious parallel: Prospects for a science of cultural evolution. *PNAS,* **114**(30), 7853–7860.
Mesoudi, A., Whiten, A., & Laland, K. N. (2006). Towards a unified science of cultural evolution. *Behavioral and Brain Sciences,* **29**, 329–383.
Mesoudi, A., & Thornton, A. (2018). What is cumulative cultural evolution? *Proceedings of the Royal Society B,* **285**, 20180712. https://doi.org/10.1098/rspb.2018.0712
Michie, D. (1985). Guest editorial. *Expert Systems,* **2**(1), 3–5.
Miłkowski, M. (2016). Unification strategies in cognitive science. *Studies in Logic, Grammar and Rhetoric,* **48**(61), 13–33.
Miller, G. A. (1956). The magical number seven, plus or minus two: Some limits on our capacity for processing information. *Psychological Review,* **63**, 81–97.
Miller, G. A. (2003). The cognitive revolution: A historical perspective. *Trends in Cognitive Science,* 7(3), 141–144.
Millikan, R. G. (1984). *Language, thought and other biological categories*. MIT Press.
Millikan, R. G. (1998). A common structure for concepts of individuals, stuffs, and real kinds: More Mama, more milk, and more mouse. *Behavioral and Brain Sciences,* **21**, 55–100.
Mills, C., Zamani, A., White, R., & Christoff, K. (2021). Out of the blue: Understanding abrupt and wayward transitions in thought using probability and predictive processing. *Philosophical Transactions of the Royal Society B,* **376**, 20190692.
Minsky, M. (1968). *Semantic information processing*. The MIT Press.
Molden, D. C., & Higgins, E. T. (2005). Motivated thinking. In K. J. Holyoak & R. G. Morrison (Eds.), *The Cambridge handbook of thinking and reasoning*. Cambridge University Press.
Moll, H., & Tomasello, M. (2007). Cooperation and human cognition: The Vygotskian intelligence hypothesis. *Philosophical Transactions of the Royal Society B,* **362**, 639–648.
Monge, P. R. (1977). The systems perspective as a theoretical basis for the study of human communication. *Communication Quarterly,* **25**(1), 19–29.
Monroe, J. G., Srikant, T., & Weigel, D. (2022). Mutation bias reflects natural selection in Arabidopsis thaliana. *Nature*. https://doi.org/10.1038/s41586-021-04269-6
Montoya, S. (2018). *Defining literacy*. UNESCO Institute for Statistics.
Moravcsik, J. M. (1979). Understanding. *Dialectica,* **33**, 201–216.

Morris, C. W., et al. (1938). Foundations of the theory of signs. In O. Neurath (Ed.), *The international encyclopedia of unified science,* **1**(2), 59. The University of Chicago Press.

Moser, E. I., Kropff, E., & Moser, M.-B. (2008). Place cells, grid cells and the brain's spatial representation system. *Annual Review of Neuroscience,* **31**, 69–89.

Mottet, T. P., Frymier, A. B., & Beebe, S. A. (2006). Theorizing about instructional communication. In T. P. Mottet, V. P. Richmond, & J. C. McCroskey (Eds.), *Handbook of instructional communication: Rhetorical and relational perspectives* (pp. 255–282). Allyn & Bacon.

Mounier, A., & Lahr, M. M. (2019). Deciphering African late middle Pleistocene hominin diversity and the origin of our species. *Nature Communications,* **10**, 3406. https://doi.org/10.1038/s41467-019-11213-w

Mueller, U. G., et al. (2005). The evolution of agriculture in insects. *Annual Review of Ecology Evolution and Systematics,* **36**, 563–595.

Mulcahy, N. J., & Dunbar, R. I. M. (2005). Gorillas (*Gorilla gorilla*) and Orangutans (*Pongo pygmaeus*). Encode relevant problem features in a tool-using task. *Journal of Comparative Psychology,* **119**(1), 23–32.

Müller, G. B. (2017). Why an extended evolutionary synthesis is necessary. *Interface Focus,* 7, 20170015.

Murray, J. (1998). Information, communication and technology—What can second order cybernetics contribute to the literate debate. *Cybernetics & Human Knowing,* **5**, 43–57.

Muthukrishna, M., Shulman, B. W., Vasilescu, V., & Henrich, J. (2014). Sociality influences cultural complexity. *Proceedings of the Royal Society B,* **281**, 20132511. https://doi.org/10.1098/rspb.2013.2511

Narvaez, D. (2011). The world looks small when you only look through a telescope: The need for a broad and developmental study of reasoning. *Behavioral and Brain Sciences,* **34**(2), 83–84.

Navarrete, M., Dıez, A., & Araque, A. (2014). Astrocytes in endocannabinoid signalling. *Philosophical Transactions of the Royal Society B,* **369**, 20130599. https://doi.org/10.1098/rstb.2013.0599

Neimeyer, R. A. (2016). Meaning reconstruction in the wake of loss: Evolution of a research program. *Behaviour Change,* **33**(2), 65–79.

Neisser, U. (1967*2014). *Cognitive psychology*. Psychology Press, New York.

Neisser, U. (1988). Five kinds of self-knowledge. *Philosophical Psychology,* **1**(1), 35–59.

Nettle, D. (2020). Selection, adaptation, inheritance and design in human culture: The view from the Price equation. *Philosophical Transactions of the Royal Society B,* **375**, 20190358. https://doi.org/10.1098/rstb.2019.0358

Newell, A. (1990). *Unified theories of cognition.* Harvard University Press.

Newell, A. (1992). Précis of Unified theories of cognition. *Behavioral and Brain Sciences,* **15**, 425–492.

Newell, A., & Simon, H. A. (1972). *Human problem solving*. Prentice Hall.

Newell, A., & Simon, H. A. (1976). Computer science as empirical enquiry: Symbols and search. *Communications of the ACM,* **19**, 113–126.

Newen, A., & Bartels, A. (2007). Animal minds and the possession of concepts. *Philosophical Psychology,* **20**(3), 283–308.

Nguyen, T. D., Kasmarik, K. E., Abbass, H. A. (2020). Towards interpretable deep neural networks: An exact transformation to multi-class multivariate decision trees. *Preprint submitted to Journal of Neural Networks*, March 12, 2020.

Nieder, A., & Dehaene, S. (2009). Representation of number in the brain. *Annual Review of Neuroscience, 2009*(**32**), 185–208.

Nishio, S., Nakanishi, H., & Fujinami, T. (Eds.). (2017). *Investigating human nature and communication through robots*. Frontiers Media.

Noble, D. (2015). Evolution beyond neo-Darwinism: A new conceptual framework. *The Journal of Experimental Biology,* **218**, 7–13.

Noordzij, M. L., Newman-Norlund, S. E., de Ruiter, J. P., Hagoort, P., Levinson, S. C., & Toni, I. (2009). Brain mechanisms underlying human communication. *Frontiers in Human Neuroscience,* **3**, 14.

Norman, M. D., Finn, J., & Tregenza, T. (2001). Dynamic mimicry of an IndoMalayan octopus. *Proceedings of the Royal Society London B,* **268**, 1755–1758.

Nour, M. M., & Barrera, A. (2015). Schizophrenia, subjectivity, and mindreading. *Schizophrenia Bulletin,* **41**(6), 1214–1219.

O'Brien, G., & Opie, J. (2004). Notes toward a structuralist theory of mental representation. In H. Clapin, P. Staines, & P. Slezak (Eds.), *Representation in mind: New approaches to mental representation* (pp. 1–20). Elsevier.

O'Keefe, J., & Dostrovsky, J. (1971). The hippocampus as a spatial map: Preliminary evidence from unit activity in the freely moving rat. *Brain Research,* **34**, 171–175.

Oaksford, M., & Chater, N. (2009). Précis of Bayesian rationality: The probabilistic approach to human reasoning. *Behavioral and Brain Sciences,* **32**, 69–120.

Oaksford, M., & Chater, N. (2020). New paradigms in the psychology of reasoning. *Annual Review of Psychology,* **71**, 305–330.

OECD. (2007). *Glossary of statistical terms*. OECD.

Ofengenden, T. (2014). Memory Formation and Belief. *DIAL PHIL MENT NEURO SCI* 2014; 7(2): 34–44.

Ogden, C. K., & Richards, I. A. (1923). *The meaning of meaning*. ARK Paperbacks.

Ong, W. J. (1982). *Orality and literacy: The technologizing of the word*. Routledge.
Osgood, C. E. (1971). Where do sentences come from? In D. D. Steinberg, & L. A. Jakobovits (Eds.). *Semantics*. Cambridge University Press.
Osgood, C. E., & McGuigan, F. J. (1973). Psychological correlates of meaning: Essences or tracers? In McGuigan F. J. & Schooner (eds). *The psychophysiology of thinking*. Academic Press
Osiurak, F., & Reynaud, E. (2020). The elephant in the room: What matters cognitively in cumulative technological culture. *Behavioral and Brain Sciences,* **43**, e156.
Overmann, K. A., & Malafouris, L. (2018). Situated cognition. In H. Callan (Ed.), *International encyclopedia of anthropology: Anthropology beyond text*. WileyBlackwell.
Parsons, T. (1937*1949). *The structure of social action: A study in social theory with special reference to a group of recent European writers*. Second Edition, The Free Press
Partridge, D. & Y. Wilks, eds., (1990) *Foundations of Artificial Intelligence: A Source Book*. Cambridge University Press.
Parvini, N. (2020). *The defenders on liberty: Human nature, individualism, and property rights*. Palgrave Macmillan.
Pask, A. G. S. (1976). *Conversation, cognition and learning: A cybernetic theory and methodology*. Elsevier.
Passingham, R. E. (2008). *What is special about the human brain*. Oxford University Press.
Patterson, O. (2014). Making sense of culture. *Annual Review of Sociology* **40**, 1–30.
Peacocke, C. (1992). *A Study of Concepts*. The MIT Press.
Pearson, J. C., Nelson, P. E., Titsworth, T., & Harter, L. (2011). *Human communication* (4th ed.). McGraw-Hill.
Pecher, D., & Zeelenberg, R. (2018). Boundaries to grounding abstract concepts. *Philosophical Transactions of the Royal Society B,* **373**, 20170132. https://doi.org/10.1098/rstb.2017.0132
Penn, D. C., Holyoak, K. J., & Povinelli, D. J. (2008). Darwin's mistake: Explaining the discontinuity between human and nonhuman minds. *Behavioral and Brain Sciences,* **31**, 109–178.
Penny, D. (2015). Epigenetics, Darwin, and Lamarck. *Genome Biology and Evolution,* 7(6), 1758–1760.
Pentland, A. P., & Fischler, M. A. (1983). A more rational view of logic, or, up against the wall, Logic Imperialists. *The AI Magazine,* **4**(4), 15–18.
Pepperberg, I. M. (1999). *The alex studies: Cognitive and communicative abilities of grey parrots*. Harvard University Press.

Pepperberg, I. M., & Nakayama, K. (2016). Robust representation of shape in a Grey parrot (*Psittacus erithacus*). *Cognition,* **153**, 146–160.

Pepperberg, I. M. (2020). The comparative psychology of intelligence: Some thirty years later. *Frontiers in Psychology,* **11**, 973.

Perreault, C. (2012). The pace of cultural evolution. *PLoS ONE,* 7(9), e45150.

Perreault, C., & Mathew, S. (2012). Dating the origin of language using phonemic diversity. *PLoS ONE,* 7(4), e35289.

Petersen, S. E., & Sporns, O. (2015). Brain networks and cognitive architectures. *Neuron,* **88**, 207–219.

Petocz, A., & Mackay, N. (2013). Unifying psychology through situational realism. *Review of General Psychology,* **17**(2), 216–223.

Phillips, S. (2019). Sheaving—a universal construction for semantic compositionality. *Philosophical Transactions of the Royal Society B,* **375**, 20190303. https://doi.org/10.1098/rstb.2019.0303

Piaget, J. (1978). *What is Psychology? American Psychologist.* (pp. 648–652). Trans and bracketed material by C. Camii. Address at the annual convention of the American Psychological Association.

Pigliussi, M., & Müller, G. B. (2010). *Evolution—The extended synthesis.* MIT Press. Pinker, S. (1994). *The Language Instinct.* Penguin Books.

Place, U. T. (1956). Is consciousness a brain process? *British Journal of Psychology,* **47**, 44–50.

Plotkin, H. (2011). Human nature, cultural diversity and evolutionary theory. *Philosophical Transactions of the Royal Society B,* **366**, 454–463. https://doi.org/10.1098/rstb.2010.0160

Pobiner, B. L. (2020). The zooarchaeology and paleoecology of early hominin scavenging. *Evolutionary Anthropology,* **2020**, 1–15.

Poole, D. L., & Mackworth, A. K. (2017). *Artificial intelligence: Foundations of computational agents.* Second Edition. Cambridge University Press.

Pool, I. S., Frey, F. W., Schramm, W., Maccoby, N., & Parker, E. B. (Eds.). (1973). *Handbook of communication.* Rand McNally College Publishing Company.

Premack, D. (1985). "Gavagai!" or the future history of the animal language controversy. *Cognition,* **19**, 207–296.

Premack, D. (2007). Human and animal cognition: Continuity and discontinuity. *PNAS,* **104**(35), 13861–13867.

Priebe, S., Dimic, S., Wildgrube, C., Jankovic, J., Cushing, A., & McCabe, R. (2011). Good communication in psychiatry—a conceptual review. *European Psychiatry,* **26**(7), 403–407.

Pulvermüller, F. (1999). Words in the brain's language. *Behavioral and Brain Sciences,* **22**, 253–336.

Pulvermüller, F. (2018). Neural reuse of action perception circuits for language, concepts and communication. *Progress in Neurobiology,* **160**, 1–44.

Putnam, H. (1983). *Realism and Reason. Philosophical Papers*, (vol. 3). Cambridge University Press.

Putnam, H. (1988). *Representation and reality*. The MIT Press.

Putnam, H. (2004). *Ethics without ontology*. Harvard University Press.

Pylyshyn, Z. W. (1984). *Computation and cognition: Toward a foundation for cognitive science*. MIT Press.

Queenan, B. N., Ryan, T. J., Gazzaniga, M., & Gallistel, C. R. (2017). On the research of time past: the hunt for the substrate of memory. *Annals of the New York Academy of Sciences*, **1396**(1), 108–125. https://doi.org/10.1111/nyas.13348

Queiroz, K. (2005). Ernst Mayr and the modern concept of species. *PNAS*, **102**(suppl. 1), 6600–6607.

Raghanti, M. A., et al. (2018). A neurochemical hypothesis for the origin of hominids. *PNAS, 115*, E1108–E1116. https://doi.org/10.1073/pnas.1719666115

Raja, S. N., Carr, D. B., Cohen, M., et al. (2020). The revised international association for the study of pain definition of pain: Concepts, challenges, and compromises. *Pain*, **161**(9), 1976–1982.

Ramachandran, V. S. (2012). *The Tell-Tale brain: Unlocking the mystery of human nature*. Windmill Books.

Ramsey, W. (2003). Are receptors representations? *Journal of Experimental and Theoretical Artificial Intelligence*, **15**, 125–141.

Range, F., & Virányi, Z. (2011). Development of gaze following abilities in wolves (*Canis Lupus*). *PLoS ONE*, **6**(2), e16888.

Raphael, B. (1976). *The thinking computer: mind inside matter*. WH Freeman and Co. San Francisco

Rendall, D. (2021). Aping language: Historical perspectives on the quest for semantics, syntax, and other rarefied properties of human language in the communication of primates and other animals. *Frontiers in Psychology*, **12**, 675172.

Rendell, L., & Whitehead, H. (2001). Culture in Whales and Dolphins. *Behavioral and Brain Sciences*, **24**(2), 309–324.

Renfrew, C. (2008). Neuroscience, evolution and the sapient paradox: The factuality of value and of the sacred. *Philosophical Transactions of the Royal Society B*, **363**, 2041–2047.

Rich, E., & Knight, K. (1991). *Artificial intelligence* (2nd ed.). McGraw-Hill.

Richerson, P. J., & Boyd, R. (2005). *Not by genes alone: How culture transformed human evolution*. University of Chicago Press.

Richerson, P. J., Boyd, R., & Henrich, J. (2010). Gene-culture coevolution in the age of genomics. *PNAS*, **107**(suppl. 2), 8985–8992.

Ricoeur, P. (1981). The task of hermeneutics. In J. B. Thompson (Ed.). *Hermeneutics and the human sciences*. Cambridge University Press, and Maison des Sciences de l' Homme.

Rilling, J. K., et al. (2008). The evolution of the arcuate fasciculus revealed with comparative DTI. *Nature Neuroscience,* **11**, 426–428.

Rilling, J. K., et al. (2012). Continuity, divergence, and the evolution of brain language pathways. *Frontiers in Evolutionary Neuroscience,* **3**, 11.

Rips, L. J. & S. L. Marcus, (1977). Supposition and the analysis of conditional sentences. In M. A. Just & P. A. Carpenter (Eds.). *Cognitive processes in comprehension*. LEA.

Rizzolatti, G., & Sinigaglia, C. (2006). *Mirrors in the brain-how our minds shape actions and emotions*. Oxford University Press.

Roberts, D. F. (1973). Communication and children: A developmental approach. In I. S. Pool, F. W. Frey, W. Schramm, N. Maccoby, & E. B, Parker (Eds.). *Handbook of Communication*, Rand McNally College Publishing Company

Roe, A. W. (2019). Columnar connectome: Toward a mathematics of brain function. *Network Neuroscience,* **3**(3), 779–791. https://doi.org/10.1162/netn_a_00088

Roediger, H. L. (2008). Relativity of remembering: Why the laws of memory vanished. *Annual Review of Psychology,* **59**, 225–254.

Rogers, D. S., & Ehrlich, P. R. (2008). Natural selection and cultural rates of change. *PNAS,* **105**(9), 3416–3420.

Rolls, E. T. (1987). Information representation, processing and storage in the brain: Analysis at the single neuron level. In J.-P. Changeux & M. Konishi (Eds.), *The neural and molecular bases of learning*. John Wiley.

Rolls, E. T. (1999). *The brain and emotion*. Oxford University Press.

Rorty, R. (1979). *Philosophy and the mirror of nature*.

Rose, S. (1999). Précis of lifelines: Biology, freedom, determinism. *Behavioral and Brain Sciences,* **22**, 871–921.

Rosenbloom, P. S. (2013). The sigma cognitive architecture and system. *AISB Quarterly,* **136**, 4–13.

Rosenblueth, A., Wiener, N., & Bigelow, J. (1943). Behavior, purpose and teleology. *Philosophy of Science,* **10**, 18–24.

Rudolph, L. (2012). *Qualitative mathematics for the social sciences*. Routledge.

Rumelhart, D. E., & McClelland, J.. L. (1985). Levels Indeed! A response to broadbent. *Journal of Experimental Psychology: General,* **114**, 193–197.

Runcan, A. (1985). Towards a logical model of dialogue. In J. Hintikka, & L. Vaina. (Ed.). *Cognitive constraints on communications: Representation and processes*, Reidel Publishing Company.

Rusakov, D. A., & Dityatev, A. E. (2014). Brain circuitry outside the synaptic cleft. *Philosophical Transactions of the Royal Society B,* **369**, 20130591. https://doi.org/10.1098/rstb.2013.0591

Russell, B. (1921). *The analysis of mind*. Allen & Unwin.
Russell, B. (1927). *An outline of philosophy*. Allen & Unwin Ltd.
Russell, B. (1946). *The history of western philosophy*. George Allen & Unwin.
Russell, B. (1948). *Human knowledge: Its scope and limits*. George Allen and Unwin, London.
Russell, S. J. & Norvig, P. (2003). *Artificial Intelligence: A modern approach*. Second Edition. Prentice Hall.
Rutz, C., Klump, B. C., Komarczyk, L., Leighton, R., Kramer, J., Wischnewski, S., Sugasawa, S., Morrissey, M. B., James, R., StClair, J. J. H., Switzer, R. A., & Masuda, B. M. (2016). Discovery of species-wide tool use in the Hawaiian crow. *Nature*, **537**, 403–407. https://doi.org/10.1038/nature19103
Rzevski, G. (1985). On criteria for assessing an information theory. *The Computer Journal*, **28**(3), 200–202.
Sadoski, M., & Paivio, A. (2007). Toward a unified theory of reading. *Scientific Studies of Reading*, **11**(4), 337–356.
Sahle, Y., et al. (2013). Earliest stone-tipped projectiles form the ethiopian rift date to > 279,000 years ago. *PLoS ONE*, **8**(11), e78092.
Sakarya, O., Armstrong, K. A., Adamska, M., Adamski, M., Wang, I.-F., Tidor, B., Degnan, B. M., Oakley, T. H., & Kosik, K. S. (2007). A post-synaptic scaffold at the origin of the animal kingdom. *PLoS ONE*, **6**(e506), 1–9.
Sakurai, Y., et al. (2018). Multiple approaches to the investigation of cell assembly in memory research—Present and future. *Frontiers in Systems Neuroscience*, **12**, 21.
Sanford, A. J. (Ed.). (2003). *The nature and limits of human understanding*. T&T CLARK Ltd.
Sanford, D. H. (1999). Inference. *The Cambridge Dictionary of Philosophy*, Second Edition, (pp. 426–27).
Sapir, E. (1921). *Language*. Harcourt Brace.
Sarkies, P. (2020). Molecular mechanisms of epigenetic inheritance: Possible evolutionary implications. *Seminars in Cell & Developmental Biology*, **97**, 106–115.
Sasaki, T., Matsuki, N. I., & T. (2011). Action-potential modulation during axonal conduction. *Science*, **331**, 599–601.
Sass, L. A. (1984*1985). Parental communication deviance and schizophrenia: A cognitive-developmental analysis. In J. Hintikka, & L. Vaina (Eds.). *Cognitive constraints on communications: Representation and processes*, Reidel Publishing Company.
Saul, J. M. (2002). Speaker meaning, what is said, and what is implicated. *Noûs*, **36**, 228–248.
Saussure, Ferdinand de (†1974). *Course in Linguistics, revised edition*. Fontana/Collins. Introduction by J. Culler. Trans from the French by W Baskin.

Savage-Rumbaugh, S. E., Shanker, S. G., & Taylor, T. J. (1998). *Apes, language, and the human mind*. Oxford University Press.

Saxe, A. M., McClelland, J. L., & Ganguil, S. (2019). A mathematical theory of semantic development in deep neural networks. *PNAS*, **116**(23), 11537–11546.

Scemes, E., & Giaume, C. (2006). Astrocyte calcium waves: what they are and what they do. *Glia*, **54**(7), 716–725.

Schank, R. C. (1972). Conceptual dependency: A theory of natural language understanding. *Cognitive Psychology*, **3**, 552–631.

Schank, R. C. (1983). The current state of AI: One man's opinion. *AI Magazine*, **4**(1), 3–8.

Scherer, K. R. (2005). What are emotions? And how can they be measured? *Social Science Information*, **44**(4), 695–729.

Schirato, T., & Yell, S. (2000). *Communication and culture: An introduction*. Sage Publications.

Schlebusch, C. M., et al. (2017). Southern African ancient genomes estimate modern human divergence to 350,000 to 260,000 years ago. *Science*, **358**, 652–655.

Schmandt-Besserat, D. (1980). The envelopes that bear the first writing. *Technology and Culture*, **21**(3), 357–385.

Schnell, A. K., et al. (2021). Cuttlefish exert self-control in a delay of gratification task. *Proceedings of the Royal Society B*, **288**, 20203161. https://doi.org/10.1098/rspb.2020.3161

Schramm, W. (1973). Channels and audiences. In I. S. Pool, F. W. Frey, W. Schramm, N. Maccoby, & E. B. Parker (Eds.), *Handbook of communication*. Rand McNally College Publishing Company.

Schyns, P. G., Goldstone, R. L., & Thibaut, J.-P. (1998). The development of features in object concepts. *Behavioral and Brain Sciences*, **21**, 1–54.

Scott, B. (1996). Inadvertent pathologies of communication in human systems. In *WOSC Tenth Congress of Systems and Cybernetics, Sociocybernetics Symposium, Bucharest Romania*, 26–31 August 1996. Reprinted in *Kybernetes*, **26**, 824–836.

Searle, J. R. (2007). Putting consciousness back in the brain: Reply to Bennett and Hacker, philosophical foundations of neuroscience. In M. Bennett, D. Dennett, P. Hacker, & J. R. Searle (Eds.). *Neuroscience and Philosophy: Brain, Mind, and Language*, (pp. 97–124). Columbia University Press.

Shackman, A. J., Fox, A. S., & Seminowicz, D. A. (2015). The cognitive-emotional brain: Opportunities and challenges for understanding neuropsychiatric disorders. *Brain and Behavioral Sciences*, **38**, e86. https://doi.org/10.1017/S0140525X14001010

Shannon, C. E. (1948*1949). A mathematical theory of communication. In C. E. Shannon, & W. Weaver (1949) *The mathematical theory of communication*. University of Illinois Press.

Shannon, C. E. (1950). Programming a computer for playing chess. *Philosophical Magazine*, 7(41), 256–275.

Sherrington, C. (1906). *The integrative action of the nervous system*. Charles Scribner's Sons.

Shettleworth, S. J. (1998). *Cognition, Evolution, and Behavior*. Oxford University Press.

Shumaker, R. W., et al. (2011). *Animal tool behavior: The use and manufacture of tools by animals*. Johns Hopkins University Press.

Simon, H. A., & Kaplan, C. (1988). *Foundations of cognitive science: Overview*. Technical Report AIP-46. Dept. of Psychology, Carnegie Mellon University.

Simon, H. A. (1990). Invariants of human behavior. *Annual Review of Psychology*, **41**, 1–19.

Skinner, M. K. (2015). Environmental epigenetics and a unified theory of the molecular aspects of evolution: A Neo-Lamarckian concept that facilitates NeoDarwinian evolution. *Genome Biology and Evolution*, 7(5), 1296–1302.

Slater, P. J. B. (1983). The study of communication. In T. R. Halliday, & P. J. B. Slater, (Eds.). *Animal Behaviour: Volume 2 Communication*, (pp. 9–42). Blackwell.

Smart, J. J. C. (1959). Sensations and brain processes. *Philosophical Review*, **68**, 141–156.

Smith, A. G. (Ed.). (1966). *Communication and culture: Readings in the codes of human interaction*. Holt.

Smolensky, P., & Legendre, G. (2006). *The harmonic mind: From neural computation to optimality-theoretic grammar. Volume 1: cognitive architecture*. The MIT Press.

Snoddy, G. S. (1926). Learning and stability. *Journal of Applied Psychology*, **10**, 1–36.

Sopher, B. (2006). A unified science of cultural evolution should incorporate choice. *Behavioral and Brain Sciences*, **29**(4), 362–363.

Solé, R., Moses, M., & Forrest, S. (2019). Liquid brains, solid brains. *Philosophical Transactions of the Royal Society B*, **374**, 20190040. https://doi.org/10.1098/rstb.2019.0040

Soucy, S. M., & Cogarten, J. P. (2017). Inteins as indicators of biocommunication. In G. Witzany (Ed.), *Biocommunication of archaea* (pp. 265–275). Springer.

Sousa, A. M. M., et al. (2017). Evolution of the human nervous system function, structure, and development. *Cell*, **170**(2), 226–247. https://doi.org/10.1016/j.cell.2017.06.036

Sowa, J. F. (1984). *Conceptual structures: Information processing in mind and machine*. Addison-Wesley.

Speaks, J. (2008). Conversational implicature, thought, and communication. *Mind & Language,* **23**, 107–122.

Sperber, D., & Wilson, D. (1995). *Relevance: Communication and cognition* (2nd ed.). Blackwell Publishing.

St. Amant, R. & Horton, T. E. (2008). Revisiting the definition of tool use. *Animal Behaviour*, **75**(4), 1199–1208.

St. John, M., & McClelland, J. (1990). Learning and applying contextual constraints in sentence comprehension. *Artificial Intelligence* **46**, 217–257.

Staats, A. W. (1981). Paradigmatic behaviourism, unified theory, unified theory construction methods, and the zeitgeist of separatism. *American Psychologist,* **36**, 239–256.

Staats, A. W. (1999). Unifying psychology requires new infrastructure, theory, method, and a research agenda. *Review of General Psychology,* **3**(1), 1–13.

Stamper, R. K. (1985). Towards a theory of information. *The Computer Journal,* **28**(3), 195–199.

Stanford, Department of Anthropology (2017). https://anthropology.stanford.edu/.

Stanier, R. Y., & van Niel, C. B. (1962). The concept of a bacterium. *Archie Für Mikrobiologie,* **42**, 17–35.

Stanyer, J. (2007). *Modern political communication*. Polity Press.

Staudenmayer, H. (1975). Understanding conditional reasoning with meaningful propositions. In R. J. Falmagne (Ed.), *Reasoning: Representation and process in children and adults*. LEA.

Sterba, J. P. (1999). Political philosophy. In R. Audi (Ed.), *The Cambridge dictionary of philosophy* (2nd ed.). Cambridge University Press.

Sterelny, K. (2011). From hominins to humans: How *sapiens* became behaviourally modern. *Philosophical Transactions of the Royal Society B*. https://doi.org/10.1098/rstb.2010.0301

Sternberg, R. J., & Grigorenko, E. L. (2001). Unified Psychology. *American Psychologist,* **56**(12), 1069–1079.

Stevenson, C. L. (1944). *Ethics and language*. New Haven.

Stich, S. P. (1978). Autonomous psychology and the belief-desire thesis. In J. L. Bermúdez (Ed.). *Philosophy of psychology: Contemporary readings* Routledge. Originally published in *Monist* **61**(4), 573–591.

Stokes, J. M., Yang, K., Swanson, K., Jaakkola, T. S., Barzilay, R., & Collins, J. J. (2020). A deep learning approach to antibiotic discovery. *Cell,* **180**, 688–702.

Stolk, A., Noordzij, M. L., Verhagen, L., Volman, I., Schoffelen, J.-M., Oostenveld, R., Hagoort, P., & Toni, I. (2014). Cerebral coherence between communicators marks the emergence of meaning. *PNAS,* **111**(51), 18183–18188.

Stonier, T. (1996). Information as a basic property of the universe. *Bio Systems*, **38**(2&3), 135–140.

Stout, D. (2011). Stone toolmaking and the evolution of human culture and cognition. *Philosophical Transactions of the Royal Society B*, **366**, 1050–1059.

Stout, D., & Hecht, E. E. (2017). Evolutionary neuroscience of cumulative culture. *PNAS*, **114**(30), 7861–7868.

Stufflebeam, R. S. (1998). Representation and computation. In W. Bechtel & G. Graham (Eds.), *A companion to cognitive science* (pp. 636–648). Blackwell.

Suddendorf, T., & Corballis, M. C. (1997). Mental time travel and the evolution of the human mind. *Genetic, Social, and General Psychology Monographs*, **123**(2), 133–167.

Sulkowski, G. M., & Hauser, M. D. (2001). Can rhesus monkeys spontaneously subtract? *Cognition*, **79**(2001), 239–262.

Sun, R. (2002). *Duality of the mind: A bottom-up approach toward cognition*. Lawrence Erlbaum Associates.

Sun, R. (2016). *Anatomy of the mind: Exploring psychological mechanisms and processes with the clarion cognitive architecture*. Oxford University Press.

Sutton, J. (2004). Representation, reduction, and interdisciplinarity in the sciences of memory. In H. Clapin, P. Staines, & P. Slezak (Eds.), *Representation in mind: New approaches to mental representation* (pp. 187–216). Elsevier Ltd.

Südhof, T. C., & Malenka, R. C. (2008). Understanding synapses: Past, present, and future. *Neuron*, **60**, 469–476.

Suzuki, T. N., et al. (2019). Syntactic rules in avian vocal sequences as a window into the evolution of compositionality. *Animal Behaviour*. https://doi.org/10.1016/j.anbehav.2019.01.009

Számadó, S., Czégel, D., & Zachar, I. (2019). One problem, too many solutions: How costly is honest signalling of need? *PLoS ONE*, **14**(1), e0208443. https://doi.org/10.1371/journal.pone.0208443

Szathmáry, E. (2015). Toward major evolutionary transitions theory 2.0. *PNAS*, **112**(33), 10104–10111.

Szathmáry, E., & Maynard Smith, J. (1995). The major evolutionary transitions. *Nature*, **374**, 227–232.

Tallis, R (2011). *Aping mankind: Neuromania, darwinitis and the misrepresentation of humanity*. Acumen.

Tarski A (1944*1969). The semantic conception of truth. In T. M. Olsewsky (Ed.). *Problems in the philosophy of language*. Holt, Rinehart and Wilson

Tauzin, T., Csik, A., Kis, A., & Topál, J. (2015). What or where? The meaning of referential human pointing for dogs (*Canis familiaris*). *Journal of Comparative Psychology*, **129**(4), 334–338.

Taylor, A. H., et al. (2007). Spontaneous metatool use by new caledonian crows. *Current Biology*, **17**, 1504–1507.

Thagard, P. R. (2002*2006). How Molecules Matter to Mental Computation. In P. Thagard (Ed.). *Hot thought: Mechanisms and applications of emotional cognition* (pp. 115–131). The MIT Press.

Thomas, L. F., & Harri-Augstein, E. S. (1985). *Self organised learning: Foundations of a conversational science of psychology*. Routledge & Kegan Paul.

Thornton, A., & Raihani, N. J. (2008). The evolution of teaching. *Animal Behaviour*, **75**, 1823–1836. https://doi.org/10.1016/j.anbehav.2007.12.014

Tokuyama, N., et al. (2021). Two wild female bonobos adopted infants from a different social group at Wamba. *Scientific Reports*, **11**, 4967.

Tomasello, M., Carpenter, M., Call, J., Behne, T., & Moll, H. (2005). Understanding and sharing intentions: The origins of cultural cognition. *Behavioral and Brain Sciences*, **28**, 675–735.

Tooby, J., & Cosmides, L. (1992). The psychological foundations of culture. In J. H. Barkow, L. Cosmides, & J. Tooby (Eds.), *The adapted mind: Evolutionary psychology and the generation of culture* (pp. 19–136). Oxford University Press.

Tooby, J., & Cosmides, L. (2005). Conceptual foundations of evolutionary psychology. In D. M. Buss (Ed.). *The handbook of evolutionary psychology* (pp. 5–67).

Tully, C. J. (1985). Information, human activity and the nature of relevant theories. *The Computer Journal*, **28**(3), 206–210.

Tulving, E. (1972). Episodic and semantic memory. In E. Tulving & W. Donaldson (Eds.), *Organisation of memory*. Academic Press.

Tulving, E. (1983). *Elements of episodic memory*. Clarendon Press.

Tulving, E. (2002). Episodic memory: Form mind to brain. *Annual Review of Psychology*, **53**, 1–25.

Turing, A. M. (1936). On computable numbers with an application to the Entscheidungsproblem. *Proceedings of the London Mathematical Society*, **2**(42), 230–265.

Turing, A. M. (1950). Computing machinery and intelligence. *Mind*, **59**, 433–460.

Tzachor, A., Whittlestone, J., Sundaram, L., & Ó hÉigeartaigh, S. (2020). Artificial intelligence in a crisis needs ethics with urgency. *Nature Machine Intelligence*, **2**, 365–366.

Vaesen, K., & Houkes, W. (2017). Complexity and technological evolution: What everybody knows? *Biol Philos*. https://doi.org/10.1007/s10539-017-9603-1. Published online: 22 November 2017.

Vaina, L. M., & Hintikka, J. (Ed). (1984*1985). *Cognitive constraints on communications: Representation and processes*. D. Reidel Publishing Company.

Valtin, R., et al. (2016). *European declaration of the right to literacy (Full version)*. European Literacy Policy Network.

Van Fraassen, B. C. (2008). *Scientific representation: Paradoxes of perspective*. Oxford University Press.

Van Gelder, T. (1998). The dynamical hypothesis in cognitive science. *Behavioral and Brain Sciences,* **21**, 615–665.

Varela, F. J., Thompson, E., & Rosch, E. (1991). *The embodied mind: Cognitive science and human experience*. MIT Press.

Vaux, F., Trewick, S. A., & Morgan-Richards, M. (2016). Speciation through the looking glass. *Biological Journal of the Linnaean Society,* **120**, 480–488.

Veldhuis, D., et al. (2014). *Human evolution: Theory and progress*. ResearchGate.

Velupillai, K. V. (2005). The unreasonable ineffectiveness of mathematics in economics. *Cambridge Journal of Economics, 2005*(**29**), 849–872.

Verheij, B. (2020). Artificial intelligence as law: Presidential address to the seventeenth international conference on artificial intelligence and law. *Artificial Intelligence and Law,* **28**, 181–206.

Vigo, R. (2013). Complexity over uncertainty in generalized representational information theory (GRIT): A structure-sensitive general theory of information. *Information,* **4**(1), 1–30. https://doi.org/10.3390/info4010001

Von Eckardt, B. (1993). *The representational theory of mind*. Cambridge University Press.

Von Frisch, K., & Lindauer, M. (1956). The "Langage" and orientation of the honey bee. *Annual Review of Entomology,* **1**, 45–58.

Vosniadou, S., & Verschaffel, L. (2004). Extending the conceptual change approach to mathematics learning and teaching. *Learning and Instruction,* **14**, 445–451.

Vygotski, L. (1934*1986). *Thought and language, second edition*. The MIT Press.

Wagoner, B. (2019). Frederic Bartlett. In: S. Bernecker & K. Michaelian (eds.). *The Routledge handbook of philosophy of memory*.

Waisbord, S. (2019). *Communication: A post-discipline*. Cambridge, Polity Press.

Wang, P. (2008). What do you mean by "AI" In Wang, P., Goertzel, B., & Franklin, S., eds. Proceedings of the First Conference on General Artificial Intelligence, 362–373.

Wang, P. (2019). On defining artificial intelligence. *Journal of Artificial General Intelligence,* **10**(2), 1–37.

Watson, J. B. (1913). Psychology as the behaviorist views it. *Psychological Review,* **20**(2), 158–177.

Watson, J. B. (1924). *Behaviorism*. W. W. Norton & Company, Inc.

Weaver, R. J., Koch, R. E., & Hill, G. E. (2017). What maintains signal honesty in animal colour displays used in mate choice? *Philosophical Transactions of the Royal Society B,* **372**, 20160343. https://doi.org/10.1098/rstb.2016.034

Wertsch, J. V., & Roediger, H. L., III. (2008). Collective memory: Conceptual foundations and theoretical approaches. *Memory,* **16**(3), 318–326.

Wetzel, L. (2008). *Types and tokens: An essay on universals*. Cambridge University Press.
Wheatley, T., Boncz, A., Toni, I., & Stolk, A. (2019). Beyond the isolated brain: The promise and challenge of interacting minds. *Neuron,* **103**, 186–188.
Whiten, A., & van Schaik, C. P. (2007). The evolution of animal 'cultures' and social intelligence. *Philosophical Transactions of the Royal Society B,* **362**, 603–620. https://doi.org/10.1098/rstb.2006.1998
Whiten, A., Ayala, F. J., Feldman, M. W., & Laland, K. N. (2017). The extension of biology through culture. *PNAS,* **114**(30), 7775–7781.
Whiten, A. & Erdal, D. (2012) The human socio-cognitive niche and its evolutionary origins. *Phil. Trans. R. Soc. B* (2012) **367**, 2119–2129.
Wiener, N. (1948*1962). *Cybernetics or control and communication in the animal and the machine. Second edition*, The MIT Press.
Wiener, N. (1950*1954*1988). *The human use of human beings: Cybernetics and Society*. Unabridged republication of his 1954 revised and updated edition initially published in 1950.
Wilde, O. (1891*1912). *The soul of man under socialism*. Edward Wiesel and Media.
Williams, G. C. (1966*2018). *Adaptation and natural selection: A critique of some current evolutionary thought*. New Foreword by R. Dawkins. Princeton University Press.
Williams, P. (2007). Quorum sensing, communication and cross-kingdom signalling in the bacterial world. *Microbiology* (2007), **153**, 3923–3938.
Williams, T., Briggs, P., & Scheutz, M. (2015). Covert robot–robot communication: Human perceptions and implications for human–robot interaction. *Journal of Human-Robot Interaction,* **4**(2), 24–49.
Williamson, T. (2006). Can cognition be factorized into internal and external components? In R. J. Stainton (Ed.), *Contemporary debates in cognitive science*. Blackwell Publishing.
Wilson, E. O. (1998). *Consilience: The unity of knowledge*. Abacus.
Wilson, E. O. (2014). *The meaning of human existence*. Liveright Publishing Company.
Wilson, M. (2002). Six views of embodied cognition. *Psychonomic Bulletin & Review,* **9**(4), 625–636.
Wilson, R. A., & Keil, F. C. (Eds.). (1999). *The MIT encyclopedia of the cognitive sciences*. The MIT Press.
Winograd, T. (1972). Understanding natural language. *Cognitive Psychology* **3**, 1–191.
Winston, P. H. (1977). *Artificial intelligence*. Addison-Wesley.
Winston, P. H. (1992). *Artificial intelligence* (3rd ed.). Addison-Wesley.
Wirth, L (1929*1954).). Preface. In K. Manheim (Ed.). *Ideology and Utopia*. Routledge & Kegan Paul, London. First published in German in 1929.

Wittgenstein, L. (1953*1976). *Philosophical investigations*. Basil Blackwell.

Witzany, G. (2017a). (Ed.). *Biocommunication of Archaea*. Springer International Publishing.

Witzany, G. (2017b). Introduction: Keylevels of biocommunication of archaea. In G. Witzany (Ed.). *Biocommunication of Archaea*. Springer International Publishing.

Woese, C. R. (2004). A new biology for a new century. *Microbiology and Molecular Biology Reviews*, **68**(2), 173–186.

Wood, B., & Collard, M. (1999). Anthropology—the human genus. *Science,* **284**, 65. https://doi.org/10.1126/science.284.5411.65

Woodford, P. (2019). Evaluating inclusive fitness. *Royal Society Open Science,* **6**, 190644. https://doi.org/10.1098/rsos.190644

Wray, G. A., Hoekstra, H. E., Futuyma, D. J., Lenski, R. E., Mackay, T. F. C., Schluter, D., & Strassmann, J. E. (2014). Does evolutionary theory need a rethink? No, all is well. *Nature,* **514**, 161–164.

Wundt, W. M. (1912*1916). *Elements of folk-psychology: Outlines of a psychological history of the development of mankind*, E. L. Schaub (trans.), London: Allen & Unwin Ltd, translation of Elemente der Völkerpsychologie: Grundlinien einer psychologischen Entwicklungsgeschichte der Menschheit, 1912, Leipzig.

Yee, E., Jones, M. N., & McRae, K. (2018). Semantic Memory. In J. T. Wixted & S. L. Thompson-Schill (Eds), *Stevens' Handbook of experimental psychology and cognitive neuroscience 4th Edition, Vol. 3: Language and Thought*, (pp. 319–356). Wiley.

Yuste, R. (2015). From the neuron doctrine to neural networks. *Nature Reviews Neuroscience,* **16**, 487–497.

Zdrazilova, L., Sidhu, D. M., & Pexman, P. M. (2018). Communicating abstract meaning: Concepts revealed in words and gestures. *Philosophical Transactions of the Royal Society B,* **373**, 20170138. https://doi.org/10.1098/rstb.2017.0138

Zeman, A. (2008). *A portrait of the brain*. Yale University Press.

Ziff, P. (1972). *Understanding understanding*. Cornell University Press.

Zuberbühler, K. (2019). Evolutionary roads to syntax. *Animal Behaviour,* **151**, 259–265. https://doi.org/10.1016/j.anbehav.2019.03.006

Index

Note: The page numbers followed by 'f' and 't' represents figure and tables.

P. A. M. Gelepithis, *Unification of Artificial Intelligence and Psychology*,
https://doi.org/10.1007/978-3-031-68319-0

T

The manufacturer's authorised representative in the EU is Springer Nature Customer Service Centre GmbH, Europaplatz 3, 69115 Heidelberg, Germany. If you have any concerns regarding our products, please contact ProductSafety@springernature.com

Printed and bound by CPI Group (UK) Ltd, Croydon, CR0 4YY
01/10/2026
02225954-0008